Charles Dickens'
Sketches by Boz

George Cruikshank

Public Dinners
[*Dickens and Cruikshank (with beard) are seen behind the
leading stewards, who may be intended for Chapman and Hall*]

Charles Dickens'
SKETCHES
BY BOZ
End in the Beginning

by Virgil Grillo

The Colorado Associated University Press
Boulder, Colorado ● 1974

THE COLORADO ASSOCIATED UNIVERSITY PRESS
BOULDER, COLORADO
COPYRIGHT 1974 BY COLORADO ASSOCIATED UNIVERSITY PRESS
ISBN: 87081-049-9

LIBRARY OF CONGRESS CATALOG NUMBER: 73-89257
PRINTED IN THE UNITED STATES OF AMERICA
DESIGNED BY PENNY L. FARON

For My Mother
Clara Grillo
(Maria Concetta Corica)
and

In Memory of My Father
Domenic Grillo

A NOTE
ON REFERENCES

ALL QUOTATIONS of the stories and sketches later collected as the *Sketches by Boz* have been checked against either the original periodical versions, or the first published version in pieces that were originally part of a collection. A bibliography of these is included in Chapter Five of this study. But because these versions are not generally available — indeed almost impossible to obtain — the parenthetical references within the text will refer to the identical passages from the Oxford Illustrated Dickens, Charles Dickens, *Sketches by Boz* (London, 1957; reprinted 1963). In cases where the Oxford Dickens differs significantly, that is, shows a deletion, or alteration which changes the meaning, the original will be cited along with an explanatory note on the differences. Minor changes in punctuation, capitalization, and replacements of words by close synonyms, have not been noted.

References to Dickens' novels will include chapter citations in Roman numerals, followed by page numbers in the Oxford Illustrated Dickens.

ACKNOWLEDGMENTS

OXFORD UNIVERSITY Press, for permission to reproduce the George Cruikshank Illustrations to *The Sketches by Boz*, from the plates prepared for the Oxford Illustrated Dickens; also, for permission to quote from their editions of the novels.

Yale University Press, for permission to quote from Volume II, of Ernst Cassirer, *The Philosophy of Symbolic Forms: Mythical Thought*, trans. Ralph Manheim (New Haven, 1955).

Holt, Rinehart, and Winston, Inc. for permission to quote from W. W. Watt's Introduction to Charles Dickens' *Hard Times* (New York, 1965).

Joan C. Stern for permission to quote from the Chapman and Hall publication of her father's (A. H. Cleaver) and Thomas Hatton's, *A Bibliography of the Periodical Works of Charles Dickens* (London, 1933).

I wish to acknowledge my indebtedness: to the Committee on Research, University of California, Berkeley, for a travel grant which enabled me to examine the *Bell's Life* sketches in the collection of Col. Richard Gimbel at the Beinecke Library, Yale University; to Col. Gimbel for making the collection available; to the Council on Research and Creative Work, University of Colorado, Boulder, for a grant to assist in preparation of typescript.

I wish to express my thanks: to Professors Masao Miyoshi, John E. Jordan, and Walter Rex, who oversaw the original version of this work; to

ACKNOWLEDGMENTS

Aladeen Smith for being the world's most literate typist; to friends, Fran-
cine Weisenberg Foltz, Robert Griffin, Marlene Griffith, Patrick McGuire,
Vivian Mercier, Elihu Pearlman, for all kinds of help and encouragement
along the way; to my wife, Joanne, for the support of her special kind of
tranquil and enduring wisdom.

V.G.

CONTENTS

ILLUSTRATIONS

PART ONE

George Cruikshank

Private Theatres

CHAPTER ONE
A BRIEF OVER-VIEW

i. Towards the later content

AMONG DICKENS' many claims to distinction — the most "widely-read," the most "loved" novelist — the fact that he is also *the* youthful prodigy of English letters has been somewhat overlooked. No other writer in English has ever stirred so wide an audience in his early twenties. Moreover, the rapidly maturing twenty-four-year-old who in 1836 gave rise to the international cult of *Pickwick* has tended to overshadow his predecessor, that struggling young reporter in his twenty-second year who began publishing short fictional pieces and sketches, in a variety of magazines and newspapers, anonymously and under pen names.

It would be a rare (and psychologically suspect) man who in his maturity could achieve a "self" that is totally discontinuous from the "self" of his twenties; but it is an equally rare man who in his twenties shows as much of his eventual maturity as does Dickens, particularly when that maturity entails so dense, so complex, and so rich and variegated a fictive world.

I should like to show that Dickens' earliest writings, those periodical pieces eventually gathered as *The Sketches by Boz*, anticipate in many ways the work of his maturity. On the one hand there are very far-reaching connections to be shown in the matters of rhetoric, of form, of vision, of thinking about the world. On the other hand there are the seemingly simple connections in "content," the repetitions at later stages of his career of things he had written in his youth.

Assuming that such a separation of "form" and "content" is possible, the problem of showing what Dickens *repeats* as he moves toward his maturity becomes an immense one when confronted by the sheer bulk of his work. From the beginning, Dickens shows a love of detail; he tends to cram a scene with vibrant precocious perceptions. Because of these tendencies, only a detailed concordance could give us the full picture of how much of the man was in the boy. But certain features do stand out.

For instance, some of the personal habits of the man were already clearly set in the boy. The incessant walking of Dickens' middle years (so fully documented throughout his correspondence and later by his biographers) certainly is connected to the reporter's need to know about city events and later describe them accurately, and in detail. Many of the sketches allude to the author's presence as a stroller of the streets, sometimes as in "The Hospital Patient" (Sketches, p. 240)[1] at all hours of the night.

As might be expected, some of the situations and settings that later become typical of the novels have their origins in the earliest writings. Even great writers have to practice, and one of the elements that Boz seems to have practiced on is the use of the dinner scene as a place to observe or expose character. Sometimes, as in "Bellamy's," Dickens delights in simply reporting in detail on the consumption of the meal and its consumer

> as he removes the napkin which has been placed beneath his chin
> to catch the superfluous gravy of the steak, and with what gusto
> he imbibes the porter which has been fetched, expressly for him,
> in the pewter pot. Listen to the hoarse sound of that voice, kept
> down as it is by layers of solids, and deep draughts of rich wine,
> and tell us if you ever saw such a perfect picture of a regular
> gourmand. (Sketches, p. 162)

Elsewhere, it may be the effects of the dinner that Boz gives his hand to describing with amusement:

> little priggish men, who have imbibed more wine than usual, kiss
> [the ladies'] hands and exhibit very distressing contortions of
> visage, supposed to be intended for ogling.[2]

And when this same dinner situation proceeds into meandering, vacuous, ceremonial speeches, we see Boz working with one of the predecessors for the kind of foolishness that was soon to delight the audience of *Pickwick*

---

1. This and subsequent references to the *Sketches* are to the Oxford edition acknowledged at the beginning of this book.
2. "Public Dinners," *The Evening Chronicle*, Tuesday, April 7, 1835. The final phrase, "supposed to be intended for ogling," was deleted from later editions.

and thereafter color almost every formal dinner occasion that he ever described.

In this same vein, it seems clear that part of Dickens' eventual finesse in satirizing the elaborate pretentiousness of the Veneerings' dinner table, where their monstrously ornate herds of camels become emblematic of a whole way of life, traces its origins to his focus on comparable decorative pretensions in his second published short story fully thirty years earlier:

> The "sit-down supper" was excellent; there were four barley-sugar temples on the table, which would have looked beautiful if they had not melted away when the supper began; and a water mill, whose only fault was, that instead of going round, it ran over the table cloth. (*Sketches*, p. 480)

Such recurrent situations in both the early periodical writings and later in the novels, though not terribly significant in themselves, begin to demonstrate a kind of continuity of detail that can be found throughout Dickens' writing. We shall see more of Boz's early dinner tables in the chapter which follows.

Perhaps a more important kind of connection between these early writings and the novels can be found in the way that they anticipate specific characters and character types. Surely the "red-headed and red-whiskered Jew, calling through the trap" in Boz's description in "Private Theatres" (*Sketches*, p. 124) has some specific connection with "Fagin" of several years later. Though the Fagin prototype here restricts itself to similarity of physical appearance, elsewhere we see hints of the psychological penetration that was to ripen into the complex characters of the novels. The depiction of the peculiarly malevolent materialism of a character like Dombey must have been assembled over a number of years, but he is clearly foreshadowed by the man in "London Recreations" whose "delight in his garden appears to arise more from the consciousness of possession than actual enjoyment of it" (Ibid., p. 93). Or even more specifically, Dombey is anticipated in the discussion of the man who will

> have his chambers splendidly furnished, collecting books, and plate, and pictures about him in profusion; not so much for his own gratification as to annoy those who have the desire, but not the means to compete with him.[3]

---

3. "Thoughts About People," *The Evening Chronicle*, Thursday, April 23, 1835. The original statement "as to annoy those who have the desire," becomes "as to be superior to those who have the desire" in later editions.

Though Dombey is much more complex than the characters implied in either of the preceding fragments, we do see what are perhaps germs of the later creation.

The early writings also show Boz's love of depicting slightly "cracked," highly idiosyncratic, elderly characters who eventually populate the novels. For instance there is the retired "half-pay captain" who lives next door to the "old lady" of "Our Parish":

> One morning he got up early and planted three or four roots of full-blown marygolds in every bed of her front garden to the inconceivable astonishment of the old lady, who actually thought when she got up and looked out of the window, that it was some strange eruption which had come out in the night.[4]

The mad "Magog" who courts his neighbor Mrs. Nickleby by hurling vegetable marrows over the wall, Captain Cuttle with his watches and silver, Mr. Dick, Miss Flite, and many others among Dickens' later senior citizenry, inherit this tendency towards baffling antics.

Other sketches show us that elements that were later to shape a given story were already present in some of the periodical pieces. For instance, two of the essential elements of Dickens' first and most successful full-dress Christmas book, "A Christmas Carol," seem to be implicit in the first piece that he ever published on the topic of Christmas. Thus the opening of "Christmas Festivities" begins by alluding to the idea of a misanthrope, almost as though Boz were rehearsing for that fictive piece in which a nay-saying "Scrooge" would help heighten his characteristically sentimental veneration of Christmas:

> That man must be a misanthrope indeed, in whose breast something like a jovial feeling is not roused — in whose mind some pleasant associations are not awakened — by the recurrence of Christmas. (*Sketches*, p. 220)

Also implicit in this early Christmas piece is a somewhat harsher version of the part that "Tiny Tim" plays in "A Christmas Carol":

> One little seat may be empty; one slight form that gladdened the father's heart, and roused the mother's pride to look upon, may

---

4. "Our Parish," *The Evening Chronicle*, Tuesday, May 19, 1835. The original "full-blown marygolds," later becomes "full grown."

not be there. Dwell not upon the past; think not that one short
year ago, the fair child now fast resolving into dust, sat before
you, with the bloom of health upon its cheek, and the gay uncon-
sciousness of infancy in its joyous eye. (*Sketches*, p. 220)

Though "Tiny Tim" is allowed to live in the story written eight Christ-
mases later, his role is already well defined here; he exists, like the dead
child in the quotation above, to color the festivities with the pathos of
death, to make the "pleasure" more exquisite with a paradoxical dash of
"pain." Christmas — a misanthrope — a dying or dead child — something
of a prototype.

Elsewhere we see faint anticipations of characters and ideas that turn
up in the novels. Turveydrop, the dancing master — "model of deportment" — of *Bleak House* probably descends from "Signor Billsmethi" in the
"Dancing Academy" (*Sketches*, p. 256). And the critiques of organized
charities and despicable tenements of the poor, both so powerfully rendered
in the "Jellybys," the "Pardiggles," "Tom-all-Alone's" in *Bleak House*, had
already been aired in different installments of "Our Parish." In "In the
Streets — Morning" we find that combination of tenderness towards the
child laborer and antagonism towards his "official protectors" that later
surfaces in the depiction of crossing sweeper "Jo." In this early instance Boz
anticipates his later tone by sarcastically approving the supposed solicitude
for the "sweep" who has been "interdicted by a merciful Legislature from
endangering his lungs by calling out" (Ibid., p. 48).

Even the idea of "spontaneous combustion" which was later to be used
so effectively in the death of Krook, was already implanted in Dickens'
consciousness. While he may have borrowed the notion of "death by spontaneous combustion" from Captain Marryat,[5] here almost twenty years
before he seriously dared to incorporate it into his fiction, he seems to be
playing with possibilities of the concept. The first time he uses it he stays
close to the scientifically understood meaning:

> while she strikes a light, [she wishes] that the principle of spon-
> taneous combustion would extend itself to coals and kitchen
> range. (*Sketches*, "The Streets — Morning," p. 49)

But within a few months Dickens uses the idea a second time and here he
starts to toy with metaphoric possibilities:

---

5. See Gordon S. Haight, "Dickens and Lewes on Spontaneous Combustion," pp.
53–63.

We revel in a crowd of any kind — a street "row" is our delight — even a woman in a fit is by no means to be despised, especially in a fourth-rate street, where all the female inhabitants run out of their houses, and discharge large jugs of cold water over the patient, as if she were dying of spontaneous combustion and wanted putting out.[6]

Many of the themes that later shape novels are explicit in the *Sketches by Boz*; themes that help structure *Hard Times* are a particularly good example. For instance there is the idea that middle class morality, as practiced by self-righteous arbiters, is really a conspiracy directed at further impoverishment of the lower classes. Boz returns to this idea at least three times in his early periodical writings. The first instance attaches to the misanthropic uncle of "The Bloomsbury Christening," who, anticipating the leaders of Coketown, "subscribe[s] to the 'Society for the Suppression of Vice' for the pleasure of putting a stop to any harmless amusements" (*Sketches*, p. 467). Similarly, "Gradgrind" is certainly to be identified with the "gentleman of enlarged and comprehensive views who proposes to Parliament a measure for preserving the amusements of the upper classes of society, and abolishing those of the lower."[7] Or again, when Boz ironically winks at alcoholism, he does it in a way that anticipates *Hard Times*:

"Let's av — drop — somethin' to drink" — we say again, can anything be more charming than this sort of thing? And what, we ask, can be expected but popular discontent, when Temperance Societies interfere with the amusements of the people?[8]

Just as in the later novel, Boz suggests that people, like Mrs. Blackpool, or the "hands," will seek out vice if their harmless pleasures are suppressed.

Other foreshadowings of *Hard Times* are sprinkled throughout the *Sketches by Boz*. Both the veneration for the tinselled imaginative workings of the circus and the disappointment towards the tawdry and diminished reality in back of the circus are announced in Boz's piece on "Astley's:"

We could not believe that the beings of light and elegance, in milk-white tunics, salmon-coloured legs, and blue scarfs, who

---

6. "The Prisoners' Van," *Bell's Life in London*, Sunday, Nov. 29, 1835. This whole passage, and more, was subsequently deleted.

7. "Thoughts About People." This passage was deleted from later editions.

8. This passage was deleted after the original publication of "The Prisoners' Van," *Bell's Life in London*, Sunday, Nov. 29, 1835.

flitted on sleek cream-coloured horses before our eyes at night,
with all the aid of lights, music, and artificial flowers, could be
the pale, dissipated-looking creatures we beheld by day. (*Sketches*,
p. 110)

Further, the symbol of imaginative flight, the "Pegasus" mounted over the
bar at the "Pegasus Arms" in *Hard Times*, seems implicit in the "fairy
courser" that Boz describes in the "Astley's" sketch. The name for one of
the more charming acrobats of *Hard Times*, "Kidderminster" (appropriately
one who along with "Childers" "ministers" to the fancies of "kids"), shows
its origins in Boz's first coining of the word as an allusion to the high
quality, mass-produced carpets of Axminster: "And such a parlour. . . .
Beautiful Kidderminster carpet. . . ." exclaims the narrator of "The Vocal
Dressmaker" (*Sketches*, p. 252).

In all, such connections between the early periodical works and the
subsequent novels are many and frequent. The greater the reader's knowledge of Dickens' novels, the more such connections he will be able to see;
there is no easy way to exhaust the topic, but the general pattern is clear.
And as the following chapters will show, virtually all of the elements of
Dickens' mature works are present in the *Sketches by Boz*. Perhaps the
singularly most valuable approach to the *Sketches by Boz* is one in which they
are studied as a record of Dickens' evolution towards maturity, and such
will be the concern of much of this study. But before proceeding, I should
like to make some further more general comments about these writings as a
whole and what they tell us about the youthful Dickens.

ii Some basic tendencies

These early writings make it quite clear that Dickens' initial literary
impulse was satiric. While there are certainly many instances of his other
side — his feeling and compassion, his social conscience — by and large,
the satiric mode tends to dominate these works, particularly in the first year
(1833–34) of the three-year period during which they were written.

When looked at as a whole, the writings suggest a keenly intelligent
awareness of the qualities of the world as it is, but an intelligence without a
center, a focus, a way of integrating disparate and contradictory feelings
about things. On the one hand there seems to be an outright rejection of
the formally philosophical as in the very early story "Horatio Sparkins"
where the protagonist speaks a garble of philosophic nonsense: "What! Is
effect the consequence of cause? Is cause the precursor of effect?" (*Sketches*,
p. 366). And the same character is made to look doubly the fool with his
frequent offerings of pretentious platitudes of debased romanticism:

7

[H]ow refreshing it is, to retire from the cloudy storms, the vicissitudes, and the troubles of life, even if it be but for a few short fleeting moments: and to spend those moments, fading and evanescent though they be, in the delightful, the blessed society of one individual — of* her* whose frowns would be death, whose coldness would be madness, whose falsehood would be ruin, whose constancy would be bliss; the possession of whose affection would be the brightest and best reward that Heaven could bestow on man. (*Sketches*, p. 359; *omitted from later editions)

While Dickens shows a rather pronounced antipathy to philosophical utterances, perhaps the vehemence of his condemnation reveals that he "protests too much."

"I say, we know that we exist," repeated Horatio, raising his voice, "but there we stop; there is an end to our knowledge; there is the summit of our attainments; there is the termination of our ends. What more do we know?" (Ibid., p. 360)

Such passages remind us, not only are we in the presence of a young man, but a man who is very much a product of his times. When Dickens began writing, the affirmative vision of the first quarter of the century had almost played itself out; it was yet to be replaced by that characteristically Victorian paradox of: 1) the necessity of work and duty to achieve the imminent universal blessings of progress and empire, and 2) the inevitability of social collapse and chaos in a culture that has lost its moorings. Eventually, Dickens helps forge and sustain that paradox, and many of its terms are implicit in the periodical writings of Boz.

One of the more conspicuous elements that later grows into the vision of Dickens' mature work is the general view of human character with which he begins. On the one hand he shows a very precocious sensitivity, a kind of Keatsian "negative capability" in the way that he projects himself into the situations of even the most minor and incidental characters. For instance, casually stopping to reflect on an old man whom he has described, Dickens tells us: "Altogether there was something in his manner and appearance which told us, we fancied, his whole life, or rather his whole day, for a man of this sort has no variety."[9] Here we have a straightforward and quiet recognition of the loneliness and boredom that befall the aged in an urban

---

9. "Thoughts About People," p. 216.

scene. Not a monumental insight, but certainly, like many comparable moments in the early writings, a revelation of a genuine and compassionate human feeling. But, perhaps even more frequently, in opposition to this gentle and feeling tone, Boz approaches his incidental characters with a very diminished, somewhat pathetic view of character. The people who populate these early stories and sketches are seen, not so much as "being," but as "pretending." Many of them are basically overwhelmed with their own insignificance, but attempting to carry on as though it were otherwise.

For Boz, the most typically human moments recorded in these early writings are those in which pretense is revealed, or the ubiquitous human actor is caught in his "act." So we see the bridesmaid in "Hackney Coach Stands" try to conceal the number on the door of the rental vehicle "evidently to delude pedestrians into the belief that the hackney-coach was a private carriage" (*Sketches*, p. 84); or we hear the compliments of an infant nurse prompted by the hope of gratuities (Ibid., p. 475). Elsewhere we read diatribes against those who devote time in a "contemptible attempt at imitation. . . of the enviable few who are privileged." [10] Or a supposed "old country gentleman" in "The House" is exposed as a lifetime inhabitant of urban Blackfriars. Characters are constantly being caught half-way between their "roles" and their "selves." The daughter in the family theater party that Boz describes in "Astley's" is typical. She is caught in a charade of filial gratitude "and whenever she could catch ma's eye, put her handkerchief to her mouth, and appeared, as in duty bound, to be in convulsions of laughter also" (*Sketches*, p. 106). The son is conspicuous for his fumbling attempts at overcoming adolescence: "George began to think himself quite a man now" (Ibid., p. 105). And the governess momentarily relaxes into an acceptance of her own significance. Each of these characters is seen as a self-conscious "actor" of a role.

The notions that people are actors, human action is a kind of comic drama, and everyplace is a stage, form one of the dominant motifs of these early writings. Many of the sketches and stories are devoted to theatrical topics and include scenes that take place in theatres.

Curiously, Boz seems to have a built-in ambivalence about the whole sense of theatre that pervades his writing. On the one hand he goes out of his way to parody and satirize the theatrical posture of his characters. In depicting actual theatrical scenes he finds the conventions that operate within the theatre laughably broad ones:

---

10. "London Recreations," *Evening Chronicle*, Tuesday, Mar. 17, 1835. The original "contemptible attempt at imitation" later becomes "in humble imitation."

"It is now nineteen years, my dear child, since your blessed mother (here the old villain's voice faulters) confided you to my charge. You were then an infant," &c., &c. Or else they have to discover, all of a sudden, that somebody, whom they have been in constant communication with, during three long acts, without the slightest suspicion, is their own child: in which case they exclaim, "Ah! what do I see! This bracelet! That smile! These documents!" (*Sketches*, "Astley's," p. 109)

Yet it is precisely the same kind of theatricality to which Boz turns when he wants to reach for a moment of pathos in a more serious sketch, as in the following melodramatic reconciliation scene from "Christmas Festivities."

A momentary pause succeeds; the girl breaks suddenly from her sister and throws herself, sobbing, on her mother's neck. The father steps hastily forward and takes her husband's hand. Friends crowd round to offer their hearty congratulations, and happiness and harmony again prevail. (Ibid., p. 223)

Moreover, one of Boz's basic tools of characterization is clothing — the costumes of his ubiquitous actors. From his first published story on, the minutiae of dress become very important announcements of the roles his characters are playing; and throughout his subsequent career as a novelist, Boz relies heavily on theatrical mannerisms of dress as a mainstay of characterization.

Obviously Dickens found clothing a very revealing outward emblem of the life within, sometimes fastening on the slightest details, as in the following example, to build a psychological portrait:

That young fellow in the faded brown coat, and very full light green trousers, pulls down the wristbands of his check shirt as ostentatiously as if it were of the finest linen, and cocks the white hat of the summer-before-last as knowingly over his right eye, as if it were a purchase of yesterday. (Ibid., "Astley's," p. 108)

Always a man with a sharp eye for pretentiousness, vanity, illusion, Dickens uses clothing throughout the *Sketches by Boz* as a sure index to the lies people tell themselves and the world; moreover, it is a sure record of the injustices that the world perpetrates on the meek. Finally, clothing itself becomes an embodiment of the basic patterns of existence in the sketch called "Monmouth Street," literally an "historical fabric" from which Dickens' imagination can reconstruct the sad stories of the wearers.

Dickens' awareness of clothes leads him into a remarkable range of observations, social, political, and economic. The whole world appears to have dressed-up for his revealing scrutiny. Whether it be the condemnation of desperate public drunkenness ("Seven Dials"), the sad spectre of "fallen women" ("The Prisoners' Van"), or pathetic attempts at maintaining an appearance of propriety ("Shabby-Genteel People"), Dickens is sure to find meaning in the costumes of the human actor.

iii Directions of this study

These preliminary remarks have tried to suggest some of the general relevance of the *Sketches by Boz* to Dickens' mature work. It is clear that habits of the man were present in the boy; that these early writings were "practice pieces" out of which grew an increasing accomplishment; that foreshadowings of later characters, situations and ideas can be found here. But the limitations of continuing in this vein are perhaps obvious. At best we might conclude that "Charles Dickens really always was Charles Dickens"; or we might decide the point at which he became "the real Charles Dickens."

In a sense, this study will pursue such notions, but hopefully with the kind of direction and clarity that makes them useful to the student of Dickens' work. Therefore, allowing that the *Sketches by Boz* are a clear intimation of the genius that was to become one of the world's favorite novelists, I will look at them in several different ways: 1) in relationship to comparable literature of the time; 2) as a record of Dickens' developing artistry; 3) as the embodiment of the predilections and problems that shape Dickens' later fiction — with emphasis on several of the early novels.

It would be sheer presumption to suggest that any book in this century will get to the "end" of Dickens, or even, that a book might with total satisfaction provide a description of Dickens' mature art, his "end." Such are not the intentions to be read into the subtitle of this study, *End in the Beginning*. Instead, the subtitle intends to summarize several of the theses pursued hereafter: the *Sketches by Boz* are far more important to an understanding of Dickens' art than has been generally credited. They reveal ways of looking at the world that can be called characteristically Dickensian. They provide valuable clues to the workings of many of Dickens' novels, but there will be no attempt here to discuss all the novels. Hopefully, however, the reader will be able to apply the conclusions herein to a richer understanding of all Dickens' novels.

George Cruikshank.

Mr. Minns and His Cousin

CHAPTER TWO
DICKENS AND THE SHORT STORY

i Prevailing assumptions about Sketches by Boz

DICKENS CRITICS tacitly assume that "Boz" the short story writer is identical with "Boz" the sketcher, who eventually becomes "Boz" the novelist. But in back of this assumption lurks a highly relevant though unexplored question: Is it possible that a novice author would attempt in all the multiplicity of situations to write in a single and sustained voice? Or might he use his various publication outlets to explore and experiment with his literary talents? Before the completion of his twenty-fourth year Dickens was writing in two genres, publishing in six different periodicals under two pen-names, as well as publishing anonymously. But if only by default, twentieth-century criticism has endorsed the first possibility, i.e. the various Boz's are identical. The highly informative differences of style, voice, and technique discernible in Dickens' early work have been overlooked, primarily because Dickens' gathering, editing, and re-arrangement of the original papers has covered up many of their most interesting features.

The standard edition of the *Sketches by Boz* (which follows the order of the 1850 "cheap edition") obscures the potential value of *Sketches by Boz* as a record of Dickens' first three years as a writer. The *Sketches by Boz* known to most readers are four revisions and fifteen years away from the originals. Even reconsidering the original versions of the papers in order of their publication chronologically does not entirely clarify the problems created by their gathering in book form. Central to understanding the relationship between *Sketches by Boz* and later Dickens is the recognition that the omnibus title brings together writings published in *different periodicals*, at *different times*. Most importantly, the *Sketches by Boz* are works written in two different genres, *short story* and *sketch*. Dickens' *sketches* purport to describe actual places, events, institutions, and occasions, without any plot or sustained focus on real or imagined characters. His *short stories* are papers written as fiction, presenting real or imagined characters in a plot. Since Dickens published short stories for almost a year before he began publishing sketches, it is Dickens the short story writer who tells us most about the first stage of his career. Most importantly, we need to see the beginning of that career in its historical perspective; we need to understand what kinds of short stories were being published at the time.

ii Boz and the fiction of his day

A perusal of the kinds of fiction being published in 1833–34 lends credence to Dickens' report that "stealthily, one evening at twilight, with fear and trembling," he dropped the manuscript for his first published work "into a dark letter-box in a dark office up a dark court in Fleet Street." [1] The stealth, fear, and trembling were all appropriate, for Dickens must have known how different his story was, both in subject matter and technique, from the kinds of stories being published in current periodicals.

Looking at a variety of periodicals from 1833–34, we find that the Scotch-Irish adventure story seems to have been particularly popular, with such magazines as *Blackwood's* and *Fraser's* featuring an abundance of titles which blend into a fuzzy, romantic, Scotsian haze: "Nora Boyle," "Shane O'Neill's Last Amour," "The Castle Elmere," [2] "The Extraordinary History of a Border Beauty." [3]

Elsewhere the romantic thrust of early Victorian short story literature shows itself in a variety of topics. Young ladies of all ages and places have sighed over stories like "The Baronet's Bride." As we might expect, the currents of the more important and innovative literature of the previous fifty years were still playing themselves out in the almost sub-literary voices of the short story. Thus there are a number of stories that approach the Gothic, such as "The Student Morgenstern, A Tale of Berne," and many stories that continue to promote the cult of near-eastern orientalism such as "A Visit to Ibrahim Pacha" and "A Remarkable Egyptian Story." Stories about the continent are very frequent, with preferences seeming to run to the polarities of warm, sunny Italy ("La Guglielma of Milan") and cold

---

1. Charles Dickens, *The Posthumous Papers of the Pickwick Club*, preface to the first "cheap edition" (1847; rpt. London: Oxford University Press, 1948), p. xi.
2. *Blackwood's Magazine*, Sept. 1833, p. 344; Feb. 1834, pp. 249–66; Mar. 1834, p. 353.
3. *Fraser's*, Jan. 1834, pp. 97–110.

austere Germany ("The Prussian Gentleman"). The sea as a subject is put to a variety of uses; on the one hand it leads to swashbuckling adventure stories such as "Freya the Fearless: The Black Buccaneer of Barbadoes;" on the other hand it becomes the vehicle for the domestic-political travelogue as in "A Seascape." [4]

Strikingly, there are very few stories that have a subject matter similar to Dickens' first stories. British periodicals in 1833–34 have very few stories of middle-class people living in contemporary London or even England. In contrast, these are precisely the kinds of stories that Dickens began with: "A Dinner at Poplar Walk," "Mrs. Joseph Porter 'over the way.'" Dickens seems to have re-discovered the British scene as a fitting subject for short fiction.

Dickens' letters of the period suggest that the predilection for British subjects was quite conscious on his part. About the time he had written more than two-thirds of the papers later gathered in *Sketches by Boz*, he wrote to J. P. Hullah, politely refusing to collaborate on a "Venetian" drama which would have catered to the popular exoticism of the day:

> What I am anxious to suggest to you is, the expediency of dropping the Venetian idea altogether, and making the Drama an *English* one. (my italics)

Dickens goes on to insist that he cannot please himself with any of the sketches he has made for the Venetian subject. Continuing in a slightly nostalgic vein, he makes his preference for English, everyday subjects quite clear:

> And remembering the popularity and beauty of many of the old english [sic] Operas I am strongly prejudiced in favor of a simple rural story. . . . [Consider] the increased ease and effect with which we could both work on an English Drama where the characters would act and talk like people we see and hear every day, and I think you will be of my opinion. [5]

Yet it is not only in his choice of subject, but also in his treatment of

---

4. These stories appeared in the following newspapers, respectively: *Blackwood's*, Jan. 1834, pp. 81–121; *Fraser's*, Mar. 1833, pp. 268–80; *Metropolitan Magazine* 9, Jan. 1834, pp. 91–96; *Fraser's*, Feb. 1833, pp. 147–57; Ibid., Aug. 1834, pp. 173–83; *Monthly Magazine*, Feb. 1833, pp. 273–76; *Metropolitan* 10, 1834: May, pp. 107–12 and June, pp. 349–52.

5. Charles Dickens, *The Letters of Charles Dickens*, vol. 1, 1820–1839, ed. Madeline House and Graham Storey (London, 1965), p. 113, 29 December 1835.

it that Dickens' first published pieces stand apart from the work of his contemporaries. Dickens always writes about his ordinary, everyday English characters from an omniscient and implicitly third-person point of view. In other contemporary authors, when we do find stories that treat contemporary Londoners (or Englishmen), most of the stories are written in the first person.

The simplicity of the categories — contemporary England and third person narrative — is entirely appropriate to the starkness with which Dickens' narrative techniques stand out from the techniques of the vast majority of his contemporaries. One need only look at the periodical fiction to be convinced of this. In turning the pages of *Blackwood's, Fraser's, Gentleman's Magazine, Monthly Magazine, New Monthly Magazine, The Mirror, The Penny Magazine*, the dominant preference for first-person narrative quickly emerges.

Of course there are thousands of pieces of contemporary short fiction that I would need to examine in order to make any rigorous and binding statements about the genre; and though such a detailed investigation goes beyond the purposes and intentions of this study, my conclusion which draws on a decade of short fiction in some of the leading magazines can be demonstrated by some observations about the fiction to be found in a typical middle-range magazine such as the *Metropolitan*.

A reading of all of the short fiction published in the *Metropolitan* during the years 1833–34, the years when Dickens began publishing, tells us the following: The *Metropolitan* published fifty-five pieces of short fiction during the two-year period. Of these, thirty-six stories, roughly 66%, are written in the first person; eighteen stories, roughly 34%, are written in the third person; only six stories, or a little more than 15% of the total, can qualify as being even remotely like Dickens' stories in their British middle-class subjects, in urban settings, told with a third-person technique. And even these similarities fade away when the contents of the stories — events, characters, situations — are examined more closely.

In an attempt to isolate the real differences between Dickens' early short stories and so much of the contemporary short fiction, let us consider the differences between the third-person narratives about middle-class urban characters that were published in our sampling of the *Metropolitan* (cited in parentheses), and Dickens' stories about the same kinds of characters in a similar narrative pattern. Unlike "The Divine Georgiana" (7, Sept. 1833, pp. 10–17) and "The Wedding Garment," (10, May 1834, pp. 143–53), both of which treat the ascension of middle-class girls to the position of "Lady," none of Dickens' stories treat such romantic-fantasy themes at all seriously. His characters always begin and end somewhere in the middle class. Though the characters in "Job Humanitas" (8, Dec. 1833, pp. 404–12) might find a place in the Dickens story world, their conduct in this story is entirely too risqué to gain admission there. (The story involves the accidental "bedding" of an unmarried couple who force Job to provide a dowry for the lady, since it was Job's attempt to rescue them from their drunkenness that brought them to bed.) Similarly, the realistic insistence in the title "Maria Hammond, A Tale of Real Life," (10, May 1934, pp. 143–52) suggests its difference from the deliberate fictive stylization of Dickens' stories, just as the subject, a story of an infamous woman, distinguishes itself from the total moral propriety of Dickens' subjects. Nor does Dickens ever try to write a serious-sentimental love story of a type like "The Physician's Visit" (8, Dec. 1833, pp. 404–12). Perhaps "Bachelor Sam" (8, Sept. 1833, pp. 162–70), a story of a bachelor who marries his cook, comes closest to being like a Dickens story; in fact Dickens tells the same story in "Love and Oysters"[6]; but whereas the author here seems to be pointing to the uniqueness of the situation, pleading the pathos and sadness caused by the events, Dickens treats the story as a laughable example of a contemporary stereotype.[7]

At the risk of being overly specific, the preceding descriptions of the kinds of fiction written about English middle-class characters, from the third-person point of view, and published in the *Metropolitan* during the first two years of Dickens career, do give us several distinctions that help put Dickens stories in perspective: 1) They are never romantic, and usually satiric; 2) their subjects are always "proper"; 3) their focus is never on the extraordinary person or event, but always on the common, familiar, mundane, and trivial. Here perhaps is Dickens' chief distinction from his contemporaries: his subjects are uncommon in their commonness.

iii The formula of Dickens' first stories

A close look at Dickens' first story will give us a clearer understanding of his first writings. "A Dinner at Poplar Walk," which was first published in *The Monthly Magazine*, December, 1833, is a very simple piece indeed:

An ordinary prim Civil Servant goes to visit his vulgar cousin and their unpleasing brat, his godson; dislikes them, wishes he had

---

6. The story was subsequently called "The Misplaced Attachment." Chapter three of this study discusses "Love and Oysters" in some length.

7. References in parentheses are all to *Metropolitan Magazine*.

obeyed his instincts and not gone to Poplar Walk at all, misses his coach home, and alters his will.[8]

In all its simplicity, the story does tell us much about where Dickens began and what he wanted to say. It points to the relationship between character and structure that shapes much of Dickens' fiction, particularly these first stories. Structurally the story has six parts. Since the same parts re-occur with only slight variation in many of Dickens' early short stories, they are worth considering in some detail.

PART I: THE CHARACTER SKETCH, IDIOSYNCRASY AS THESIS.

The first of these recurring parts is the character sketch of the protagonist, in this case, Augustus Minns. Minns, like most of the characters in the early stories and even many of those in the novels, has very few character traits. Minns is a bachelor of "about forty," a "clerk in Somerset House," the "most retiring man in the world," "very precise," "and tidy" (Sketches, p. 312). With these few details, Dickens has exhausted Minns' character. The protagonist is a stereotype of a familiar kind of priggish, fastidious bachelor.

The striking thing about Minns and the other characters who inhabit this story is that they have an existence as *ideas* prior to their existence as characters. The ideas they represent always surmount and precede any dramatic representation of the ideas. Thus, once Dickens' narrator has advanced the idea "Mr. Minns was very clean, precise and tidy," an unlimited number of observations can be marshalled in evidence of his hyperfastidiousness. And Dickens proceeds to give them to us: he wore "a frockcoat without a wrinkle," "light inexplicables without a spot," and a "neat neckerchief with a remarkably neat tie." Because Dickens belabors Minns' compulsive neatness, the stereotype acquires a peculiar vitality: the reader if he wishes can extend the notion of neatness *ad infinitum*. We all know and feel that Minns undoubtedly wore black patent leathers polished to a blaze, and a high white collar, starched to perfection and so on. Dickens need not tell us.

In effect, Dickens' ability to establish the idiosyncratic stereotype, and our ability to extend it, places character idiosyncrasy at the center of

---

8. The summary is from F. J. Harvey Darton's *Dickens, Positively the First Appearance*, p. 71. Darton summarizes the story in its revised form, even though the primary purpose of his book was to reprint the original story. In the original, Minns changes his residence, but there is no mention of a changed will.

the story. Idiosyncrasy becomes a kind of thesis out of which the story will evolve.

PART 2: COUNTERING-AGENTS TO CHARACTER IDIOSYNCRASY AS ANTITHESIS.

The story advances with the logic of a dialectic. Where character has been contracted into an idiosyncratic obsession for neatness, the surest and simplest way of generating a semblance of dramatic conflict arises out of the introduction of characters and situations antithetic to such neatness. In Dickens' first story, as in subsequent stories, the antithesis is given very explicit formulation:

> [Minns] had but two particular horrors in the world, and those were dogs and children. His prejudice arose from no unamiability of disposition, but that the habits of the animals were continually at variance with his love of order, which might be said to be equally as powerful as his love of life.[9]

The reader immediately recognizes that by a process of fictive logic Minns will be faced with dogs, children, and general violations of his compulsive need for order. Thus structurally the second part of the story is a dialectical response to the first.

With Minns firmly in mind, we are introduced to his antithesis in the persons of his cousins, the Bagshaws.[10] Though the quality of the Bagshaws' counter-idiosyncrasy is not explicitly described, we do get a foreshadowing of their eventual violation of Minns' fastidiousness. Mrs. Bagshaw closes the second scene with ominous instructions to her son: "Alick my dear, take your legs off the rail of the chair."

PART 3: THE PRELIMINARY ENCOUNTER.

The third part of the story brings the characters together, attempting an abortive synthesis of the antithetical characters. Since the characters have

---

9. "A Dinner at Poplar Walk," *Monthly Magazine*, Dec. 1833, XVI, p. 617. The story was radically revised for inclusion in the Second Series. In later editions Minns is described: "There were two classes of created objects which he held in the deepest and most unmingled horror; these were dogs, and children. He was not unamiable, but he could at any time, have viewed the execution of a dog, or the assassination of an infant, with the liveliest satisfaction. Their habits were at variance with his love of order; and his love of order was as powerful as his love of life" (see *Sketches*, p. 312).

10. After the original publication in the *Monthly Magazine*, Dickens changed the cousin's name from Bagshaw to Buddens. Kathleen Tillotson, with John Butt, explains the change in *Dickens at Work*, p. 52.

such shallow dimensions, the only available matter for their encounter must be the conflict of their idiosyncrasies. Bagshaw must be sloppy where Minns is neat, boisterous and vulgar where Minns is quiet and decorous, aspiring and pretentious where Minns is self-effacing but arrogantly modest. Accordingly, Bagshaw enters and violates Minns' fastidious world in the following ways: he pays a call at breakfast, unannounced; sends in a diminutive calling card engraved with indecorously large print; comes up to the breakfast room without waiting to be ushered in by the servant; announces his hunger, invites himself to breakfast, and orders Minns to send for more food; he dusts his road-dirtied boots with a table napkin; brags about his house immodestly; cuts the ham in the wrong way, in "utter violation of all established rules"; he requests (rather than waits to be offered) more tea and sugar; and finally demands that his cousin come to dinner on Sunday, punctually at five.

As if this were not enough, Minns' annoyance is increased by the presence of his cousin's large, uncouth dog. In terms of the story-structure the dog discharges the obligation established in making dogs one of Minns' "particular horrors," part of the counter-idiosyncrasy. Thus the dog also proceeds to violate Minns' fastidiousness by standing

> with his hind-legs on the floor, and his forepaws resting on the table [and] dragging a bit of bread and butter out of a plate, preparatory to devouring it, with the buttered side next the carpet. (*Sketches*, p. 314)

The dog then spoils Minns' curtains, and when finally placed on the landing outside the door maintains an "appalling howling." At this point it should be painfully clear that Dickens' first story shows a real inventiveness in making the same point over and again. The incessant violations of Minns' compulsive need for order are the only action of the story thus far. Yet, for all its seeming redundancy the story escapes being entirely heavy-handed through deftness and compression. Though Dickens only has one point, he succeeds in engaging us through his ability to re-make that point in a dazzling number of ways.

PART 4: FORESHADOWING THE CLIMAX.

Thus far the development of the story has followed an almost inevitable pattern. The fourth part, however, is more arbitrarily related to the obligatory story considerations. Here Dickens chooses to delay the climax of the story by tracing the protagonist's journey to his fateful dinner engagement. In a number of stories Dickens uses either an aside on transportation or a commentary on street activity as a prelude to the climax. In this particular instance, Mr. Minns' obsession for order continues to be at variance with the ways of the world. He boards a coach, anticipates departure in three minutes, and is forced to suffer a quarter-hour's wait followed by three successive five-minute delays. His anxieties are increased by the arrival of new passengers, a mother and her son; the boy proceeds to wipe his shoes on Minns' "new drab trousers" thereby engaging Minns' second "particular horror," children.

PART 5: THE DRAMATIC CLIMAX.

The fifth part of the story is conceived of as the climax and grand encounter between Dickens' opposing parties. Since Dickens has thoroughly worked Minns' fastidiousness in prior scenes, much of the climactic scene is given to exploiting Minns' only other characteristic, the pretentious decorum of the "most retiring man in the world." The scene opens with a description of the Bagshaw house and its too obvious aspirations to elegance, all of which are undercut by its diminutiveness. Coerced by his vulgar cousins, Minns is made to play the social lion to the dozen assembled guests. (In a manner that reveals the novice author at work, significantly, only two of these guests are given names, and none of them is given even the slightest degree of characterization. They exist as a backdrop for the encounter between the opposing parties.) Minns, despite his "position in Somerset House," i.e., clerk, embarrassedly disclaims any knowledge of whether or not "the ministers will go out." The company proceeds to a "usual dinner" at which Minns suffers the inflated praises and empty toasts of both Bagshaw and his friends; he finally musters the courage for a reply. He endures the performance of his godson Alick, who, after reciting on cue, smears his godfather with jam and reveals his parents' ulterior motive in courting their cousin Minns: "Ma says I am to coax you to leave me all your money."

PART 6: THE NARRATIVE ANTI-CLIMAX.

The sixth and final part of the story shows a shift in technique. Where the preceding parts were at least in some degree dramatic, relying on dialogue and culminating in the climactic revelation of the Bagshaws' ulterior motives, the final part is the narrator's very rapid summary of the ensuing action. Minns leaves precipitiously, having been offered the last remaining seat in the last coach to town. He misses the coach, walks home arriving at three A.M., is thoroughly soaked by rain, and subsequently changes his residence in order to evade his relatives.[11] The comparable technique of ending with a narrative summary runs all the way through both Dickens' stories and novels.

In all, "A Dinner at Poplar Walk" demonstrates a relationship between character and structure which also runs through Dickens' stories and well into his novels. Dickens begins with an abstract, stereotyped character. A frustration of the character's personal idiosyncrasies provides the matter for the story. Because Dickens relies entirely on character-idiosyncrasy to generate action and to create structure for his stories, these first stories have almost no plot. The stories are concerned with the ludicrous catastrophes that arise out of the clash of antithetical idiosyncrasies.

If we turn to a consideration of what is said in this first story, we find that in many ways it anticipates ideas, subjects, and attitudes Dickens was to treat in subsequent stories as well as the novels. Preciousness, excessive fastidiousness, pretentiousness, false decorum are frequent objects of satire in both early and later Dickens. The first ten stories (and in a way all of the stories published in *Sketches by Boz*) are concerned with these qualities.

The characters, their actions and preoccupations, their configurations with respect to one another all anticipate later work. For instance, if we look on Mr. Minns as an uncle-figure who frustrates his relatives' plans, we find him very soon reappearing in Dickens' second published story, "Mrs. Joseph Porter 'over-the-way,'" and again in the fourth published story as the dour, sardonic uncle-godfather in the "Bloomsbury Christening," and again in the sixth story as the uncle of the late Mr. Bloss, in "The Boarding House," Chapter II.

The arrangement of the characters with respect to one another and to the central conflict, i.e., the configuration of the uncle and the prospect of disinheritance which occurs in this first story, can be said to be only one satiric-ironic dimension removed from the melodramatic plights of the waifs of the novels. Oliver without parents in captive hands, Nicholas Nickleby without his patrimony, Little Nell banished from the Curiosity Shop, are in a sense the serious versions of the disinheritance we see in Dickens' very first story. A rigorously psychological study of this first story might show that it is in essence a sublimated version of the configuration that was later to fascinate Dickens so.

---

11. In Dickens' 1836 revision for the Second Series of *Sketches by Boz*, Minns immediately changes his will, cutting off his relatives, but there is no mention of a change of residence, cf. *Sketches*, p. 322.

In a less speculative vein, however, Alick Bagshaw in this first story is quite clearly the direct ancestor of Dickens' child heroes. His linguistic and social ingenuousness are more than a faint anticipation of his most famous descendant, Pip. Alick, like Pip, has "expectations," though much diminished. And again, his performance for the dinner guests has its counterpart in Pip's performance for Pumblechook. It recalls children throughout the novels who are required to make similar displays and answer their elders' inane questions. Alick is also the first in the line of children who have difficulty with the ambiguities of the English language: "Alick . . . tell me the meaning of *be*." "Be?" said the prodigy, after a little hesitation — "an insect that gathers honey."

Another detail of the first story, the vacuous toasts of the dinner guests, and the dinner scene itself, is played over and again throughout the stories and the novels. Dickens devotes a whole sketch to "Public Dinners" fairly early in his career, and his delight in satirizing the meaningless noise of dinner speakers moves through *Pickwick Papers* to *Our Mutual Friend*, resplendent in the clicking of Podsnappery.

Given the fact that *Sketches by Boz* is a collection of fifty-nine separate papers, perhaps the repetition of characters, structures, incidents and configurations is more or less inevitable. Similarly, it appears only natural that some of these materials would re-appear in the novels. Most likely the number of this kind of correspondences has precluded any really thorough study of them. But the important observations about this first story really reside in how, in all its simplicity and redundancy, it foreshadows both typical Dickensian subject matter and technique.

iv Repeating the formula

Dickens' second, third, and fourth published stories do show him working with the same story elements in much the same pattern. However, some of the differences that occur in these stories reveal Dickens' very rapid development of more sophisticated techniques in telling a story. For instance, from the second story on, Dickens was careful to allow for some dramatic exposition of character before his narrator summarizes it. In several of the stories the dramatic exposition is accomplished by placing the foreshadowing scene (Part 4, in the analysis of Dickens' first story) very near to the opening of the story. Thus, though the narrator's pronouncements of character are just as explicit in later stories as they were in the first story, the reader has a chance to experience the character's idiosyncrasies before being *told* them. Dickens is learning to *show*.

As in the first story, characterization through idiosyncrasy continues to operate as a *thesis* for the story; concomitantly, Dickens is always careful to give an explicit antithesis for each character. Thus, in the second story, "Mrs. Joseph Porter 'over-the-way,'" the Gattleton family is entirely given to the achievement of social success. But, Mrs. Gattleton's antithesis is so baldly stated as to suggest a novice author using formulas to write stories. Mrs. Gattleton fears three things: 1) other people's unmarried daughters, 2) ridicule in any form, and 3) Mrs. Joseph Porter over-the-way. With these announcements the fate of the amateur theatrical around which the story revolves becomes quite clear. It will necessarily be a continuous embarrassment arising from the three named antithetical elements which she fears. Similarly, in the third story, "Horatio Sparkins," the Malderton family fears "anything low," thereby requiring that their fate take the form of embarrassment through something low. Thus the starry-eyed Malderton girls and their aspiring mother are forced into a painful confrontation with their princely romantic ideal, Horatio Sparkins, who turns out to be a partner and assistant in a contemptible "cheap shop."

But by the fourth published story, "The Bloomsbury Christening," we begin to see a less formulary use of the antithesis. As in previous stories Dickens assigns his protagonist, a misanthropic Mr. Dumps, a very explicit series of antitheses: children, cabs, and doors that will not close. True to form, the story shows Mr. Dumps being annoyed by each of these things he despises. But Dickens' use of these elements reveals precisely how he has grown as a story teller. The series of annoyances is no longer at center of the story as it was in the first story. Instead, Dickens uses the antitheses and the annoyances they produce to fill out his plot rather than to make the point of his story. The real point of the story revolves around the opposition between Mr. Dumps' sardonic misanthropy and his nephew's simpering gullibility.

From the second story on, another move towards mature techniques is apparent in Dickens' improved ability in sharpening the focus of his climactic scenes. In the first story, Mr. Minns and his vulgar cousins play out their counter-annoyance against the vague background of a dozen anonymous, dramatically unrealized "guests." But from the second story on Dickens is careful in setting the climactic events against a background of more concrete characters. If there are new characters in the climactic scene, the reader is already familiar with them before important events begin. Thus in the second story, Mrs. Porter and the Gattleton's Uncle Tom provide a counterpoint of satiric exposure to the vain pretensions of the amateur theatrical at the Gattleton's. Significantly, Dickens makes the motives of the two exposing characters quite different. Mrs. Porter's exposures of the farce at the Gattleton's are calculated and aggressively spiteful, while Uncle Tom's exposures are innocent and unknowing. The effect is quite complex with both the accidental and intentional exposures combining to increase the over-all satiric thrust of the story.

Similarly in the third story Dickens uses the identical technique, focussing the crucial scene by entrapping the objects of the satire in the crossfire of different characters, only here he adds a third speaker. One of the speakers, Flamwell, exposes both himself and the Maldertons by catering to their social climbing; he foolishly puffs up Horatio Sparkins, implying that Horatio is a nobleman *incognito*. On the opposite side, the Maldertons' shopkeeper cousin continues their exposure by juxtaposing their pretentiousness to his own mercantile crudity. Meanwhile the simple honesty of the Maldertons' younger son, whom all the Maldertons dismiss as grossly inept and retarded, negotiates between the satiric polarities, excessive inflation and deflation, of the other speakers; he sees Horatio for what he is, a rather conceited unremarkable pretender.

In a very few months as a publishing author of short stories Dickens had learned a considerable amount; he had learned to allow for a dramatic exposition of character; he had learned to handle several concrete characters simultaneously; he had learned how to add depth to his satire through the juxtaposition of several points of view.

v Moving beyond the formula

By the time Dickens published his fifth story, "The Boarding House," Chapter I, he achieved a level of technical finesse which in some respects he was never to surpass throughout the remaining stories in *Sketches by Boz*. Although the story uses elements and techniques that Dickens had experimented with in the previous four stories, nowhere else does he exceed the complexity of structure or the economical compression attained here.

To some extent, all of the first four stories rely on direct retribution of character idiosyncrasy for their structure. In the first Mr. Minns' fastidiousness and false modesty become vehicles for his discomfiture. In the second, the Gattletons' social pretensions turn back on them in the abortive theatrical; in the third, Horatio Sparkins proves to be unspeakably low, thereby frustrating the Maldertons' aspirations. The fourth story begins to move away from the formula, but by the fifth story Dickens is really capable of structuring a story that does not simply rest on the negation of his characters' idiosyncrasies. Because "The Boarding House" represents a significant advance in technique, it is worth considering in some detail.

It opens with the introduction of Mr. and Mrs. Tibbs and their idiosyncrasies. She is distinguished by her fastidiousness, he, by his hen-pecked introversion. Because of his wife's aggressive dominance, Mr. Tibbs has never finished telling his only army story. If Dickens had not pro-gressed considerably by the time he wrote this story, we might have here another version of his first story. Since Mrs. Tibbs shares the obsessive fastidiousness of Dickens' first character Minns, the whole action might have consisted of an elaborate and farcical dirtying of the Tibbs' house, and the perpetual forestalling of Mr. Tibbs' anecdote. Instead, although idiosyncrasy continues to be the chief element in characterization, here idiosyncratic characterization ceases to be the dictator of story structure.

Following the presentation of the Tibbs and their background Dick-ens introduces a plot element that changes the story structure radically. At the tail-end of a scene in which the Tibbs dramatize their idiosyncrasies — she worries about tidiness, he tries to tell his story — Mr. Tibbs comments on the pleasant and natural possibility of a marriage taking place between their newly acquired boarders. Mrs. Tibbs is horrified by the suggestion. The reader immediately recognizes the suggestion of marriage as a foreshadowing of the climax. In this respect "The Boarding House" is like the previous stories; but structurally there is an important difference. The story must now move away from a focus on the Tibbs' idiosyncratic charac-ters.

In a sense the story closes off the Tibbs from any willful participation in their own fate. They become a kind of frame for the action that will eventually turn back on them. Instead of foreshadowing retribution for the Tibbs' personal idiosyncrasies, the action turns to foreshadowing the in-evitability of marriage amongst the boarders. With an innovative spurt, in very short order, Dickens introduces six new characters into his story. In keeping with his already established manner of characterization, each character has a conspicuous idiosyncrasy. Although the preceding stories show Dickens introducing new characters into the middle of his stories, partly to relieve the monotony of his characterization, and partly to extend the range of the satire, this is the first time that the new characters monopolize the action so completely. Further, instead of serving mainly to continue the exposure of the protagonists, here they act as fully as the protagonists themselves.

The introduction of the new characters is accomplished with consider-able more grace than in earlier stories. Although Dickens continues to have stereotypes in mind for each character, the actual narrative presentation of the stereotype in a character sketch is much less intrusive than formerly. When the sketches are presented, they are different from his earliest manner of presentation in one of two ways: 1) Before summarizing the characters' idiosyncrasies he allows us to experience them dramatically; such is the case with Mrs. Mapleson's hovering-mother anxieties, her daughters' maiden romanticisms, Mr. Calton's superannuated vanities. 2) Or, Dickens presents the formal character sketch parenthetically, following a short dramatic introduction of the character which may for the time being skirt his idiosyncrasy entirely; such is the case with Mr. Hick's obsession with *Don Juan*, and Mr. Simpson's preoccupation with fashion.

The story drives towards assembling the diverse cast in an hilarious dinner scene. Structurally the scene corresponds to the *climactic* scene in earlier stories. But whereas the comparable scenes in previous stories are an end in themselves, here, the scene is a prelude to the increasing complication of plot. Probably the best of its kind in Dickens' early work, the dinner scene satirizes the pathetic attempts at conversation among the Boarding House tenants. Missed conversational connections, embarrassing silences, trivially inflated egos, attempts at "one-upmanship," namedropping, all of the inanities of "polite conversation" are excoriatingly satirized as the assembled characters each dramatize their own idiosyncrasies. Mrs. Tibbs vainly tries to maintain the pretence of elegance and abundance in the face of her sparsely furnished table; she is forced to cope with a husband and servant who are too unsophisticated to aid her in masking her stinginess. The Mapleson girls present an absurdly exaggerated facade of female delicacy while their anxious mother works full time at promoting their already too obvious eligibility. Mr. Hicks persists in quoting *Don Juan*, the only book he has ever read. Mr. Simpson shows that his fashionable foppishness is the extent of his character or interests, and Mr. Calton "knocks" his way through dinner, punctuating the conversation with meaningless interjections which reveal his tenuous contact with the world and the conversation. Poor Mr. Tibbs vainly finds an oblique opening for his single anecdote, only to lose it in the conversational crosscurrents.

In its brevity, this scene demonstrates the ground that Dickens had covered in his first six months of publication. With less than a thousand words he is able to separate and dramatize the disjunctive idiosyncrasies of nine different characters. The scene has the quality of an abortive attempt at musical harmony, the separate idiosyncratic voices of the characters aspiring to a harmony they are incapable of, ironically verifying the solipsistic limitations of the human state where the equivalent of music is at best a raucous simultaneity.

Part of the excellence of this scene derives from the fact that Dickens' writing is cumulative. Some of the elements he uses here had been introduced in previous stories. For example, this was the fourth time, out of a total of five stories thus far published, that he had worked with a dinner scene. Similarly, his ability to work with three varieties of bachelors in this story must in part derive from the fact that the idiosyncrasies of bachelors had made up parts of all the first four stories. Or again, the finesse in handling the anxious mother must flow from his use of the same stereotype in his second, third, and fourth stories.

Very small details that in previous stories might have made for an aside by the story's narrator reappear in this story. And Dickens reaps comedy from his earlier sowing. For instance, the narrator in the fourth story, "The Bloomsbury Christening," offers the following comment on the eating habits of the guests at the christening party:

> The young ladies didn't eat much for fear it shouldn't look romantic, and the married ladies ate as much as possible for fear they shouldn't have enough. (*Sketches*, p. 481)

In turn, part of the same idea recurs in the dinner scene of the "Boarding House," the next story:

> "Miss Julia, shall I assist you to some fish?"
> "If you please — very little — oh! plenty, thank you"
> (a bit about the size of a walnut put upon the plate). (Ibid., p. 282)

A similar overhauling of details occurs throughout the stories by Boz.

In contrast, the other highly successful scene in "The Boarding House" derives little from the stories Dickens had already written. It has a very strong echo of Restoration comedies and probably reflects, at least in its content, what were still current motifs in drawing-room comedy. Dickens' narrator rushes us from the dinner to a scene that supposedly takes place six months later. The scene deals with the secret marriage plans, mistaken identities, confusion of partners that are so common in Restoration comedy. It opens with Mr. Calton and Mr. Hicks very gingerly broaching the topic of marriage, only to find that they both plan to marry Matilda Mapleson the following day — an impossible situation that resolves itself in their realization that they are talking about different Maplesons, mother and daughter. With much circumspection, Calton and Hicks request that Mr. Tibbs act the father for the marriages. Abashed at Tibbs' whimsical nonchalance toward the impending secret marriages, Calton and Hicks discover that they have been talking at cross-purposes with Tibbs; he has confused their marriages with the impending third marriage between Mr. Simpson and Julia Mapleson. They are left with the bizarre circumstance of three marriages apparently secretly and independently planned for the same day. The story ends with the narrator's explanation of the coincidences — conspiracy among the women — and his rapid summary of the disastrous outcome of the marriages. None of them is remotely successful. The Tibbs' boarding house has been emptied, and they must begin anew.

In all, Dickens' development in six months as a short story writer is impressive. His increasing reliance on dialogue in "The Boarding House" results in a greater dramatic integrity in both the presentation of characters and the working of the plot. The story shows a relaxation of the formula that had controlled the first four stories. Dickens learns to substitute a daring diversity of characters for the redundancy of incident that had marred the first few stories. Here for the first time Dickens comes close to his mature comic statements in which the comedy arises from the disjunctive encounters, the potential union that never succeeds among characters who occupy different worlds. The Tibbs, the bachelors, the Mapleson women, never really understand how their solipsistic limitations and their abortive conspiracies have mis-fired into the absurdities of their fates.

Yet even despite his accomplishment here, Dickens is still very much an apprentice writer. He has not yet learned to suppress his frequently obtrusive witticisms. More importantly, he does not really know how to effect fluid transitions between scenes and across time. The "Boarding House" rather glaringly exposes the author's uneven accomplishment. The two great scenes are spliced together with very awkward narrative transitions. Nevertheless, though some of the later stories are more graceful in the writer's chores of moving characters around, opening and closing scenes, and generally creating a fluid story line, the later stories are not necessarily better. "The Boarding House" gains in energy what it lacks in fluidity. The angular joints of its structure make for a more startling display of Dickens' early genius than the more smoothly structured stories that were to follow it within a year. Most importantly, in "The Boarding House" we see Dickens working with his earliest imaginative forte: building a story out of a variety of idiosyncratic characters who are immeshed in a complicated plot that ends in comic catastrophe for all.

Though a scrutiny of the techniques in Dickens' first published stories reveals his rapid growth as a literary craftsman, comparable consideration of the "world" of these stories suggests almost a stasis. The world of the earliest stories in *Sketches by Boz* is the same as the world in the latest ones. Most significantly the characteristics of that world are very much like those in the world of myth, as the next section of this study shall demonstrate.

Mr. John Dounce at the Oyster-Shop

CHAPTER THREE
A HOLLOW
MYTHIC WORLD

i. Defining mythic literature

Perhaps a discussion of mythic elements in Dickens' early writings can be given the clearest rendering by carefully tying this elusive subject to one of the more thorough critical discussions of it. Ernst Cassirer's volume, *Mythical Thought* (p. 21),* describes the epistemological principles that support primitive myths. Cassirer explains the differences between two kinds of consciousness: 1) the primitive "mythical consciousness" versus 2) the modern "empirical" (or "rational" or "scientific") consciousness. In effect Cassirer's discussion produces a dichotomy between epistemology of primitive peoples as derived from their literatures (oral and written), and epistemology based on empirical data. Cassirer's concerns are epistemology and "consciousness," not literature *per se*. But his discussion provides an interesting framework for looking at literature. Implicit within Cassirer's discussion is the notion that all literature will remain by its very nature on the mythic side of the dichotomy "mythic versus scientific." But within the category of the "mythic" we can point to a continuum which runs, at one extreme, from literature dependent on a primitive "mythic" epistemology to literature, at the opposite extreme, that takes cognizance of a more "empirical" or "scientific" view of the world.

Cassirer explains that both modes of consciousness, the empirical and the mythical, are obliged to arrive at some coherent explanation or description of the physical world, to reformulate and order a "rhapsody" of perceptions into a coherent way of looking at the world. Cassirer contends that

* *The Philosophy of Symbolic Forms, Vol. II.*

each consciousness has its own way of representing reality and in its own way provides an explanation for it. There are two chief categories which separate the mythic from the empirical mode of consciousness: 1) the way in which each consciousness attempts to assimilate the object, and 2) the way in which each mode explains causality.

According to Cassirer, the *mythic view* of the world is dominated by a fascination with the object, *per se*. Although the *empirical view* of the world begins with the perception of the object, the whole point of the empirical view of reality is to isolate, abstract, and intercalate the various constant qualities of the object world that will allow us eventually to apprehend the more permanent and unvariable aspects of reality, that is, the empirical reality. In doing this, an empirical view of the world ceases to contemplate the object in and of itself and by eliminating the arbitrary, temporary, and accidental traits and occurrences, seeks to establish a clear and consistent notion of the object, and seeks to relate it to other objects that constitute reality. In opposition, the mythic view of the world is dominated by the arbitrary, accidental, and temporal traits of the object. The mythic view of the world is controlled by "facticity." It is manifestly concrete in its observations about the world, primarily because the *thing*, as it is viewed from a mythic point of view, not only *is*, but *means*; objects carry meaning and significance in and of themselves. "The two factors, thing and signification, are undifferentiated because they merge, grow together, concresce into an immediate unity" (Cassirer, p. 24).

Cassirer goes on to tell us, partly as a consequence of this unrelenting belief in the meaning of the *thing*, the mythic view attaches peculiar significance to words and names.

> Word and name do not designate and signify, they are and act. In the mere sensuous matter of language, in the mere sound of the human voice, there resides a peculiar power over thing. (Cassirer, p. 40)

In Dickens' short stories, as in most of Dickens, we can see clearly his rapt fascination with things in themselves. While many of the things named in a typical story do entail what we would ordinarily call symbolic import, the notion of literary symbolism does not adequately explain the density of named objects in a typical short story published in the *Sketches by Boz* or in Dickens generally. While it would be a decided over-statement to contend that Dickens is operating on the level of primitiveness in which Cassirer traces out the "mythical consciousness," nevertheless, Cassirer's distinctions between the mythical and the empirical consciousnesses provide an interesting analogical framework for understanding Dickens' early-style fictive world. Significantly enough, if we compare the qualities of Cassirer's "mythical consciousness" with the way that Dickens represents reality in his short stories, we find there are some striking similarities.

Certainly Dickens love of objects is too well known to require extensive documentation here. Any description of Dickens' style inevitably discusses the ubiquitous presence of the "object" in Dickens' world: chairs, tables, bedsteads, cups, saucers, tankards, punchbowls, bottles, carriages, carriage whips — every scrap and tatter of the material world seems to have been recorded.

In addition to the sheer numbers of objects we see in Dickens' writing, the peculiar power that objects have over his imagination is suggested by several of his sketches. "Meditations in Monmouth Street" is essentially the re-counting of the imaginative flights that occur to Dickens upon contemplating a room full of second-hand clothing. The clothes tell their former owners' stories and even conjure up their presences: Clothes become the man. Or conversely, the end of "The Parlour Orator" shows us Dickens' narrator waiting for the objects that surround him in an old inn to tell their story, which in this instance they fail to do. Or again, in "Hackney Coach Stands" we see the narrator imagining the stories that could be told by an old coach. Other sketches reveal that their origins flow from associations with objects: reflections on a certain kind of roman lettering in "Astleys" lead to anecdotes out of a schoolboy past.

The reader of Dickens finds the novel landscapes strewn with objects that seriously affect characters' lives: the borrowed coat that leads to the duel in *Pickwick*, Oliver's picture of his mother, the clocks and watches in *Dombey*, the sawed-off manacle in *Great Expectations*, and the monumental dust-heaps of *Our Mutual Friend* are just part of a fictive world where objects, character and fate are frequently bound together.

The very dominance of objects in Dickens' world, the "homogeneous" and "undifferentiated" blend of things (Cassirer, p. 35), establishes a correspondence between the concreteness and facticity of what Cassirer calls the mythic consciousness, and the way in which things are looked at in Dickens. It is almost as though Dickens were attempting to exercise some kind of *primitive word-magic* with which the world could be controlled through the naming of the objects in it. Taylor Stoehr has described this quality:

> Dickens having conjured up an imaginative world. . . hastens
> to bind it with a charm of words. His rhetoric is akin to that spell
> and incantation, which serves man's desire to exercise control over

the world by organizing experience (*as it is the function of science to do*) under the formulae that ritually names its parts and thus presumably ensure its obedience to law and order.[1] (my italics)

Stoehr is correct in describing the incantatory power that Dickens derives from the naming of objects; but he is speaking analogically in comparing the organizing of experience in Dickens with the scientific method of organizing experience. For as Cassirer argues, both the mythic consciousness and the empirical or scientific consciousness must take their shapes according to the way in which the perceptions of objects and configurations are organized into a coherent system; but it is the mythic system *alone* which seizes on the object itself and seems to find meaning in the presence of the object. In Cassirer's view the "scientific consciousness" makes a very different use of the object.

Although the aim of scientific thinking "consists in a supreme universal *synthesis*, in the comprehension of all particulars in the thorough-going unity of experience, still the only method by which it can obtain to this goal seems to point in the opposite direction" (Cassirer, p. 32). In order to make meaningful statements about the physical world, the scientific consciousness must give up the facticity and simplicity of sensory experience, and seek instead to establish a description of the essential and constant reality, as opposed to the accidental and variable. The synthesis which the empirical consciousness applies to sensory data, in itself only a conglomerate of things, must be achieved by bringing the sensory apprehension of the world of things to rest on a ground in which a reticulated network of explanatiory conditions makes it meaningful; that is, the objects and configurations of sensory experience must be mounted in a network of causal explanation. Keeping well in mind the basic correspondence between the object-centered, concrete, mythic consciousness and Dickens' object-centered style, let us consider the second major category in Cassirer's system: causality.

ii An example of rational literary vision

The transformation of Cassirer's epistemological framework into a framework for discussing Dickens' style and rhetoric necessarily entails some interpretation. But perhaps we can get a better idea of the relevance of Cassirer's distinctions to Dickens by first considering a passage from George Eliot whose more "rational" or "empirical" or "scientific" fictive world in *Middlemarch* will set Dickens' mythic one clearly in relief. Our

---

1. Taylor Stoehr, *Dickens: A Dreamer's Stance*, p. 87.

interest here will be primarily in the notion of causality implicit in the way each author tries to explain occurrences.

Significantly, the *consistency* of Eliot's "rational" fictive world dispenses with any objections we might make to comparing a selection from her enormous novel with a selection from one of Dickens' little short stories. Since a "rational" vision informs all parts of Eliot's novel, many individual parts of it are self-contained (i.e., partake of that pervasive rationality). The selection reproduced below could well be the opening paragraph of a story. Although the paragraph is dense in detail, it does not presume any prior knowledge of the story or characters. I am only interested in what the paragraph tells us about Eliot's way of representing reality. Comparable statements might be extracted from any paragraph, in any genre, by any author. I am not opposing the novel *Middlemarch* to a short story by Dickens. Rather I am examining the way in which short selections from each can inform us of an author's way of looking at the world.

Perhaps the most striking quality of Eliot's "rational or empirical" fictive world is her obdurate refusal to accept any simple explanations of the motives of her characters. For Eliot, there are no absolutes; there are no simple ways of apprehending the complexity of experience. Instead, we see demonstrated that "analytical dissection of reality into independent partial factors, and partial conditions with which the scientific approach to nature begins and which remains typical of it" (Cassirer, p. 51).

> Lydgate found it more and more agreeable to be with her, and there was no constraint now, there was a delightful interchange of influence in their eyes, and what they said had that superfluity of meaning for them, which is observable with some sense of flatness by a third person: still they had no interview or asides from which a third person need have been excluded. In fact, they flirted; and Lydgate was secure in the belief that they did nothing else. If a man could not love and be wise, surely he could flirt and be wise at the same time? Really, the men in Middlemarch, except Mr. Farebrother, were great bores, and Lydgate did not care about commercial politics or cards: what was he to do for relaxation? He was often invited to the Bullstrodes'; but the girls there were hardly out of the schoolroom; and Mrs. Bullstrode's *naive* way of conciliating piety and worldliness, the nothingness of this life and the desirability of cut glass, the consciousness at once of filthy rags and the best damask, was not a sufficient relief from the weight of her husband's invariable seriousness. The Vincys' house, with all its faults, was the pleasanter by contrast; besides, it nourished Rosamond — sweet to look at as

a half-opened blushrose, and adorned with accomplishments for the refined amusement of man. ([Boston: Houghton Mifflin, 1956] ch. 27, p. 198)

Although the Eliot paragraph quoted above undertakes to explain Lydgate's increasing attentions to Rosamond Vincy, no one thing, or even no one sequence of interrelated things adequately explains his attentions. Each sentence, perhaps each phrase, seems to argue against the possibility of a simple explanation.

First of all, as an explanation of a *change* in Lydgate's behavior, Eliot subtly, but necessarily, points to the fact that changes occur within a temporal context. The paragraph opens by asserting that Lydgate "found it more . . . agreeable" to be with Rosamond, but Lydgate's new-found pleasure is modified by a temporal reference. He finds it agreeable partly because "there was no constraint *now*." Thus, while the rest of the paragraph will be concerned with clarifying Lydgate's willingness to spend time with Rosamond, the whole notion is framed by a suggestion of the disparity between Lydgate's conduct *now*, and the implication that *earlier* there was "constraint." The retention of the temporal dimension is characteristic of and crucial to the empirical notion of causality. And Eliot is careful in suggesting that changes occur over time.

In keeping with the principles of an empirical notion of causality, Eliot's paragraph is very much concerned with representing different "planes" of reality. The narrative is careful in distinguishing the internal, subjective plane from the external, objective plane. One plane of subjective reality is set out in the intimacy of the lovers' conversations. We are told that "there was a delightful interchange of influence in their eyes." Yet Eliot is careful to point out that this is a subjective plane only relevant to the lovers' mutual feelings; that although the lovers find "a superfluity of meaning" in their new rapport, most observers would not be aware of this. Eliot introduces, on a second plane, an objective plane of reality by suggesting that the "superfluity of meaning" would only appear as a sense of "flatness" to a third person. Additionally, the *objective* "propriety" of the interviews between Lydgate and Rosamond is vouched for by the creation of a hypothetical "third person."

Eliot introduces a third plane in isolating Lydgate's subjective consciousness. It is apparently only Lydgate who is "secure in the belief" that he and Rosamond are only engaged in flirting. Similarly, both Lydgate's hopeful supposition that flirtation and wisdom mix, and his rationalization that "commercial politics" and "cards" do not provide adequate relaxation are clearly set off as subjective observations — they are framed as questions and, consequently, never attain the status of being objectively true.

A fourth, and mixed, perspective is introduced in the second half of the paragraph; here we see a combination of Lydgate's subjective consciousness and statements that are more or less objectively demonstrable in view of the reader's prior experience of the novel. Still anxious to clarify Lydgate's willingness to flirt with Rosamond, Eliot carefully sets up a complex intermingling of reasons: it is partially the youth of the Bullstrode girls, partially the oxymoronic intermingling of "piety" and "worldliness" in Mrs. Bullstrode's "naive" philosophy; it is partially the heavy "seriousness" of Mr. Bullstrode's views and the way in which they outweigh the ridiculous levity of his wife's views, that lead Lydgate finally to seek the company of Rosamond. Only after *all* of these considerations does the paragraph culminate in a very tentative and less than absolute conclusion. That is, Lydgate visits the Vincy's because he finds it "pleasanter by *contrast*" than any of his other alternatives.

If we were to attempt to deduce a principle of causality from Eliot's paragraph, we would find it to be a very complicated one indeed. The response to the question "Why does Lydgate visit Rosamond Vincy?" is in no way a simple response; and the principle of causality which provides an answer to the question is concomitantly complex. The paragraph from *Middlemarch* entails implicitly a *scientific* or *empirical* causal judgment which "dissects an event into constant elements and seeks to understand it through the complex intermingling, interpenetration and constant conjunction of these elements" (Cassirer, p. 47).

For Eliot there is no possibility of reducing cause and effect to a series of absolutes. Changes in human behavior must be seen as taking place over time. Eliot's mode of apprehending reality necessarily admits that reality is complex. In order to attain the truth of a given event we must allow that the event has a multifaceted existence: it exists internally and subjectively as well as externally and objectively; it exists uniquely for each individual, and it exists differently for combinations of individuals. In order to legitimately pretend to an accurate description of reality, the empirical consciousness must submit itself to the configuration produced by the intermingling of diverse planes of reality.

iii Dickens' mythic literary vision

In moving from a selection out of *Middlemarch* to a selection out of a short story by Dickens, what is perhaps the most apparent is the stark simplicity with which Dickens attempts to explain his characters' motivation, as opposed to the complexity we have seen in Eliot. But the distinction is more than just the distinction between a simple style and a complex style. Eliot's complexity is complex in the way that an empirical view of reality is complex. In the following excerpt from "The Misplaced Attachment" [2] we shall attempt to show that Dickens' story is *simple* in the ways that a mythic vision of causality and reality is simple.

[Mr. John Dounce is a "steady old boy" as opposed to a "gay old boy." Dickens describes the regular tavern dinners of John Dounce and his friends, and their occasional attendance at theatres, where they spend much time commenting on the ladies.]

The decrees of Fate, and the means by which they are brought about, are mysterious and inscrutable. John Dounce had led this life for twenty years and upwards, without wish for change, or care for variety, when his whole social system was suddenly upset, and turned completely topsy-turvy — not by an earthquake, or some other dreadful convulsion of nature, as the reader would be inclined to suppose, but by the simple agency of an oyster; and thus it happened.

Mr. John Dounce was returning one night from the Sir Somebody's Head, to his residence in Cursitor Street — not tipsy, but rather excited, for it was Mr. Jenning's birth-day, and they had had a brace of partridges for supper, and a brace of extra glasses afterwards, and Jones had been more than ordinarily amusing — when his eyes rested on a newly-opened oyster shop, on a magnificent scale, with natives laid, one deep, in circular marble basins in the windows, together with little round barrels of oysters directed to Lords and Baronets, and Colonels and Captains, in every part of the habitable globe.

Behind the natives were the barrels, and behind the barrels was a young lady of about five-and-twenty, all in blue, and all alone — splendid creature, charming face and lovely figure! It is difficult to say whether Mr. John Dounce's red countenance, illuminated as it was by the flickering gas-light in the window before which he paused, excited the lady's risibility, or whether a natural exuberance of animal spirits proved too much for that staidness of demeanor which the forms of society rather dictatorially prescribe. But certain it is, that the lady smiled; then put her finger upon her lip, with a striking recollection of what was due to herself; and finally retired, in oyster-like bashfulness, to the

---

2. Originally called "Love and Oysters," in *The Morning Chronicle*, Oct. 18, 1835. Revised as "The Misplaced Attachment," *Sketches*, p. 244.

very back of the counter. The sad-dog sort of feeling came strongly upon John Dounce: he lingered — the lady in blue made no sign. He coughed — still she came not. He entered the shop.

[Dounce, ordering oysters one at a time, consumes a dozen of "those at eight pence," eats an additional half-dozen, and after sending the girl for a glass of brandy-and-water, prevails upon her to sit down with him and share the drink, whereupon he flirts with her. Following a courtship of unspecified duration, the young lady declares]

she "wouldn't have him at no price"; and John Dounce, having lost his old friends, alienated his relations, and rendered himself ridiculous to everybody, made offers successively to a schoolmistress, a landlady, a feminine tobacconist and a housekeeper; and being directly rejected by each and every of them, was accepted by his cook, with whom he now lives. (*Sketches*, pp. 246–48)

While Eliot is very careful in setting her explanation of Lydgate's flirtation with Rosamond Vincy in a temporal framework, we see that Dickens very readily abandons the framework of time in offering a causal explanation of John Dounce's behavior. Even though the first half of "The Misplaced Attachment" is devoted to describing Dounce's way of life for *twenty years*, the radical alteration that he undergoes is simply disconnected from what has gone before. Yesterday's ritualistic widower very easily becomes today's foolish suitor.

"Whereas empirical thinking speaks of 'change' and seeks to understand it on the basis of a universal rule, mythical thinking knows only a simple metamorphosis" (Cassirer, p. 46). So while Eliot is "essentially directed toward establishing an unequivocal relation between *specific* 'causes' and *specific* 'effects'" Dickens has a "free selection of causes" at his disposal (Ibid.) and the cause that Dickens points to is very peculiar: "Without wish for change, or care for variety," John Dounce's "whole social system" was "turned completely topsy-turvy . . . by the simple agency of an oyster." John Dounce does not change; he undergoes a metamorphosis.

Dickens does not literally believe that radical changes in John Dounce's life are traceable to an oyster (although he may be playing with the reputed aphrodisiacal qualities of oysters).[3] The important point is

---

3. T. W. Hill, "The Oyster: A Close-up," *Dickensian*, 36 (1940), pp. 139–46, traces Dickens' use of oysters from *Sketches by Boz* through *Pickwick, David Copperfield, Nicholas Nickleby, Martin Chuzzlewit, Bleak House, Dombey, Little Dorrit, Great Expectations*, and *Our Mutual Friend*; Hill points to several instances in which Dickens uses oysters in amorous situations.

. that, to the extent that he needs causal explanations, he is willing to offer them in absolute terms, in the same way that pre-scientific myth does.

Dickens' willingness to attribute causality to an oyster is typical of the "physics of mythical causality" in several ways:

> It has even been called a principle of mythical causality and of the "physics" based on it that one take every contact in time and space as an immediate relation of cause and effect. The principles of *post hoc, ergo propter hoc* and *juxta hoc, ergo propter hoc* are characteristic of mythical thinking. (Cassirer, p. 45)

These are certainly the causal principles that preside in "The Misplaced Attachment" as in other *Sketches by Boz*. First it is precisely the *post hoc, ergo propter hoc* principle that Dickens resorts to here. No intermingling of subtly differentiated reasons explains Dounce's violent amorous attack. Secondly, Dickens shows an affinity with the mythical notion of causality in attributing the cause to a material (concrete and physical) object, i.e., "an oyster."

Despite the comic tone of the episode, Dickens' simplistic explanation of causality represents a very important tendency of his early short stories. The reduction of human motivation to objective and mechanical terms possibly pre-supposes ironic responses on the part of the reader. But the point here is not that most readers would implicitly recognize that causality and human motivation are really more complicated than the story suggests, but that Dickens would choose to represent them in the simple manner that he does. The impulse of the story is reductive. Rhetorically, the reader is not encouraged to reflect on the complexity of internal causes that explain the process of "falling in love;" rather he is encouraged to accept an external and mechanical cause, a material embodiment of the mysteries that lie within. Though the tone may invite us to chuckle at the explanation of why John Dounce falls in love, significantly, the story suggests no explanation beyond this very simple one.

Besides attributing the change in John Dounce to the arbitrary agency of an oyster, "The Misplaced Attachment" shows other similarities to the mythic predilection for explaining causality materially. Later in the story, Dickens "seeks to create a kind of continuity between cause and effect by intercalating a series of middle links between the initial and the ultimate states" — between John Dounce "old boy," and John Dounce henpecked spouse of his cook. "But even these middle links preserve a merely material character" (Cassirer, p. 55).

The subsequent changes in Dounce are evidenced by certain *material* changes that he undertakes.

He bought shirt-pins; wore a ring on his third finger; read poetry; bribed a cheap miniature-painter to perpetrate a faint resemblance to a youthful face, with a curtain over his head, six large books in the background, and an open country in the distance (this he called his portrait). (*Sketches*, p. 248)

Here in Dickens, just as in the "mythic consciousness," the materialization of causality is ultimately traceable to the concept of the object. "The form of causal thinking determines the form of objective thinking, and vice versa" (Cassirer, p. 43). John Dounce, as an intelligible personality, is no more real, perhaps less real, than the objects that Dickens allows to make up his environment.

The resultant picture of reality lacks the dimension of depth — the differentiation of foreground and background so characteristically effected in the scientific concept with its distinction between "the ground" and that which is founded on it. (Cassirer, p. 36)

Thus in Dickens' stories people exist on the same plane as objects. Frequently, he presents them in verbal "still-lives," arrested in a blend of objects where each object has an equivalent existence. In "The Misplaced Attachment," John Dounce's fate is sealed by an encounter with "natives," "circular marble basins," "round barrels of oysters," and a "young lady," whose presence is subsumed and dominated by the objects surrounding her. In Dickens' stories, as in myth, there are no varying degrees of objective certainty. The characters are simply additional objects in a uniform world of objects. The apprehension of personality here is as absolute as the apprehension of the chairs, tables, oysters, red silk curtains that make up the rest of the environment.

Although Dickens does give us an occasional glimpse into the subjective life of Dounce, what we see is not subjective in the way that Eliot's presentation of Lydgate is. Eliot dissects the event into constant elements, into different planes of fact and consciousness. She seeks to understand the event through the "complex intermingling, interpenetration and constant conjunction of these elements" (Cassirer, p. 47). Just as the mythical thinker does, Dickens "clings to the total representation as such" and contents himself "with picturing the simple course of what happens" (Ibid.). We are never forced to consider the disparateness between what is subjectively true for the character and what *is true*. Instead, subjective experience, when it is treated, monopolizes the narrative. It is thoroughly seen and acquires an objective character.

We have seen how Eliot is careful in distinguishing objective, external reality from subjective internal reality; but in Dickens' short stories, all objects merge. Subjective experience acquires an objective character; it is revealed in the narrative with the same absoluteness that objects acquire. Whereas the "empirical vision" in Eliot is concerned with carefully setting out and distinguishing the various objective and subjective planes that intermingle to create "reality," the "mythical vision" in Dickens is concerned with merging all levels of reality:

> For mythical thinking all contents crowd together into a single plane of reality; everything perceived possesses as such a character of reality. (Cassirer, p. 42)

Dounce's appearance, friends, habits, dreams, and fate are all treated with the absoluteness of concrete objects, all existing on a "single plane" of reality.

John Dounce as one of the "objects" in the created environment acquires many of the qualities that the object has in the mythic view. Dounce is described in the first section of the Sketch as one of the *species* of the *genus* "old boy." Rather than acquiring his personal and material characteristics from a series of carefully isolated qualities that are universal in "old boys," Dounce is subjected to the already preconceived notion of the genus, "old boy."

> He was a short, round, large-faced, tubbish sort of man with a broad-brimmed hat, and a square coat; and *had that grave, but confident, kind of roll, peculiar to old boys in general. (Sketches*, p. 245, my italics)

In Dickens' stories, distinguishing characteristics are enmeshed in a circular logic. Anything that occurs in the genus "old boy" is immediately attributed to its representation in the species — here, John Dounce. And conversely, traits that would ordinarily be individualizing, that would separate out the species, are immediately offered as typical of the "genus." Cassirer has described this quality of the mythic consciousness:

> The genus, in its relation to the species or individuals it comprises, is not a universal which logically determines the particu-

lar, but is immediately present, living and acting in this particular. Here we have no more logical subordination but an actual subjection of an individual to its generic concept. (Cassirer, p. 64)

The point here is that John Dounce is not conceived of as a peculiarly unique, and avowedly idiosyncratic human individual, but rather as an example of the presiding genus, "old boy." Rather than bestowing on him the uniqueness of human personality that comes with idiosyncrasy in the empirical view, each of Dounce's distinguishing characteristics renders him more lifeless, more of an object in Dickens' mythically objective world. His fate is set out as a "melancholy monument of antiquated misery," and "a living warning to all uxorious old boys."

In mythical thinking any similarity of sensuous manifestation suffices to group entities in which it appears into a single mythical "genus." Any characteristic, however external, is as good as another; there can be no sharp distinction between "inward" and "outward," "essential," and "nonessential," precisely because for myth every perceptible similarity is an immediate expression of an identity of essence. (Ibid., p. 67)

Many of the characters in Dickens' stories demonstrate this feature of mythical consciousness. They announce an essence, become part of a genus, through the specification of rather arbitrary, external characteristics.

Finally, the principle of unity operative in "The Mistaken Attachment" is characteristic of the kind of unity found in mythical thinking. In Dickens' stories "all reality is smelted down into concrete unifying images" (Ibid., p. 62). People, objects, dreams, conversations all exist on a single objective plane, which is supposed to provide an explanation of what happened:

Indeed the proposition that nothing in the world happens by accident and everything by conscious purpose has sometimes been called fundamental to the mythical world view. (Ibid., p. 48)

Significantly, the peculiar metamorphosis of John Dounce is not conveyed as an arbitrary or accidental occurrence. Instead, Boz attributes Dounce's transformation to the agency of an oyster acting in accordance with the "decrees of Fate." While acknowledging that such decrees are "mysterious and inscrutable," Boz argues for the *purposiveness* of the event. Throughout the Dickens stories, and his novels, we see the "kind of hypertrophy of the causal 'instinct' and of a need for causal explanation" (Ibid.) that are typical of the mythic consciousness. The arbitrary and accidental occurrences in Dickens' fiction are frequently subsumed into an "intuition of purposive action" (Ibid., p. 49). Whereas Eliot is satisfied in leaving a "certain sphere of indeterminacy surrounding the particular" event, Dickens attempts to explain it away with the principle of purposive occurrence. In Eliot the "why" of the situation does not give way to any universal rule. Although Lydgate's courting of Rosamond has been explained, the narrative preserves the indeterminacy of cause. We are not left with an explanatory rule, but with a process, a way of understanding reality that has no rules. For Eliot the process of describing reality necessarily entails the separation of what is objectively true from what is only subjectively true. Dickens writes in such a way as to give all perceptions a uniformly real existence.

While the story of John Dounce does not exhaust the similarities between Cassirer's "mythic consciousness" and Dickens' mythic fictive world, perhaps we have established some notion of the correspondences between the two. The details of "The Misplaced Attachment" have a peculiarly precise alignment with the mythic reality described by Cassirer. Although not all of Dickens' stories could be shown to line up, the stories are similar in their use of objects and causality; the object-centered vision of Dickens' fiction dismisses change in favor of metamorphosis; it merges all planes of reality into a uniformly objective plane; it invests causality materially; it seeks to establish a purposive universe by explaining away the accidental as a manifestation of fate.

Moreover a kind of pervasive indifference to both empirical time and empirical space colors many of Dickens' early short stories and subsequently his novels. Dickens' use of space frequently has the arbitrary plasticity of mythic space. Though the short stories are set in London and frequently use actual place names as points of reference, Dickens is not always concerned with establishing a consistent set of space and time coordinates. Instead, space and time expand and contract according to the events in the story. For instance, as T. W. Hill points out, Mr. Minns in Dickens' first story takes over five hours to walk home in the rain even though his cousin makes the same walk before breakfast only a few days previous.[4] The discrepancy is disturbing. Has the distance between the two houses changed or has time? A comparable indifference to space-time coordinates exists in many of Dickens' novels.

---

4. T. W. Hill, "Notes on *Sketches by Boz*," *Dickensian*, 46 (1950), p. 216 ff.

In contrast, even though Middlemarch is primarily an imaginative place, and only secondarily a re-creation of the real place, Warwickshire, Eliot maintains a rigorous space-time coordination.

Despite the similarities between Dickens' story world and the world of myth, no one would want to call these stories myths. At best, Dickens records reality in a manner that might set the stage for the affirmative actions of myth. That such actions fail to take place perhaps gives us a clue to both what Dickens might have done within the dimensions of his story world, and the course he was to follow in the successive fiction.

The next section of this study will suggest general ways in which the kind of reality represented in the early short stories is connected to their immense success; additionally we will focus on the ways in which Dickens collapses the mythic potential inherent in his way of representing the world.

iv A refreshingly simple vision

The preceding discussion of differences between Dickens and Eliot can be used to answer questions that go beyond the style of the two authors. One such question attaches to the matter of Dickens' phenomenal early success: What made these transparently simple writings so popular? Why did they achieve such a conspicuous place in the view of contemporaries?

We have already noted the technical distinctions that made Dickens' early stories somewhat unusual — the third-person omniscient narration of the fictive situations of ordinary people. Moreover, the mythic simplicity of the world that Dickens describes must have struck his readers as a refreshingly different kind of view, particularly if we consider the contexts in which both the stories and sketches were originally read.

The assumptions that shape the view of the world expressed in Dickens' earliest writings are radically different from the views expressed in the journals, magazines and newspapers that surrounded them in their original published form. Although Dickens published his first work in journals, he was, from the beginning, much more than a journalist. In contrast to Dickens' fiction, much of the fiction in British magazines of the early 1830's is simply journalism, idle words, chatter, writing nonsense, for people who are bored and need to fill up time. Dickens, from the very first, shows himself as a man with something he really wishes to write, and to judge from the impact he made on his first audience, there were definitely people who wanted to read it. What was it? The answer resides in Dickens' stories.

First of all, the stories implicitly contradict many of the prevailing notions of the short fiction in the early 1830's. Implicitly, Dickens' stories are an answer to his contemporaries. Where their stories assert that the world is opaque and mysterious, Dickens' stories say it is transparent and simple. Where their stories assert that the profound passion and nobility of human character are unfathomable, Dickens' stories assert that the trivial motives and superficiality of human character are laughably plain. Where their stories hold up an individual's uniqueness in evidence of sublime human capability, Dickens' stories hold up an ubiquitous idiosyncrasy in testimony to human limitations.

In a sense, Dickens' stories import wholesale the prevailing assumptions of much 18th-century satiric literature into the romantically colored fiction of the early 1830's. Though it is ultimately the satiric force of those notions which controls the rhetoric of Dickens' early fiction, the world view on which those notions rest is extremely important in understanding Dickens intentions as an artist.

Dickens' short stories (and later his sketches) first came to the public sandwiched in with fiction and news — in newspapers and magazines. If the short fiction in the early 1830's had given itself over to expositions of the unique and unusual in human affairs, the non-fiction accounts in both the newspapers and magazines suffered a comparable limitation.

The contemporary newspapers and magazines are relentlessly factual in their non-fiction reporting. In a manner corresponding to the romantic obscurantisms that shape the fiction, the news reporters seem reluctant and incapable of making meaningful generalizations. Although in 1833–34 the readers of the *Morning Chronicle* had daily access to an unsigned, *verbatim* transcript of proceedings in Parliament, written by Charles Dickens, doubtless there was more understanding of the world to be had in the same paper's columns signed "Boz." The not-yet "mass media" seem to have been bent on inundating the world with a Gradgrindian flood of facts. For instance the following excerpt is from a *Morning Chronicle* account of the fatal injuries suffered by a "waterman" in an alleged instance of police brutality; it grotesquely typifies the relentless detail that British periodicals regularly inflicted on their readers in the reporting of both trivial and significant news.

> On examining the bones of the skull, a circular portion of bone,
> an inch in diameter at the very top of the head was fractured and
> depressed to the extent of the eighth of an inch, and a fissure
> extended from the fore part of this broken piece of the bone to
> within an inch of the root of the nose and another fissure extended

towards [sic] about an inch. About an ounce of bloody serum escaped from the cavities of the brain. A considerable quantity of blood was effused into the anterior part of the substance of the brain, full an ounce. From an ounce and a half to two ounces of coagulated blood was found under the external membrane of the brain on the right side. The arteries of the brain were healthy. About an ounce of bloody serum was found at the base of the brain; but there was no fracture of the skull in that direction. There was nothing to account for death in the cavities of the chest and body. The viscera was sound. (*Morning Chronicle*, Monday, July 15, 1833)

In other words, the man's head was pretty badly "bashed." In place of the *Chronicle's* compulsively detailed account with its measured blood and fissures, a modern newspaper would most likely find it sufficient to state that the "victim died of multiple head injuries." Our point here is more than a matter of changed "taste" in journalistic reporting. The significant fact is that the newspapers and magazines of the early 1830's showed a propensity for eliminating the news, destroying its vivacity and immediacy, through an information over-load. The same quality of relentless detail seems to have pervaded the reporting of most accessible newsworthy events. Perhaps this tendency is traceable to the sparsity of news-gathering facilities, and the need to fill the pages of the newspaper. Whatever the reasons, the effects of such a journalistic style are quite conspicuous.

The attitudes implicit in the *Morning Chronicle* account above are only a reflection of the attitudes that were to shape British society for the next fifty years. The relentless detail of the *Chronicle* story is only part of a pattern in a society that was already obsessed by facts.

The typical reforms of the two decades following the Reform Bill of 1832 were not the result of hit-or-miss humanitarianism; they followed widespread investigations by Parliamentary Committees and Royal Commissions, which enshrined their findings in mountains of "blue books" cluttered with statistical tables. Local inquiries supplemented those on a national basis. After the establishment of the first English Statistical Society, in Manchester in 1834, similar organizations broke out all over England. The year 1836 saw the beginning of the practice of selling parliamentary blue books to the public. Compiling, publishing, and reading statistics about the condition of England assumed the proportions of a national fad. In a few years' time the treatment of national affairs had been transformed — to use G. G. Young's phrase —

from a polemical to a statistical basis, from Humbug to Humdrum.[5]

Both the newspapers and magazines of the 1830's are filled with the products of this statistical craze. It is precisely Dickens' ability to restore vitality to that "humdrum" world already far too grey, a world far too well dissected, analyzed, and tabulated that makes Dickens stand out among his contemporaries. While the newspapers and periodicals in which Dickens first published his stories and sketches are filled with minutely detailed accounts of the *malaise* and *progress* of the British scene, in very few other places does one get the comprehensive assertion of an understandable and understood world — a world with certain affinities for the world of myth — that exists in Dickens' short stories and later his sketches.

v Undercutting mythical possibilities

The qualities that make the world of Dickens' stories like the world of myth culminate in a powerful omniscient narrative intelligence. The voice in back of these stories has the appeal of the "generalist" in a world already dominated by "specialists." On the one hand, there is a presumptive nonchalance in that voice which distinguishes it from the voices in the comparable fiction. Dickens' narrative voice constantly implies "I know, I see, I understand all of my world." But on the other hand that voice is finally too clear and too knowing. Although the short stories seem to operate in a mythic world, and thereby offer their readers a powerfully omniscient vision lacking in much of the contemporary fiction, the mythic vision in the stories is only a partially satisfactory one — in effect it is a negative myth. Rhetorically there are many elements that undercut the mythic possibilities of Dickens' story world.

The distinction here is a real one. If for the moment, we can isolate the *way* Dickens' narrator sees (as we have in the previous sections of this study) from *what* the narrator sees, the mythic possibilities of that way of seeing should be, by now, clear. But when we admit a comprehensive picture of *what* the narrator sees, as of course we must if we are to accurately describe his "vision," the mythic possibilities of these stories dry up and shrivel away.

The stories fail to provide either an explicit or implicit moral framework for the actions they depict. They fail to make the important distinctions of good and evil relevant to the stories.

---

5. William W. Watt, ed., Introduction to *Hard Times*, by Charles Dickens, p. xvi.

Rhetorically these stories reach for only one response, laughter. In their world all events are equally funny. In the first story we are asked to laugh at Mr. Minns' fastidiousness and his cousins' vulgarity — they are laughable enough. So are the Maldertons, the Gattletons, Mr. Dumps, the Tibbs, and the Boarding House tenants. But frequently the stories go beyond the description of events that would ordinarily be considered laughable. Consider the following details from the closing paragraphs of "The Boarding House."

> Mr. Septimus Hicks having walked the hospitals, took it into his head to walk off altogether. His injured wife is at present residing with her mother at Boulogne. Mr. Simpson, having the misfortune to lose his wife six weeks after marriage (by her eloping with an officer during his temporary sojourn in the Fleet Prison, in consequence of his inability to discharge her little mantua-maker's bill), and being disinherited by his father, who died soon afterwards, was fortunate enough to obtain a permanent engagement at a fashionable hair-cutter's. (*Sketches*, p. 290)

Perhaps the preposterous density of calamities outlined above is funny, but consider what we are asked to laugh at: abandonment, adultery, bigamous elopement, *imprisonment for debt*, disinheritance, and death. Nor is this an isolated example of Dickens recourse to "black humor." The previous story, "The Bloomsbury Christening," relies almost entirely on a comparable sardonicism. For instance, how are we expected to respond to the following account of the vaccination of the "christened" child?

> He has been vaccinated, but in consequence of the operation being rather awkwardly performed, some small particles of glass were introduced into the arm with the matter. Perhaps this may in some degree account for his being rather fractious. (Ibid., p. 470)

Here too, perhaps the artistry of the pun of "fractious," is expected to cancel out the reader's recoil from the sardonic humor called for. Again, in a later story which concerns the pathetically unsuccessful amorous adventures of "Mr. Watkins Tottle," Dickens closes with a paragraph exploiting the irony of his protagonist's suicide:

> A few weeks after the last-named occurrence, the body of a gentleman unknown, was found in the Regent's Canal. In the

49

trousers-pockets were four shillings and threepence halfpenny; a matrimonial advertisement from a lady, which appeared to have been cut out of a Sunday paper; a toothpick, and a card-case, which it is confidently believed would have led to the identification of the unfortunate gentleman, but for the circumstance of there being none but blank cards in it. Mr. Watkins Tottle absented himself from his lodgings shortly before. A bill, which has not been taken up, was presented next morning; and a bill, which has not been taken down, was soon afterwards affixed in his parlour window. (Ibid., p. 466)

The narrator deliberately avoids any appeal to pathos. So what if Watkins Tottle commits suicide? Everything is funny, ironic.

G. K. Chesterton has attempted to explain this quality biographically. He sees the pervasive irony as:

the peculiar hardness of youth; a hardness which in those who have in any way been unfairly treated reaches even to impudence. It is a terrible thing for any man to find out that his elders are wrong. And this almost unkindly courage of youth must partly be held responsible for the smartness of Dickens, that almost offensive smartness which . . . sometimes irritates us like the showy gibes in the tall talk of a schoolboy.[6]

But if we consider the pervasive ironies of Dickens' stories from a rhetorical perspective, their implications are much broader than the adolescent impudence that Chesterton sees in them.

In effect, Dickens' narrator, with his "cocksure jibing," "flip puns," and "knowing word plays" undermines and negates the affirmative possibilities of the mythically simple world he creates for his stories.[7]

The narrator's rhetorical tricks tear at fictive illusion of his stories. He is constantly in search of the ironic effect. Consider his use of the following devices:

(1) PARALLEL PHRASES AND CLAUSES:

Mr. Augustus Minns was a bachelor of about forty as he said — of about eight-and-forty as his friends said. . . . He was a clerk in

---

6. G. K. Chesterton, *Appreciations and Criticisms of the Works of Charles Dickens*, pp. 6–7.

7. Edgar Johnson, *Charles Dickens: His Tragedy and Triumph*, p. 112.

Somerset house, or, as he said himself he held "a responsible situation under government." (*Sketches*, p. 312)

In each of the cases above, through the use of parallel structures the narrator ironically points to the discrepancy between Minns' vain notion of himself, and the narrator's ability to see through that vanity. What exists for Minns and what the narrator knows about him are played against one another in ironic counterpoint.

(2) THE APOSITIVE:

Mr. Minns found himself opposite a . . . house with . . . "a garden" in front, that is to say, a small loose bit of gravelled ground, with one round and two scalene triangular beds, containing a fir tree, twenty or thirty bulbs, and an unlimited number of marigolds. (Ibid., p. 317)

The aposition of "a garden" and "loose bit of gravelled ground" works rhetorically to suggest that at best the motley collection of growing things is a parody of a real garden.

(3) THE PARENTHETICAL PHRASE:

[he hung] his hat on one of the dozen brass pegs which ornamented the passage, denominated by courtesy, "The Hall." (Ibid.)

Here we are forced to see that a passage with a few pegs is by no means a hall, a term that is meant to retain baronial connotations in this instance.

The foregoing devices all have the same effect rhetorically. They create a schism between the matter of the story, the things that could be said to exist and happen in the story world and the narrator's presentation of them. The narrator in effect sets up an opposition between his world and the story world. The reader is constantly forced to acknowledge the discrepancies between: a bachelor of forty versus a bachelor of forty-eight, a responsible situation under government, versus a clerk, a garden versus a bit of gravelled ground, a Hall versus a passage with pegs.

The schism here should not be mistaken for approximating the different subjective and objective planes of reality we have seen in connection with George Eliot's fiction, for in effect the two presentations are quite different. Eliot is always careful in pointing to the several perspectives that exist *within* her story world. She presents us with the complexities that are part of the lives of her characters. The reality she reports allows its inhabitants varying degrees of consciousness and awareness of its complexity. In contrast, in Dickens' stories, there is always an opposition between the flat, limited, unconscious level of reality in which the characters exist, and the external complexity of the narrator's vision. Where Eliot insists that differing views of the world be contained within the dramatic line of her narrative, Dickens never allows that an inhabitant of his story world could be aware of such complexities.

The narrator's world and the story world exist in counterpoint, but they are fundamentally disparate. He usurps and retains as part of his own world everything decorous: the government position, the garden, the hall. The story-world proper is left with only diminished echoes of the decorous world the narrator inhabits. If characters in the story-world aspire to elegance and refinement, they are cut down by the narrator's commonsensical colloquial diction. If characters in the story world speak colloquially, they are put at the mercy of the narrator's elegance and refinement.

Other rhetorical devices are used to establish the narrator's *superiority* to the story world he has created. Sometimes the effect is achieved through a pun:

> His eyes appeared fixed on the wall . . . in short there was no catching his eye and perhaps it is a merciful dispensation of Providence that such eyes are not catching. (*Sketches*, p. 468)

Elsewhere the effect arises from the narrator's zeugmatic construction: "Mrs. Tibbs bustled out of the room to give Tibbs his clean linen — and the servant warning" (Ibid., p. 279). Here, just as in the narrator's frequent similes and occasional metaphors, the rhetorical figure points back to the narrative voice in testimony of the narrator's wit.

Even syntactical patterns become a rhetorical tool used to effect the diminution of the story world through ironies that also establish the narrator's superiority to it. The following sentence from "The Boarding House" is a good example:

> Mr. Simpson, having the misfortune to lose his wife six weeks after marriage (by her eloping with an officer during his temporary sojourn in the Fleet Prison in consequence of his inability to discharge her little mantua-maker's bill) and being disinherited by his father, who died soon afterwards, was fortunate enough to obtain a permanent engagement at a fashionable haircutter's. (Ibid., p. 290)

Here the narrator is using the sentence form itself in a highly ironic fashion. His grammar is entirely correct. But his syntax is an ironic denigration of the events he records. The impossible melodrama of the forty-six-word subject in the sentence — with all its catastrophes — pushes to a bathetic low, the anticlimactic revelation of the predicate — the man has become a haircutter. Although the sentence contains its facts elegantly, logically, it cannot contain them emotionally. The rhetoric of the sentence demands that either we dismiss as insane a narrator who speaks this way — and of course we won't do that, he's too charming — or we accept the implications of his syntax: the events it records are trivial and laughable.

In all, Dickens' short stories project a curiously mechanical and transparent physical world, where character, change, time, and causality are reminiscent of the world of myth. The stories dramatize for their readers a powerfully omniscient intelligence, a kind of intelligence that was lacking in both the fiction and the news of the day. But rhetorically, Dickens cuts across the underpinning of his potentially mythic world. Syntax, language and tone, the whole texture of his narration, culminate in a negative, sardonic, and ironic voice that precludes the affirmative vision Dickens later showed he really aspired to. Because the presiding rhetorical thrust of the short stories is a satirical and negative one, Dickens creates a mythic world without mythic relevance. While the rhetoric presents the reader with a comfortable superiority to the world of the stories and the trivially involved characters who inhabit them, the stories fail to suggest the existence of any viable alternative to their own comic-satiric world. Except for echoes of an Augustan decorum (which are never stated explicitly or given any locus in the stories) the reader is left with the disquieting possibility that, although he feels superior to the story world, it *is* after all his own world — trivial, mechanical, and finally absurd. The characters in the stories occupy a representational world; they, like the reader, are excluded from the rhetorically decorous and ideal world of the narrator.

Dickens' short stories imagine no possibilities for heroic action, disinterested behavior, or dignity. Though Dickens shows himself an accomplished ironist, in the short stories there are no indications of his mature compassion, warmth, and straightforward sentiment. He does not yet have at his disposal a syntax for unembarrassed feeling. In effect, he creates a mythic world without a mythic center — a hollow or negative myth that repudiates rather than affirms the society he depicts and informs.

The supercilious aloofness that shapes all of the stories by Boz emerges as the fundamental impulse of Dickens' earliest imaginative work. That Dickens sustained one tone for so long suggests both the primacy of this tone and his satisfaction with it. However, the overall development of Dickens' work suggests he also recognized his limitations. By the end of his first year as a publishing writer, when Dickens began publishing sketches, his initial "uniformity" began to fade away. Dickens was never again capable of presenting such a simplified attitude towards reality as he reveals in the stories by Boz, particularly the earliest stories.

CHAPTER FOUR
FILLING
IN THE CENTER

i The sketch form — Pierce Egan

DICKENS BEGAN writing sketches fully a year after his debut as a short story writer. As with any two pieces from the same hand, Dickens' *sketches* have much in common with his *stories*. Though the following pages will point to the similarities between Dickens' efforts in the two genres, it is primarily their differences that give us the best understanding of Dickens' growth and changing intentions as an artist.

Before proceeding to a study of the differences between Dickens' sketches and stories, however, it is important to understand Dickens' relationship to the other sketch writers and the tradition of sketch writers at the time Dickens began. Dickens was really only one of many "sketchers" grinding out pages to fill the void of interesting prose in the early 1830's. Yet his writings were received with considerable acclaim, surfacing in a round of popular applause, despite the legions of competitors. His contemporaries saw in him a descendent of Pierce Egan, and a rival of Thomas Hood and Theodore Hook. More recently, John Butt and Kathleen Tillotson have suggested that Boz's sketches are most like those of John Poole.[1] And while Robert Browning,[2] a twentieth-century critic, has compared Boz rather cursorily to all of the contemporaries mentioned above (in addition to Leigh Hunt) no one seems to have gotten at the subtle, but

---

1. John Butt and Kathleen Tillotson, *Dickens at Work*, p. 37 n. After asserting the likeness, Mrs. Tillotson dismisses it as a likeness "merely of substance." But a reading of Poole's *Sketches and Recollections* (London, 1835) fails to suggest even that minimal similarity.

2. "Sketches by Boz," in *Dickens and the Twentieth Century*, ed. John Gross (London, 1962), p. 11.

profound rhetorical differences that are revealed in Boz's version of the sketch.

The writers whom both Dickens' contemporaries and more recent critics have cited as his "rival" sketch writers operate in very different rhetorical frameworks, and as such, help clarify and define the much broader scope and implications of Boz as a writer of sketches. What follows will be an attempt to analyze the rhetorical considerations that shape a typical sketch by Boz, as distinguished from the sketches of his "rivals."

As a literary form, a sub-genre of the essay, the sketch in the 1830's was primarily comic; it sought to amuse, occasionally to inform its readers. The subject matter of the sketch ranged from the depiction of a particular person or character type, to a description of a building, a neighborhood, a town, a social event, an institution, or even a peculiarly contemporary phenomenon.

Within this broad subject matter, we can view the sketch writer as one who processes his subject in any of a variety of ways. The sketch, as the product of authorial process, is amenable to rhetorical analysis in so far as it reveals the author's assumptions about his subject and audience, his expectations of his readers, and his range of effects, both deliberate and accidental. More specifically, in undertaking a rhetorical analysis of several sketch writers, we shall be interested in *how* a given version of the sketch seeks *to involve* the reader.

The following pages will examine excerpts from sketches of Greenwich Fair and its environs by Egan, Hood and Hook, moving on to a more detailed analysis of Dickens' treatment of the same subject. While the presentation of four contemporary views of Greenwich Fair is illuminating in itself, we shall be concerned primarily with pointing out rhetorical differences in the sketches, particularly the varying degrees of *involvement* or *participation* that each sketch allows *to*, or demands *from* its readers. The questions here are: How does each author's treatment act on the reader? Has the author processed his subject in such a way as to exclude, to pacify, to disinvolve the reader?

Pierce Egan's sketches of London were immensely popular, despite what has been called their "superficial realism."[3] And because they cleverly conferred "glamour on the sordid and the squalid,"[4] we encounter an amusing, but rhetorically *uninvolving* version of the sketch. Consider the following excerpt from his "The Frolics of Greenwich Fair."

---

3. See note 2 above.
4. Ibid.

Greenwich Fair

"Greenwich," said Tom, "is not a very long journey, nor do I know, speaking of the town itself, independent of its surrounding attractions, particularly to be admired, though it is a neat town, about five miles from London Bridge in the County of Kent with a market on Wednesdays and Saturdays. It is however famous for an hospital for decayed Seamen, the brave defenders of their native soil, who have fought and bled for their King and country; thought to be the finest structure of the kind in the world and for an observatory built by Charles II on the summit of a hill, called Flamstead Hill, from the astronomer of that name, who was here the first astronomer Royal: and we compute the longitude from the meridian of this place. It is also a place of great resort at holiday time, for being so near London. The lads and lasses move off in groups to Greenwich Fair, and the amusements at those times are of so varying a kind as almost defy description.

> The hills and dales are lined
> With pretty girls all around.

And there are but few who have had an opportunity but have occasionally enjoyed a roll down this hill. The roads leading to the sporting spot are to be seen clogged with coaches, carts, and waggons decorated with laurel, and filled with company, singing their way down or up to participate in the frolics of Greenwich Fair. It is however, much more celebrated for its once having been a Royal Palace, in which Edward VI died and Queen Mary and Queen Elizabeth were born. On a part of the site of it, now stands the house belonging to the Ranger of the Park at Greenwich, also a College called the Duke of Norfolk's College, for the maintenance of 20 decayed Housekeepers, and another called Queen Elizabeth's as well as a Royal Naval Asylum for the orphans of Sailors and Marines."[5]

Primarily, the sketch seems to have been aimed at providing a kind of tourist's guidebook knowledge of Greenwich and its institutions. The information has been strung together on a fictive thread with the historical and scientific facts, and the identification of donors of buildings and monuments being offered as the supposed dialogue between characters. In addition to the impressive array of factual material presented, Egan provides intermittent relief from the guided tour by stopping his characters for a hot lunch and some spirits, thereby setting the stage for drinking songs and poetry recitations.

---

5. *Real Life in London* (London, 1821; rpt. London, 1905), II, pp. 155–56.

While the combination of guidebook and high-jinx is a very workable format for a long series of papers directed to a somewhat starved and indiscriminate reading public, rhetorically Egan's sketches operate under a number of strained assumptions. First of all, as an internal consideration, there is the question of verisimilitude. Who but a paid and licensed professional guide would have as much detailed information about a particular locale? Egan's speaker in the above quotation is supposedly an elegant gentleman. And even if we allow that such an encyclopedic gentleman might exist, the form of his speech is radically at odds with the context. No man ever spoke that way. The syntax of Egan's speaker contradicts the illusion of dialogue that he attempts to impose on it.

In fact, all of Egan's principle characters speak in the same inflated *written* (as opposed to oral) syntax. Egan's narrator is indistinguishable from his characters. Thus, at the end of the Greenwich sketch the narrator describes the chapel at the Seaman's Hospital in the following manner:

> Tallyho was delighted with a view of the Chapel, which is 111 feet long, and 52 broad, and capable of accommodating 1000 Pensioners, nurses and boys, exclusive of pews for the Directors, the several officers of the establishment, & c.—.

This compound-complex sentence, loaded with detailed information, is precisely like the sentences that Egan's characters speak. The fact that the sentence is supposedly *not* dialogue is as arbitrary as the fact that comparable sentences *are*. Secondly, if we consider the external implications of Egan's rhetoric, how Egan affects the reader, we find he is very uninvolving. His approach to the sketch is a perfect example of a kind of erudite posture which makes the reader a subject to be acted upon by the writer. Although the sketch appears to inform its audience, it does so without conceding that the audience has, or might have, any prior knowledge of the subject. Certainly any literate Londoner (and most literate Englishmen) would have known that Greenwich was a suburb of London, and that besides an annual fair, the town is renowned for an observatory, a naval hospital, a hill, etc.

Egan attempts to fuse the fictive and the factual in an harmonious blend of sweetness and light. But he mistakes the requisite simultaneity in the adage that literature should delight and instruct. While the reader may learn about London by reading Egan, the rhetorical assumptions that shape his presentation anticipate a very passive audience which is prepared to accept and remember, rather than participate, in what he reports.

ii Thomas Hood, Theodore Hook, and the sketch

Another of "Boz's rivals," Thomas Hood, seems to have shaped his sketches exclusively for the "delight" of his audience. He was renowned for his verbal trickery and puns. As his description of a Greenwich Parishioner quoted below will prove, his strength resides in a mastery of facetious devices. A Greenwich Parishioner is:

> A sort of stranded marine animal, that the receding tide of life has left high and dry on the shore. He pines for his element like a Sea Boar, and misses his briny washings and wettings. What ocean could not do, the land does, for it makes him sick: he cannot digest properly unless his body is rolled and tumbled about like a barrel-churn. Terra firma is good enough he thinks to touch at for wood and water, but nothing more. There is no wind, he swears ashore — every day of his life is a dead calm — a thing above all he detests — he would like it better for an occasional earthquake. Walk he cannot, the ground being so still and steady that he is puzzled to keep his legs; and ride he will not, for he disdains a craft whose rudder is forward and not astern.[6]

Here, Hood gives us a derivative version of the seventeenth-century character sketch. Although he reproduces the exaggerated style — wit, fancy, and conceit — that the English character sketch had acquired by the time of Sir Thomas Overbury's collection in 1614, Hood lacks the moral point of view and social concern that gives the genre its chief historical significance. His intention is obviously to amuse by exploiting the displacement suffered by the retired sailor. While the sketch may persuade the reader to laugh, rhetorically its assumptions are rather simple. Once the reader concedes the appropriateness of the subject, that the Greenwich parishioner is a funny thing, the writer leisurely prosecutes his point of view for the amusement of his audience. But the land-sea polarity over-dominates the sketch. The reader quickly sees, and subsequently withdraws from his point. Similarly, when Hood undertakes a sketch on Greenwich Fair itself, the reader rapidly seizes the premise that shapes the whole sketch: Greenwich Fair is an artificial and contrived reduction of the real spirit of a country Fair:

> Only a Toy shop out of Town with a gals skool looking after it, without a Guvverness and al Oglein like Winkin. . . . Am blest

---

6. *The Works of Thomas Hood*, edited "by his Son and Daughter" (London, 1869), I, pp. 184–85.

if our hone littel Fare down a Goos Grean don't lick it all to Styx.
Bulbeating, Baggerdrawing, Cuggleplaying, Rastlin, a Soped
pigtale, a Mane of Cox Jackasreacing jumpin in Sax, and a Grand
Sire Peal of Trouble Bobs puld by the youths by way of givn a
Bell's life to the hole. Call that Fancy. Too wild Best Shoes, fore
theaters besides a Horseplay A Dwarft A She Giant, a fat Child a
prize ox five carriboo savidges, a lurned Pigg a Albany with wite
Hares, a real see Murmaid a Fir Eater and lots of Punshes and
Juddis. Call that a Fare. . . . Now for Lonnon. No sanderses —
no Richardsens no wummils menageris no bacy boxys to shy for
— no luch Boxis. No poster makin no jugling or dancing. Prest
one Yung laidy in ruge cheaks and trowsers verry civelly for a bit a
caper on the tite rop — But miss got on the hi rop, and call'd for a
conestubble. Askt annother in a ridding habbit for the faver of a
little horsemanship and got kiced out of her Booth. Goos Grean
for my munny! Saw yung laidy there that swallerd a Sord an
wasn't too Partickler to jump threw a hoop. Dutchesses look dull
after that at a Fare. Verry dignified, but Prefer the Wax Wurk, as
a Show. Dont sea anny thing in Watch Pappers cut out by
Countisses that have been born with all their harms and
leggs. . . . Have a notion Perressis that keep Booths would take
moor Munny if they wasn't abuv having the dubble drums and
speaking trumpets and gongs. There's nothin like goin the hole
Hog![7]

Here, in contrast to Egan, Hood does assume that his readers are familiar
with the regular establishments of Greenwich Fair, and his sketch plays off
their knowledge. Yet a good deal of the humor resides in being able to
penetrate the phonetic orthography of the rustic persona. The point of the
sketch is to satirize the genteel pretensions of the ladies who maintain
charity booths at the fair: their useless "Watch Pappers," and their stultify-
ing dignity that falls short of the ironically ideal lifelessness of a "wax
work." The effect of the sketch does rest on the reader's recognition of the
events alluded to, but it also requires a willingness to submit to a very
contrived stance on the part of the author.

Similarly, when Theodore Hook undertakes a diminutive satiric
sketch of Greenwich, he shapes his presentation with a rhetoric that relies
on the readers' familiarity. He purports to view the fair and its activities as
part of a larger pattern of dissolution described in a paper on "National
Distress."

---

7. Ibid., pp. 353–56.

To us who remember Greenwich park in the year 1792, what a reverse! — then there were gaiety and sunshine, and fun and amusement. In the first place, Whit-Sunday this year was a wet Sunday, — a circumstance which, we are bold to say, never occurred before the late Mr. Pitt's accession to office, and very rarely even during his ruinous administration. . . . Our readers may conceive the gloom this oppressive mismanagement, and evident disregard for the comforts of the poor, threw over the quondam scene of gaiety; the people surely might have been allowed to meet, and weep in comfort in one of the Royal parks!

But if Sunday filled us with this feeling, what must Monday have done, when nature interfering, to triumph over the tyrants, gave the people a fine day? Then did we see them loading every sort of vehicle, on the inner and outer sides, driving horses, and donkeys, and ponies, and riding them with all their speed and energy, to reach the once-loved spot they had known in former days, and grieve all together at our deplorable state.

When arrived there how did they conduct themselves? They threw themselves into the most extravagant postures, rolling down hills, and running up again, throwing sticks even at oranges and cakes, in hopes of getting something to allay their hunger and thirst — some indeed we saw, decent looking persons, devouring with avidity fish, called eels who themselves (poor victims!) are driven to wallow in mud for their food, and first skinned alive, are next cut to pieces and finally exterminated by the hands of cooks as men are by ministers. — What a striking resemblance there is between an Eel and an Englishman.[8]

As in Hood's sketch, Hook's humor is basically a function of the persona — in this case a persona who is a curious blend of the naive and sophisticated. Hook's narrator is presumably bemoaning the lot of the poor and attributing their desperation at Greenwich to changes in the political climate since 1792. But of course the irony of the sketch operates to disqualify the narrator and his lamentations. The reader is expected to see that the fair progresses as it always has; that is, anyone who remembers "Greenwich park in the year 1792" would not be puzzled by the "extravagant postures, rolling down hills." (Both Egan's sketch and later Dickens' sketch describe rolling down hills as one of the more popular free amusements at the fair.) Similarly, the narrator's distraction at people "throwing sticks at . . . oranges and cakes," is an ironically naive description of people playing at games of chance. Comparably, eel eating, at which the narrator

---

8. *The Choice Humourous Works* (London: John Camden, n.d.), pp. 345–46.

pretends to be aghast, was a regular delicacy at the fair, which Dickens also reports. Thus the reader's response is not an acceptance of the narrator's presentation, but rather an evaluation and reconstruction of it. The success of the sketch rests on the reader's responding to the narrator's posture by seeing through his literal statements. At the same time, the point of the political satire in Hook's paper rests on the reader's willingness to accept his literal statements about the grotesque behavior of the people at Greenwich as evidence for the political ineptness producing the conditions of "national distress." Thus the success of the sketch rests on some rather complicated rhetorical reactions; Hook does not expect his reader to accept the presentation in any literal way. In a sense his sketch is only incidentally about Greenwich. It serves as a vehicle for very broad satirical purposes, one of which is the disqualification of the narrator's political commentary based on Greenwich Fair.

iii Boz and the other sketch writers

In contrast to these contemporaries, Boz's general approach to the sketch can be easily distinguished. He is never so presumptuously informative as Egan; he always assumes his audience has a basic familiarity with the subjects of his sketches. He is never so facetiously ironic as Hood is, nor does he ever use the sketch as obliquely as Hook does. In turning to Boz's treatment of Greenwich Fair, we will see that he does not attempt to present an idiosyncratic or private view of the fair. Rather, his purpose is to distill the essence of the fair, and report it as Everyman might see it, and contain and control the experience of the fair by relating to his audience through a fictive persona.

The excellence of *The Sketches by Boz* does not reside in the superior realism of the sketches, as both contemporary and more recent critics have insisted, but rather in the relationship Boz establishes with his readers in such a way as to promote their active participation in the vision of his sketches. In support of this thesis, we shall consider Boz's treatment of Greenwich Fair from three related perspectives: 1) The persona of Boz as a rhetorical device; 2) Boz's techniques in describing the fair; 3) Boz's techniques which effect active participation in the vision of the sketch.

The persona of Boz is of primary importance in understanding the kind of relationship between author and reader generated by the *Sketches*. Where Hood and Hook have their *ad hoc* ironic masks, Egan his encyclopedic guide, Dickens has a skillfully created persona who manipulates the effects of the sketch with a genial, mature, omniscient voice; a reassuring voice that is oracular in wisdom, prophetic in vision; it is a voice that dominates and controls the reader's responses throughout the *Sketches*.

In opening "Greenwich Fair" Dickens seems anxious to put the reader at ease by investing the narrator's voice with authority. Here, as in other *Sketches*, the narrative voice seeks to identify itself as being considerably more mature than the voice one might attribute to a speaker twenty-three years old, which Dickens was at the time the sketch was published: "In our earlier days we were a constant frequenter of Greenwich Fair, for years. . . ." In fact, the speaker deliberately tries to sound middle-aged:

> We have grown older since then, and quiet, and steady: liking nothing better than to spend our Easter, and all our other holidays, in some quiet nook, with people of whom we shall never tire. (*Sketches*, p. 111)

In terms of establishing a friendly and relaxed relationship with his reader, Dickens' technique in implying the speaker's age has several valuable rhetorical implications. It at once allows him to endorse attendance at the fair for those readers who retain some of the vitality and exuberance of youth and simultaneously, it allows him to suggest a wise sobriety and maturity as good reasons for abstention. Going to the fair and staying home are established as equally valuable alternatives. The reader is at ease in that his own attendance at the fair will not conflict with the narrator's views. Here we begin to see one of Boz's most discrete rhetorical techniques. He controls the reader's responses in such a way as to neutralize all opposition to what is being said.

In contrast to Egan, Boz is not trying to use Greenwich as a compendium of historical facts; nor does he make the fair a satiric object as Hood and Hook do, thereby requiring that the reader laugh at the foolish vanity of the fair, at the society that supports it, and at the person (perhaps himself) who attends it. Instead, "Greenwich Fair" becomes a vehicle for establishing a relationship with Boz's readers; the base of this relationship is a shared belief in the knowability of the world, a faith in the penetrability of the confusing surface of life.

In considering Boz's techniques in describing the fair, it is important to notice that Boz purports to be comfortably indifferent to the concrete events of a particular Greenwich Fair. Supposedly, Boz is writing from memory: ". . . but we think we remember enough of Greenwich Fair, and those who resort to it, to make a sketch of this seasonable period."[9]

---

9. *Evening Chronicle*, Apr. 16, 1835. The later revised version increases the sense of an old person writing from memory: "but we think we still remember something of Greenwich Fair, and those who resort to it. At all events we will try" (*Sketches*, p. 111).

Rhetorically, the supposition that Boz can report on the fair without attending it has very affirmative implications. Dickens' stance assumes a certain stability about its subject; it implies that the annual fair, resurrected *ad hoc*, has a permanence despite its hurly-burly atmosphere.

At the same time Boz's admission that he is not reporting on a specific Greenwich fair establishes an omniscient, almost oracular, predisposition towards the experience in which he invites the reader to participate. The oracular voice of Boz knows, and thoroughly understands Greenwich Fair — and all of the subjects of his sketches. He offers the reader an opportunity to share a vision in which the world is transparent and all action attaches itself to pattern and ritual.

Boz's tendency to see all action as ritual shapes his entire presentation. It is almost as though he were attempting to provide that dimension of order which ritual provides for more primitive societies. Thus in integrating the fair into a natural cycle, Boz represents it as a

> periodical breaking out, we suppose, a sort of spring rash: a three days' fever, which cools the blood for six months afterwards, and at the expiration of which London is restored to its old habits of plodding industry, as suddenly and completely as if nothing had ever happened to disturb them. (*Sketches*, p. 111)

The humorous intention of Boz's simile is inescapable. But the humor is finally subservient to the presiding rhetorical purpose of presenting the fair as an annual ritual, which is divided into smaller rituals repeating themselves endlessly. Thus the dancers in the ballroom, with their "scrambling and falling, and embracing, and knocking up against the other couples" becomes part of a scene "repeated again and again (slightly varied by an occasional 'row') until a late hour at night." (Ibid., p. 118). Or at the theatre, we are told:

> A change of performance takes place every day during the fair, but the story of the tragedy is always pretty much the same. (Ibid., p. 116)

Boz's omniscient voice is peculiarly slanted in the direction of ritual. Northrop Frye tells us that a ritual is a "temporal sequence of acts in which the conscious meaning or significance is latent: it can be seen by an observer, but is largely concealed from the participants themselves."[10] With

---

10. Northrop Frye, *Anatomy of Criticism*, p. 154.

a kind of oracular sagacity, Boz discerns and describes the latent meaning of little rituals at the fair:

> You will see a sunburnt woman in a red cloak "telling fortunes" and prophesying husbands, which it requires no extraordinary observation to describe, for the originals are before her. Thereupon, the lady concerned laughs and blushes, and ultimately buries her face in an imitation cambric handkerchief, and the gentleman described looks extremely foolish, and squeezes her hand, and fees the gipsy liberally; and the gipsy goes away perfectly satisfied herself . . . and the prophecy, like other prophecies of greater importance, fulfils itself in time. (*Sketches*, p. 113)

The oracular Boz has observed the world in such a way as to discern its rituals and prophesy the accuracy of prophecies. Here Boz hovers over the scene, knowingly commenting on the way of the world, taking a God's-eye view of the fortune-telling ritual that will culminate in another genial but cosmically insignificant marriage. Boys will be boys, and girls, girls.

Because of Boz's peculiar narrative stance and omniscience, there are no primary moments of experience in his report of the fair. Nothing is reported as having happened, rather everything happens, over and over again: all events are plural, so on the road to Greenwich Fair,

> turnpike men are in despair; horses won't go on, and wheels will come off; ladies in "carawans" scream with fright at every fresh concussion, and their admirers find it necessary to sit remarkably close to them, by way of encouragement. (Ibid., p. 112)

Nothing is emblematic of itself, but rather stands for one of the many patterns which Boz has discerned, penetrated and offers to his readers. Concrete details, which in the rhetoric of most authors are the evidence of the peculiar and idiosyncratic event, in Boz become evidence of the typical:

> Little old men and women, with a small basket under one arm, and a wine-glass, without a foot, in the other hand tender "a drop o' the right sort" to the different groups. (Ibid., p. 113)

Here, the broken wine glass and the snatch of colloquial dialogue are not intended to describe a peculiar and unique wine vendor, but rather, the details are offered as the characteristics of a whole genus of vendors at the fair. Similarly, the details of the couple who consult the fortune-teller in the quotation above make them emblematic of a whole class of people: "the imitation cambric handkerchief," the gentleman's "foolish" looks, his hand squeeze and liberal "fee" make him a stereotype rather than an individual. In a sense Boz controls the world by refusing to allow that anything is idiosyncratic.

Even events that would ordinarily smack of the improper or indecorous are neutralized by Boz's rhetorical predisposition towards the actions. He omnisciently traces the amorous behavior of "love sick swains" to the influence of "gin and water" as well as "the tender passion." And, when the swains "become violently affectionate, and the fair objects of their regard enhance the value of stolen kisses by a vast deal of struggling and holding down of heads and cries," Boz neutralizes the impropriety of public love-making and drunkenness with his benign and genial rhetorical stance. The lovers become another of the many rituals of the fair.

We have already seen how Dickens' early stories rely on idiosyncrasy as a basis for characterization, and in some instances for plot. Although the bulk of our comparison between Dickens' stories and his sketches will be in a later section of this study, it is worthwhile to observe now that the rhetorical effect of Dickens' use of idiosyncrasy in the sketches as opposed to the stories is quite different. In the stories, the characters are *reduced to* their idiosyncrasies, exhausted by them. The reader is also bludgeoned by them. He cannot help but feel that a life we know in this way is both dull and a lie. The contracted possibilities of character that Dickens allows in his stories demean human potential. Rhetorically such an approach denies the affirmative assumptions about human character that make individuality, dignity, and ultimately heroism possible. Accordingly, and largely because of this technique, the stories culminate in an absurdist vision. But in the sketches Dickens' use of character idiosyncrasy has a very different effect. The ability to fabricate or isolate idiosyncratic details of dress, posture, mannerism, or speech, typifying individuals, or classes of individuals, is a specialized, but not unique accomplishment. Even the most generous assessments would call such an approach to human character "superficial." Strikingly, in a manner quite different from his stories, Dickens' sketches allow that the reduction of human character to generic idiosyncrasies *is* very superficial. The depiction of idiosyncratic characters becomes only part of a vision that places such superficial observation in a more honest and, rhetorically, far more affirmative perspective. Implicitly, Dickens' stories assert: "This is human character, uniformly idiosyncratic, trivial, absurd." But his sketches make a much more complicated, and modest statement. The benign and genial narrator of Dickens' sketches seems to be saying: "As I look around me the romance of real life is perpetually revealing itself. Details of dress and speech, and mannerism, and gestures make the classes, the pursuits and the preoccupations of our society quite clear. Look for yourself! It's all there, awaiting your observation. It all makes sense."

In contrast to the relatively passive expectations of Egan's, Hood's, and Hook's sketches of Greenwich Fair, Boz's assumptions about his audience, his expectations of his readers, and his range of effects work in such a way as to enforce the reader's active participation in Boz's vision of experience. Boz's pluralistic vision that reports action as ritual, his elimination of primary moments of experience (i.e., the reporting of the highly abstract "what happens" in lieu of the more concrete "what happened") increase the reader's participation in the rhetorical process. As long as the narrator restricts himself to a presentation of "what happened," his observations are a series of either true or fictive facts to which the reader responds rather passively, as a recipient. When the narrator moves away from "what happened" and the level of abstraction is stepped up to the more generalized "what happens," the reader's involvement is increased by an opportunity and obligation to measure and validate the abstractions with his own experience. The readers of Boz's sketches are constantly called in to validate the accuracy of his reporting. In contrast Egan requires that his readers sit for lectures that combine the commonplace with the erudite. Rhetorically, in both instances Egan's reader is at a disadvantage. He is not given credit for what he does know, and he is subjected to a barrage of information that he could not possibly know. Thus he is constantly excluded from an active participation in and identification with, the narrative. Similarly, though both Hood and Hook presume a greater knowledge on the part of their readers, their rhetoric assigns the readers the role of reconstructing their literal statements, seeing through to implied meanings, and thereby excluding them from participation in the narrator's literal, non-ironic point of view. Boz's sketches anticipate a reader who shares the narrator's knowledge and viewpoint.

Additionally, if we consider the tense of Boz's reporting, we find further evidence of his ability to anticipate and control the reader's participation. Most readers will have noticed that Boz's reporting is primarily in the present tense. But curiously he has already admitted he is writing from memory. However, his choice is a discreet one in that it has at least two rhetorical advantages. First of all his use of the present tense much more actively involves the reader in perception and judgment than would a more usual narrative stance in the past tense. Rhetorically, events described in the past tense are over and done with. But events described in the present tense elicit our attention; they demand our attention to things that are happening before us. Secondly, while the present-tense narrative increases the reader's sense of immediacy, concomitantly it diminishes the dominance of the narrator's presence. As in the following statement, the narrator merges with his observations, thereby allowing the reader to enter the narrative more actively. "Pedestrians linger in groups at the roadside, unable to resist the allurements of the stout proprietress of the 'Jack-in-the-box, three shies a penny.'" The use of the historical present, "pedestrians linger," rather than the past, "pedestrians lingered," diminishes the presence of the narrative voice. The use of the past tense in such instances would call our attention to the narrator as an eye-witness. He would be highlighting what he *had* seen. But with the benign, genial, omniscience of the narrator firmly established, he is no longer interested in pointing to himself as eye-witness. Instead, he uses the present tense to open up the narrative and allow the reader's own memory or imagination an opportunity to perceive and validate the occurrence. Frequently, as in the above example, Boz guarantees his desired effect by requiring the reader to fuse a statement in the historical present with snatches of interpolated dramatic dialogue; the net effect is one of immediacy, as the reader negotiates the rapid transition from the historical to the dramatic present.

Further, Boz allows and even exhorts his readers to do a good part of the structuring of his sketch for themselves. While the sketch of "Greenwich Fair" moves in time and setting from afternoon on the road to Greenwich, to dusk at the entrance to the fair, and finally to a wee-hours-of-the-morning conclusion at the ballroom, there is relatively little attempt to orient the reader spatially. In contrast, Pierce Egan belabors his readers with copious notations on spatial relations: "to the right, left, above below, facing, opposite," all of which may be useful in a piece intended as a guide. But Boz recognizes intuitively that such indications are both intrusive and useless. If the reader is familiar with the site, they are unnecessary and presumptuous. If the reader is unfamiliar, unless he plans to re-read the sketch "on location," they simply slow down and confuse his reading. Boz's assumption is that the reader knows, or can put together the spatial relationships of the various places of amusement being described. This indifference to spatial order throws the familiar reader into a producer role. The reader has to process the experience for himself; he has to co-create, to cooperate in the creation of the work. This quality of Dickens' rhetoric calls for the direct participation of the reader. Occasionally this activity on the part of the reader is demanded quite explicitly where the narrator uses imperatives in lieu of less obtrusive structural and transitional devices:

> *Imagine* yourself in an extremely dense crowd, . . . *See* with what ferocious air the gentleman who personates the Mexican chief paces up and down. (*Sketches*, pp. 114–15, my italics)

Rhetorically, the imperatives draw the reader into the narrative. They presume either his familiarity with the subject, or his capacity for imagination and vision.

In an allied manner, Dickens describes some of the other highlights of the fair, proceeding elliptically, always presuming the reader's intelligence or experience will enable him to keep up:

> See . . . with what an eye of calm dignity the principle tragedian gazes on the crowd below, or converses confidentially with the harlequin! The four clowns, who are engaged in mock broadsword combat, may be all very well for the low-minded holiday-makers; but *these* are the people for the reflective portion of the community. *They* look so noble in *those* Roman dresses, with their yellow legs and arms, long black curly heads, bushy eyebrows, and scowl expressive of assassination, and vengeance, and everything else that is grand and solemn. (Ibid., p. 115, my italics)

Here the use of pronouns without antecedents, and the rapid juxtaposition of the various actors who flow into a panorama of activity, suggest the narrator's eye, snatching at details of the scene. The deliberate omission of transitions with rapidly shifting subjects forces the reader into actively organizing such passages while the passages themselves skillfully re-create the energy and confusion of the fair.

In all, Dickens' sketch of "Greenwich Fair" has very different intentions and effects than the sketches of his "rivals." While Dickens' rhetorical stance entails a slight though good-natured condescension towards the fair, the condescension does not extend to his readers. Instead, through a skillful variety of techniques, he enlists his readers' participation in a shared affirmative vision of Greenwich Fair.

iv Stories and sketches, a difference in vision

The same quality that distinguishes Dickens' sketches from those of his rivals also distinguishes his sketches from his stories. Although Dickens' sketches are inhabited by the same curiously transparent figures who people his short stories, the world they move in, in the sketches, is considerably more complex. Where the stories prosecute a negative vision of society, the sketches culminate in a far more positive vision. The remainder of this chapter will be given to showing how the techniques Dickens uses in his sketches effect a radical reconstruction of the vision and rhetoric of his short stories.

Dickens published his first sketch more than nine months after he published his first short story. Though "Greenwich Fair," the sketch I have discussed in the preceding pages, was published midway in Dickens' sketch-writing career (April 7, 1835), many of the qualities I have observed in it are present in the very earliest sketches. The most conspicuous of these is the narrator. The short stories are told by a highly ironic narrator whose condescension, superciliousness, and sardonic tone end in a contempt towards his subjects and an undermining of his own way of seeing the world. In contrast, from the very beginning the narrator of the sketches presents himself as a genial, urbane, omniscient intelligence, a compassionate apologist for a far more complex and coherent world. In and of itself, the narrative voice of the sketches effects a radical shift in the rhetoric that has presided in Dickens' short stories.

Further, the characteristic structures that Dickens developed for writing the sketch provided him with a form for presenting a vision of a far more complex world, with a much broader range of affective relevance and appeals than the world that had existed in the short stories.

To begin with we have seen that the world of Dickens' short stories is one-dimensional. The world of a given story takes its shape from the protagonist's character; the events are directed towards an exposure of the protagonist's shallow pretensions, his inability to transcend the pathetic limitations of his idiosyncrasies; his idiosyncrasies seem to be at odds with the sardonic forces of a humiliating world. Except for the sensibility of the narrator, who never enters the story dramatically, there are no possibilities of dignity or unpretentious decorum in the stories. All of the story characters occupy a ludicrously transparent and trivial world that locks up all experience in a single plane. Rhetorically the stories reach for only one response, a sardonic laughter.

In contrast, Dickens' sketches make rhetorical appeals to many emotions and reach for many responses. Instead of the uniformly simple and ironic stance of the short stories, the sketches present a new complexity of tone and attitude, much of which derives from Dickens' use of comparisons as a framework for discussing his subject. The technique of comparison

- eventually becomes the base of a form that allowed Dickens to approve and disapprove of his society simultaneously. Let us consider Dickens' use of comparison in some of his earliest sketches.

v Comparison and the complex sketch mode

Though Dickens' first published sketch, "Omnibuses," does not show the final form that Dickens developed for the sketch, it does illustrate some of the technical differences that make for the very different rhetoric of the sketch. First of all, though Dickens' title and topic is "Omnibuses," he begins the sketch with a discussion of stagecoaches and then proceeds to a comparative discussion of his real topic. The technique here, in itself, is unremarkable; it is undoubtedly the outgrowth of a schoolboy's exercises in classic definition whereby he offers first the *genus* and then the *differentia* of the object to be defined. But ultimately the effect of this comparative technique on both the texture and rhetoric of the sketch is most important.

Thus in the sketch "Omnibuses," Dickens begins by listing the inconveniences of stagecoaches. His narrator makes the following complaints: 1) stagecoaches have "no change, no variety in passengers;" 2) the passengers "get cross and sleepy" on bumpy roads and excessively "prosy" on smooth ones; 3) one may have to suffer the company of a man who drinks rum and water at every stop; 4) and not infrequently, one shares company with a "small boy of pale aspect with light hair and no perceptible neck" who is enroute to school. Having set out the disadvantages of stagecoach travel, Dickens proceeds to his real topic, carefully answering his objections to stagecoaches with the differing correlative attributes of omnibuses.

> Now you meet with none of these afflictions in an omnibus; sameness there can never be. The passengers change as often in the course of one journey as the figures in a kaleidoscope, and though not so glittering, are far more amusing. We believe there is no instance on record, of a man's having gone to sleep in one of these vehicles. As to long stories, would any man venture to tell a long story in an omnibus? and even if he did, where would be the harm? nobody could possibly hear what he was talking about. Again; children, though occasionally, are not often to be found in an omnibus; and even when they are, if the vehicle be full, as is generally the case, somebody sits upon them, and we are unconscious of their presence. Yes, after mature reflection, and considerable experience, we are decidedly of opinion, that of all known vehicles, from the glass-coach in which we were taken to be christened, to that sombre caravan in which we must one day

make our last earthly journey, there is nothing like an omnibus. (*Sketches*, p. 138)

The rhetorical effect here is very significant. The sketch has opened with a wry critique of stagecoaches. In turning to his real topic, Dickens at least temporarily suggests an amelioration of every specific disadvantage of stagecoach travel. In contrast to the confinement of a stagecoach, the omnibus offers a variety of passengers and a breath of freedom; freedom from children, snoring old men, and the tedium of long stories. Though the description of the omnibus' advantages has its own wry insinuations of disadvantages (which are developed in the rest of the sketch) for a moment at least the reader has been presented with an affirmative alternative to the unpleasantness of stagecoach travel. The negative qualities of stagecoach travel seem cancelled and overcome by the comparative advantages of omnibuses. Thus, the world of the sketches begins to take on a complexity which was lacking in the short stories. For once, the narrator allows himself to look two ways before issuing pronouncements about the value of things. Omnibuses are seen within the context of stagecoaches.

Though this first sketch finally culminates in the flip and sardonic tone that Dickens had used in his short stories, the technique of opening with a comparison led the way to developing a much greater variety of tones in subsequent sketches. Either by accident or intention Dickens had hit upon a device for presenting a much more complicated picture of reality, and a form that could contain varying attitudes toward it while eliciting very different rhetorical responses.

That Dickens recognized implicitly the value of this technique is borne out by a perusal of the succeeding sketches. Of Dickens' first eight published sketches, six open with the technique of comparison: "Omnibuses," "Shabby Genteel People," "Brokers' and Marine Store Shops," "Hackney Coach Stands," "Gin Shops," "Early Coaches." (The remaining two sketches use an allied, but different, form of comparison for their openings.)

In the third published sketch, "The Old Bailey," Dickens' use of comparison is much less direct. Yet he proceeds to discuss his subject by breaking it into a number of discrete parts, in each of which he assumes a slightly different tone. The three major parts of the sketch are: 1) a reminiscence of Dickens' youthful attitude towards prison; 2) a tableau in which Dickens describes the wayward son; and 3) a description of the two courts at the Old Bailey, the Old Court and the New Court. Though there is some use of both implicit and explicit comparison within the sketch, its

˙most noteworthy quality arises from the great diversity of tones that Dickens experiments with here.

"The Old Bailey" may well have unlocked a sensibility which heretofore had only broadcast itself in a presidingly ironic and supercilious tone. For whatever reason, unmistakably this sketch reveals new concerns, new directions, and new seriousness in Dickens' writing. The first two paragraphs of "The Old Bailey" have a confessional tone and seem to anticipate a much more private confession that Dickens was later to make to only one person in his whole life; neither his wife nor children were ever to be privy to the dark secret he shared with Forster — the agony of being a debtor's son, the shame of visiting his father in prison, the fear of the Marshalsea and the neighborhood of the blacking warehouse that brought tears to his eyes and left him shaken and disoriented even as a mature adult. The weight of all these memories seems to be coloring the first two paragraphs of "The Old Bailey" (revised as "Criminal Courts").

> We shall never forget the mingled feelings of awe and respect with which we used to gaze on the exterior of Newgate in our schoolboy days. How dreadful its rough heavy walls, and low massive doors, appeared to us — the latter looking as if they were made for the express purpose of letting people in, and never letting them out again. Then the fetters over the debtors' door, which we used to think were a *bona fide* set of irons, just hung up there, for convenience sake, ready to be taken down at a moment's notice and riveted on the limbs of some refractory felon! We were never tired of wondering how the hackney-coachmen on the opposite stand could cut jokes in the presence of such horrors, and drink pots of half-and-half so near the last drop.
>
> Often have we strayed here, in sessions time, to catch a glimpse of the whipping-place, and that dark building on one side of the yard, in which is kept the gibbet with all its dreadful apparatus, and on the door of which we half expected to see a brass plate, with the inscription "Mr. Ketch"; for we never imagined that the distinguished functionary could by possibility live anywhere else! (*Sketches*, p. 196)

The paragraphs above are the most personal and emotional writing Dickens had published to date. Though there is some attempt to distance the memories he describes by setting them in his boyish past, still the allusions to fear, horror and dread are the closest Dickens had yet come in appealing to pathos directly. Significantly, the paragraphs that follow these are the first published writings in which Dickens focuses on a public institution, anticipating the "awe," "dread," and "horror" of institutions that was to find its way into Dickens' novels and to spur his subsequent humanitarian activities. In the stories he had already published, Dickens had found it fairly easy to fend off his deeper feelings about prisons — we are asked to laugh at Mr. Simpson in "The Boarding House," who goes to prison for debt; or later, Mr. Watkins Tottle's detention in a sponging house is seen as a fitting punishment for his timidity, and a prelude to his ironic suicide. But in "The Old Bailey," for the first time we see Dickens straightforwardly describing his feelings about a prison, and this sketch inaugurates a new diversity of tones in Dickens' writings.

In fact, the rest of "The Old Bailey" suffers from a confusion of tone. It seems that having stumbled onto his feelings about prisons, Dickens is unable to find his customary sustained attitude towards his subject. The sketch moves from the reflection on prisons to an unabashed sentimental reflection on "the wayward son," an archetype that reappears frequently in *Sketches by Boz*.[11] Dickens records a tableau of a young man leaving prison:

> The boy was her son, to whose early comfort she had perhaps sacrificed her own — for whose sake she had borne misery without repining, and poverty without a murmur — looking steadily forward to the time when he who had so long witnessed her struggles for himself might be enabled to make some exertions for their joint support. He had formed dissolute connexions; idleness had led to crime; and he had been committed to take his trial for some petty theft. He had been long in prison, and, after receiving some trifling additional punishment, had been ordered to be discharged that morning. It was his first offence, and his poor old mother, still hoping to reclaim him, had been waiting at the gate to implore him to return home. . . . The woman put her hand upon his shoulder in an agony of entreaty, and the boy sullenly raised his head as if in refusal. . . . Perhaps the wretchedness of his mother made some impression on the boy's heart; perhaps some undefined recollection of the time when he was a happy child, and she his only friend, and best companion, crowded on him — he burst into tears; and covering his face with one hand, and hurriedly placing the other in his mother's, walked away with her. (*Sketches*, pp. 197–98)

---

11. Other "wayward sons" appear in "The Black Veil," pp. 371–81, and "Meditations in Monmouth Street," pp. 74–81.

Here again we have the emergence of a new tone in Dickens' writing. The melodramatic situation and the operatic gesturing of the newly released prisoner are an outgrowth of, but very different in feeling from, the preceding reflections on the prison.

A third tone enters the sketch as Dickens shifts abruptly from the wayward son to a description of the two "courts at the Old Bailey." At the "Old Court" he contemptuously points to the "calm indifference" of "the proceedings," to the excess of "form but no compassion; considerable interest, but no sympathy" (*Sketches*, p. 198). He indignantly berates the "body of the Court — some wholly engrossed in the morning papers . . . carelessly conversing, . . . quietly dozing away an hour" (Ibid.). Dickens proceeds with an ominous melodramatic voice as he describes the prisoner in the dock:

> Mark how restlessly he has been engaged for the last ten minutes, in forming all sorts of fantastic figures with the herbs which are strewed upon the ledge before him; observe the ashy paleness of his face when a particular witness appears, and how he changes his position and wipes his clammy forehead, and feverish hands. (Ibid.)

This part of the sketch concludes with the climactic report of "a shriek" that "bursts from a female in the gallery" when the verdict of guilty is delivered. The very last part of this "Old Court" section of the sketch returns to the tone of the opening critique of the court's indifference: "and fresh business is proceeded with, as if nothing had occurred" (Ibid., p. 199).

Dickens concludes the whole sketch by describing the "New Court" and assuming another new tone, a righteous indignation towards the "cunning and pertinacity of juvenile offenders" (Ibid.). Dickens implicitly condemns the defendant in "New Court" who

> asserts that all the witnesses have committed perjury, and hints that the police force generally have entered into a conspiracy "again" him. (Ibid.)

He continues using snatches of the defendant's dialect to enforce his own righteous attitude towards the defendant's flippancy. The final sentence of the section and the sketch closes with an underscoring of the narrator's impatience with the defendant:

He gives vent to his feelings in an indignant cry of "Flare up, old big vig!" and as he declines to take the trouble of walking from the dock, he is forthwith carried out by two men, congratulating himself on having succeeded in giving everybody as much trouble as possible.[12]

In all, the complexity of narrative attitudes and variety of tonal effect in "The Old Bailey" are a long way from the uniform irony of Dickens' short stories. More importantly, both the structure of the sketch and the complexity of narrative viewpoint that arises from the structure underscore a distinct development that was to influence many of Dickens' sketches and many of his novels. The structure and tonal variety of "The Old Bailey" present the reader with perplexing questions: What finally is Dickens' attitude toward the prison and court system he describes in this sketch? How does the grim opening of the sketch where Dickens recalls his youthful fear of prisons mesh with the self-righteousness of the closing section where Dickens seems to side with the abused dignity of the court — totally indifferent to seeing a man carried off to prison. Or, in the second part of the sketch, how does Dickens' compassion for the "wayward son" and his long-suffering mother relate to his condescension and self-righteousness towards the "pertinacious urchin" — undoubtedly another wayward son — whose sentencing closes the sketch? Given the level of archetypal generality that the sketch operates on, they are for all intents and purposes the same boy. Why the different attitudes towards them? Similarly, how do the criticisms of the "Old Court's" overly expeditious indifference to the defendant being tried mesh with the implicit indignation at the "New Court's" having to waste time with an impudent defendant? Dickens seems to reject both the expeditious and the patient courts!

Instead of the single attitude of the ironic short stories, "The Old Bailey" presents us with a variety of attitudes that are impossible to synthesize into a single point of view. Implicit in the structure of the sketch is a very complex attitude about which we can say several things. First of all, the answer to the question "What is the narrator's attitude towards the court and prisons in 'The Old Bailey'?" can only be found through a *comparison* of conflicting attitudes scattered through the sketch. Secondly, although the sketch does make some very explicit criticism of the judicial

---

12. *Evening Chronicle*, Oct. 23, 1834. Later versions have changes in the first line: "he gives vent to his feelings in an imprecation bearing reference to the eyes of 'old big vig!'" (*Sketches*, p. 200).

·and penal systems, overall, the rhetoric of the sketch is calculated to effect an affirmative endorsement of the systems, for the following reasons: Though Dickens does strike a new note in the opening of the sketch, recalling his childish fears of prisons, he is careful to see that these fears do not dominate his attitude towards the subject. Before moving on to the next section of the sketch he cancels out the relevance of those childish fears by setting them in a comparative temporal framework: "The days of these childish dreams have passed away, and with them many other boyish ideas of a gayer nature" (*Sketches*, p. 196). Thirdly, though the sketch moves through a critique of the courts, the final section is given over to an implicit endorsement of them, their dignity and their patience, a repudiation of those scalawags who would make a mockery of the benign workings of justice. Thus, because only a synthesis of conflicting attitudes that the sketch presents will lead us to the narrator's overall attitude, and because of the shape Dickens gives to the sketch, he is able to have it both ways. No casual reader of Boz's sketches would bother to add it up, to ask "What does this come to?" Hence Dickens can both negate and affirm the subject of his sketch.

This is not to blame Dickens for not being a polemicist, to demand that he present a single and dogmatic attitude towards all of his subjects. Rather the attempt here is to point out a characteristic way that Dickens developed for working with his subjects and to suggest that the techniques he developed give us a fundamental insight into the rhetoric, artistry, and vision of both his early and mature writings.

vi A pattern emerges

After "The Old Bailey," Dickens' comparative introduction, and his accompanying divergent attitudes towards each member of the comparison become a way of reconciling a critique of society with an affirmation of the *status quo*, a way of both condemning and approving the various subjects of his sketches, a way of saying both "Isn't it deplorable?" and "It's O.K." Thus in the fourth published sketch "Shabby Genteel People," Dickens begins by separating out from the subject of his discussion two classes: the purely shabby and the purely genteel. He proceeds to balance the melancholy pathos of the "shabby genteel" against the assurance that the phenomenon is not widespread; it exists only in London: "this shabby gentility — is as purely local as the statue at Charing Cross, or the pump at Aldgate" (*Sketches*, p. 262). In the manner of a social-geneticist he assures his readers that shabby-gentility is a sex-linked characteristic:

It is worthy of remark, too, that only men are shabby-genteel; a woman is always either dirty and slovenly in the extreme, or neat and respectable, however poverty-stricken in appearance. (Ibid.)

At this point the sketch has narrowed down its focus through the exclusion of four comparative classes: 1) the genteel, 2) the shabby, 3) non-Londoners, 4) all women. The narrator explicitly and implicitly announces different attitudes towards the classes. Finally, before proceeding to the real topic, the narrator carefully directs us to exclude from our sympathies an unnamed, comparative species of impoverished man who is likely to be confused with the "shabby genteel;" the species might be called the faded dandy-about-town:

If you meet a man, lounging up Drury Lane, or leaning with his back against a post in Long Acre, with his hands in the pockets of a pair of drab trousers plentifully besprinkled with grease-spots: the trousers made very full over the boots, and ornamented with two cords down the outside of each leg — wearing, also, what has been a brown coat with bright buttons, and a hat very much pinched up at the sides, cocked over his right eye — don't pity him. He is not shabby-genteel. The "harmonic meetings" at some fourth-rate public-house, or the purlieus of a private theatre, are his chosen haunts; he entertains a rooted antipathy to any kind of work, and is on familiar terms with several pantomime men at the large houses. (*Sketches*, pp. 262–63)

The most striking thing about the above description is the length that Dickens goes to, to exclude the subject from the reader's sympathy, "don't pity him." He tells his readers implicitly, "Don't waste your sympathies on any old derelict." He is antagonistic to the man's leisurely, somewhat cocky style; offended by his faded foppishness and condescending towards the man's ability to salvage some kind of ego, self-respect, and social pretense; he encourages his reader's contempt for this kind of shabbiness.

Thus, the comparative framework having been established, the sketch can proceed to its real subject, inviting the reader's sympathy for a sub-class of derelicts, those who are ashamed of their own poverty, those who with a "timorous air of conscious poverty, will make your heart ache" (*Sketches*, p. 263). In great detail Dickens sketches out the pathos of a shabby-genteel man's feeble attempts to hide his poverty, concluding that such a man "is one of the most pitiable objects in human nature" (Ibid., p. 265). But just as in "The Old Bailey," if we pause and ask ourselves what the sketch comes to, we are faced with a similar kind of confusion and ambiguity. On the one hand the sketch encourages contempt for the irreverent poor, the man whose dress and actions announce his indifference to middle-class society's judgments of him and his ability to carry off a self-vindicating façade. The narrator implies that such men should be ashamed of themselves, their immodestly foppish trousers "besprinkled" with grease, and their antipathy to work. Yet on the other hand, when the sketch turns to a contemplation of a man who has entirely submitted to the shame of poverty and is obviously haunted by his diminishing ability to maintain genteel appearances, we are asked to advance our compassion. In a sense the' sketch is saying: "Any man who is poor and ill-kempt should be ashamed of himself, but isn't it a shame when the poor and ill-kempt are ashamed." The tonal variety in the sketch ranges from smug superiority to patronizing compassion. Rhetorically the sketch encourages the reader to exclude from his compassion all those who are not conspicuously burdened with their inability to meet middle-class notions of decency; and that group includes the simplistic category of women who are always "dirty and slovenly in the extreme" as well as the faded, would-be dandies. Dickens has carefully controlled the social and political ramifications of his sketch. Though the sketch is about the grotesqueness of poverty, he restricts the reader's sympathies to a very special and localized kind of poverty — the shabby genteel; others can fend for themselves.

Nor is this to say that Dickens had no genuine compassion for the poor. Rather we see that a real, if somewhat patronizing compassion co-exists with a supercilious detachment, just as in the previous sketch a self-righteous indignation to "pertinacious urchins" co-exists with a melo-dramatic compassion when the "urchin" is presented as the "wayward son." Dickens' old uniformly ironic vision is breaking up. He continues using comparisons as a means of containing contradictory attitudes.

Two out of the next three sketches Dickens published follow exactly the same pattern of announcing a topic for discussion, excluding various comparative sub-categories, and attributing different values to the sub-categories while shaping the reader's responses to them. Thus in the fifth published sketch, "Brokers' and Marine Store Shops," we find the familiar opening pattern. The narrator begins by showing his wholehearted approval of the merchandise in first-class brokers' shops:

> Perhaps when we make use of the term "Brokers' Shop," the
> minds of our readers will at once picture large, handsome

warehouses, exhibiting a long perspective of French-polished dining-tables, rosewood chiffoniers, and mahogany wash-hand-stands, with an occasional vista of a four-post bedstead and hangings, and an appropriate foreground of dining-room chairs. (*Sketches*, p. 177)

But such elegant warehouses are really not the subject of the sketch, so the narrator moves on to another category of shops, those that would most likely cater to the lower middle classes, with their "groves of deceitful showy-looking furniture," with "goods . . . adapted to the taste, or rather to the means, of cheap purchasers" (*Sketches*, p. 177). And again, dismissing this category of shop, just as in the previous sketches, the narrator moves on to his real subject: "small dirty shop[s], exposing for sale the most extraordinary and confused jumble of old, worn-out, wretched articles, that can well be imagined" (Ibid., p. 178). He proceeds to describe several different kinds of this lowest class of shop, carefully enumerating their respective merchandises, and finally concludes the sketch with a pronounced appeal to pathos in reflecting on some used garments exposed for sale:

> There they are, thrown carelessly together until a purchaser presents himself, old, and patched and repaired, it is true; but the make and materials tell of better days; and the older they are, the greater the misery and destitution of those whom they once adorned. (*Sketches*, p. 181)

Though the subject of "Brokers' and Marine Store Shops" is very different from the previous two sketches, Dickens' techniques, the structure he uses for the sketch, and even his variety of affective appeals are identical. He presents his topic with a discretely categorized but finally unsynthesized series of comparisons. Between Dickens' unabashed admirations of fine shops and his solicitous compassion for the poorest shops, the reader is faced with the problem of integrating his condescending contempt for the middle range of shops. The three divergent attitudes do not make for a consistent position towards material well-being in society as reflected in the quality of goods available to various classes of people; perhaps such consistency can only come from a social philosopher. Instead, Dickens surveys his subject in a way that induces the reader to share his admiration, laughter, and compassion for various aspects of his society, with no necessity of seeing things whole.

Thus the use of comparisons, categorization, and stratification in dealing with his sketch topics led Dickens to a variety of tones in his writing. Where his short stories present a one-dimensional world subjected to the levelling omniscience of an ironic narrator, his sketches present a multi-dimensional world, constructed from the varying attitudes of a much more sympathetic and complex narrator.

The limitations of the short stories, their uniformity, their mythic vision undercut by ironic humor, are overcome in the sketches. Where the stories can only present an anti-hero in a one-dimensional universe — pratfalling through an apparently cosmic pratfall — the sketches respond with a hero in the person of the narrator, a reassuring, compassionate, knowing seer and apologist for a far more complex world.

Significantly, the differences in Dickens' early sketches brings them closer to what we have called an empirical view of reality. We have discussed an empirical view of reality in the following ways: 1) An empirical view of reality, whether it be focused on the object, time, space, change, or causality, always dissects its subject into *partial factors* and *partial conditions*. 2) It seeks to understand its subject through the complex intermingling, interpenetration, and constant conjunction of these partialities. 3) It is always left with a certain sphere of indeterminancy surrounding its subject. Rhetorically, the techniques of Dickens' early sketches move in the direction of supporting an empirical view of the world. The subjects are always dissected into *"partial factors* and *partial conditions."* We understand the subject of the sketch through a complex intermingling, interpenetration, and conjunction of these partialities, thereby leaving a certain indeterminacy surrounding the subject. Dickens' sketches present a vision of reality in which even the most banal subjects, omnibuses, prisons, courts, shops, classes of people are seen in a framework of partiality and tentativeness. Of course a truly empirical view of reality aspires to a "universal synthesis in the comprehension of all particulars." But it is at this point that Dickens' sketch techniques fail to produce a truly empirical view of reality; what they produce is pseudo-empirical. The dissected subject in Dickens' early sketches is never re-synthesized as a more truly empirical approach would require.

His sketch techniques leave Dickens halfway between two views of the world — which is probably where he wanted to be. On the one hand, the new techniques allow him the appearance of having come more firmly into conjunction with an empirical reality, a reality that partakes of something more complex than the diminished and trivial possibilities of the stories. On the other hand, having created the illusion of dealing with a more complex reality, a pseudo-empirical one, Dickens is freed to pursue conflicting impulses, to carry on the illusion of mythic clarity and simplicity.

Curiously, the pseudo-empirical world of the sketches achieves an affirmation of society through what appears to be, in places, a more rigorous and explicit denunciation of it. While the narrator of the sketches is more vehemently condemnatory of society than the story narrator, in overall rhetorical effect his sketches are more roundly consolatory and approving of it. The narrative of the stories explores the ludicrous, false, shallow, pretentious involvements of idiosyncratic characters culminating in a negative vision and a disdainful chortle. In contrast to this anonymous deprecation in the stories, the narrator in the sketches is able to assure his readers that though there are some things wrong with the world, there are also things right with it. One of the grand consolations of the sketches is the narrator's own sensibility. In a sense, the narrator and the new techniques of the sketches provide a center or core for the hollow vision of the short stories.

Our Next-door Neighbour

CHAPTER FIVE
REVISIONS
FOR SYNTHESIS

OUR INTEREST in Dickens' early stories and sketches is ultimately directed towards acquiring a continuous perspective on his art. While Boz and his periodical works were a literary event of some local interest, at this remove in time any realistic assessment of their worth would have to rest on their value as "early-Dickens." Therefore, by way of transition to the second half of this study, in which our focus shifts to the novels, this chapter will be concerned with filling out the picture of the *Sketches by Boz* in several different ways.

First of all, a consideration of these short pieces within their bibliographic contexts suggests a number of interesting facts about the evolution of both Dickens' writing techniques and sensibility; accordingly, the largest part of this chapter will look at the rather complicated bibliography of the *Sketches by Boz*, for the light it sheds on Dickens' growth and development as an artist.

Secondly, the critical response to the publication of Dickens' first book adds another dimension to our understanding of both what his readers saw and expected in him and what kinds of literary goals he might accordingly have set for himself as a result of their expectations.

Thirdly, because Dickens' next periodical writings (the periodical parts of the *Pickwick Papers*) were being published simultaneously with the book versions of *Sketches by Boz*, not unexpectedly they reveal an interesting parallel with much we have seen in the *Sketches by Boz*, and finally much that will be of interest in those subsequent works which Dickens consciously designed as novels. Thus using an admittedly heterogenous approach, this chapter will attempt to pave the way for a discussion of several of the novels.

i Publication chronology

The *Sketches by Boz* available to twentieth-century readers are the rearranged and edited version of fifty-nine separate papers. In order to understand the relationship of the original papers to their later edited versions and, in turn, the relationship of *Sketches by Boz* to the later writings, we must be able to see the chronology of the papers, their groupings into series in various periodicals, their rearrangement and regrouping in subsequent book versions and periodical numbers, culminating in the final version of 1850. An accurate bibliography cannot be reconstructed by drawing on the several sources which have attempted to offer such a bibliography (Eckel,[1] Hatton and Cleaver,[2] Butt and Tillotson[3]), though the Pilgrim edition of the letters does list the proper chronology in Appendix F.[4]

Of primary importance is the chronological arrangement of the stories and sketches. The chronology is useful for the light it sheds on several aspects of the original *Sketches by Boz*: redundancy of character, subjects and theme; expansion and contraction of details within the papers; periods of tonal experimentation; connections between papers. Each of these aspects will be discussed in the material following the chronology reproduced below.

The commentary on the bibliographic materials which follow necessarily entails a radical shift in our analytic perspective. Because the preceding chapters have been concerned with describing rhetorical intention in the stories and sketches, we have necessarily presumed the reader's unfamiliarity with those materials; but here our attention, for the most part, shifts

---

1. John C. Eckel, *The First Editions of the Writings of Charles Dickens* (London, 1932).
2. Thomas Hatton and Arthur H. Cleaver, *A Bibliography of the Periodical Works of Charles Dickens* (London, 1933), pp. 93–103.
3. John Butt and Kathleen Tillotson, *Dickens at Work*, pp. 35–61.
4. See Madeline House and Graham Storey, eds., *The Letters of Charles Dickens* (London, 1965), I, 1820–1839, pp. 692–694. My corrections, which achieve a chronological numbering identical to House and Storey's, are based on the observations of Butt and Tillotson, who point out that "Brokers' and Marine Store Shops," reported as Item 47 in Hatton and Cleaver should actually be Item 13, since it was originally printed as No. V of Dickens' "Street Sketches" for the *Morning Chronicle*, Dec. 13, 1834. Additionally, H. Nielsen, "Some Observations on *Sketches by Boz*," points out that "Sentiment" reported as Item 50 in Hatton and Cleaver should actually be Item 6, since it was first published in *Bell's Weekly*, "Original Papers," June 7, 1834.

to much more obvious matters of content in which a familiarity with at least the twentieth-century version of the *Sketches by Boz* and a briefer kind of documentation are necessary.

SKETCHES BY BOZ,
IN ORDER OF THEIR PUBLICATION CHRONOLOGICALLY [5]

Key

M.M.   *The Monthly Magazine or British Register of Politics, Literature, Art, Science and the Belles Lettres.* New Series, 1833–35

B.W.   *Bell's Weekly Magazine,* 1834

M.C.   *The Morning Chronicle,* 1834–36

E.C.   *The Evening Chronicle,* 1835–36

B.L.   *Bell's Life in London and Sporting Chronicle,* 1835–36

C.C.   *The Carlton Chronicle of Politics, Literature, Science and Art,* 1836

L.F.   *The Library of Fiction, or Family Storyteller,* 1836
      Sketches, First Series, Vol. 1, 1836
      Sketches, First Series, Vol. 2, 1836
      Sketches, Second Series, 1837 (actually December, 1836)

(1) Dec. 1833.   M.M.   Vol. XVI, pp. 617–624
     A Dinner at Poplar Walk
         Reprinted as "Mr. Minns and his Cousin" in Second Series, Dec. 1836, pp. 257–282

(2) Jan. 1834.   M.M.   Vol. XVII, pp. 11–18
     Mrs. Joseph Porter "over the way"
         Reprinted as "Mrs. Joseph Porter" in First Series, Vol. 2, Feb. 1836, pp. 253–272

(3) Feb. 1834.   M.M.   Vol. XVII, pp. 151–162
     Horatio Sparkins
         Reprinted in First Series, Vol. 2, Feb. 1836, pp. 110–141

(4) Apr. 1834.   M.M.   Vol. XVII, pp. 375–386
     The Bloomsbury Christening
         Reprinted in First Series, Vol. 1, Feb. 1836, pp. 242–275

(5) May 1834.   M.M.   Vol. XVII, pp. 481–493
     The Boarding House
         Reprinted in First Series, Vol. 1, Feb., 1836, pp. 147–180

(6) June 7, 1834.   B.W.
     Original Papers
         Reprinted in First Series as "Sentiment," pp. 319–342

---

5. See note 4 above.

(7) Aug. 1834. M.M. Vol. XVIII, pp. 177–192
The Boarding House, No. II
Reprinted in First Series, Vol. 1, Feb. 1836, pp. 181–223

(8) Sept. 26, 1834. M.C.
Street Sketches No. I. OMNIBUSES
Reprinted in First Series, Vol. 2, Feb. 1836, pp. 244–252

(9) Oct. 1834. M.M. Vol. XVIII, pp. 360–376
The Steam Excursion
Reprinted (a passage omitted) in First Series, Vol. 2, Feb. 1836, pp.
273–318

(10) Oct. 10, 1834. M.C.
Street Sketches No. II. SHOPS AND THEIR TENANTS
Reprinted in First Series, Vol. 1, Feb. 1836, pp. 88–96

(11) Oct. 23, 1834. M.C.
Street Sketches No. III. THE OLD BAILEY
Reprinted as "Criminal Courts" in Second Series, Dec. 1836, pp. 51–62

(12) Nov. 5, 1834. M.C.
Street Sketches No. IV. SHABBY-GENTEEL PEOPLE
Reprinted in First Series, Vol. 2, Feb. 1836, pp. 101–109

(13) Dec. 13, 1834. M.C.
Street Sketches No. V. BROKERS' AND MARINE STORE SHOPS
Reprinted in First Series, Vol. 2, pp. 233–241

(14) Jan. 1835. M.M. Vol. XIX. pp. 15–24
Passage in the Life of Mr. Watkins Tottle. Chapter the First.
Reprinted in First Series, Vol. 2, Feb. 1836, pp. 1–29

(15) Jan. 31, 1835. E.C.
Sketches of London No. I. HACKNEY-COACH STANDS
Reprinted in First Series, Vol. 1, Feb. 1836, pp. 224–232

(16) Feb. 1835. M.M. Vol. XIX. pp. 121–137
Passage in the Life of Mr. Watkins Tottle. Chapter the Second.
Reprinted in First Series, Vol. 2, Feb. 1836, pp. 30–76

(17) Feb. 7, 1835. E.C.
Sketches of London No. II. GIN SHOPS
Reprinted in First Series, Vol. 1, Feb. 1836, pp. 276–287

(18) Feb. 19, 1835. E.C.
Sketches of London No. III. EARLY COACHES
Reprinted in First Series, Vol. 2, Feb. 1836, pp. 171–181

(19) Feb. 28, 1835. E.C.
Sketches of London No. IV. THE PARISH
Reprinted as "The Beadle — The Parish Engine — The Schoolmaster" in
First Series, Vol. 1, Feb. 1836, pp. 1–11

(20) Mar. 7, 1835. E.C.
Sketches of London No. V. THE HOUSE
Reprinted in conjunction with "Bellamy's" as "A Parliamentary Sketch —
with a few Portraits" in Second Series, Dec. 1836, pp. 227–255

(21) Mar. 17, 1835. E.C.
Sketches of London No. VI. LONDON RECREATIONS
Reprinted in First Series, Vol. 1, Feb. 1836, pp. 136–146

(22) Apr. 7, 1835. E.C. Issue No. 29.
Sketches of London No. VII. PUBLIC DINNERS
Reprinted in First Series, Vol. 1, Feb. 1836, pp. 288–299

(23) Apr. 11, 1835. E.C.
Sketches of London No. VIII. BELLAMY'S
Reprinted in conjunction with "The House"; as "A Parliamentary Sketch
— with a few Portraits" in Second Series, Dec. 1836, pp. 227–255

(24) Apr. 16, 1835. E.C.
Sketches of London No. IX. GREENWICH FAIR
Reprinted in First Series, Vol. 1, Feb. 1836, pp. 314–330

(25) Apr. 23, 1835. E.C.
Sketches of London No. X. THOUGHTS ABOUT PEOPLE
Reprinted in First Series, Vol. 1, Feb. 1836, pp. 97–106

(26) May 9, 1835. E.C.
Sketches of London No. XI. ASTLEY'S
Reprinted in First Series, Vol. 1, Feb. 1836, pp. 300–313

(27) May 19, 1835. E.C.
Sketches of London No. XII. OUR PARISH
Reprinted as "The Curate — The Old Lady — The Captain" in First
Series, Vol. 1, Feb. 1836, pp. 12–23

(28) June 6, 1835. E.C.
Sketches of London No. XIII. THE RIVER
Reprinted in First Series, Vol. 2, Feb. 1836, pp. 182–195

(29) June 18, 1835. E.C.
Sketches of London No. XIV. OUR PARISH
Reprinted as "The Four Sisters" in First Series, Vol. 1, Feb. 1836, pp.
24–33

(30) June 30, 1835 E.C.
Sketches of London No. XV. THE PAWNBROKER'S SHOP
Reprinted in First Series, Vol. 2, Feb. 1836, pp. 142–157

(31) July 14, 1835. E.C.
Sketches of London No. XVI. OUR PARISH
Reprinted as "The Election for Beadle" in First Series, Vol. 1, Feb. 1836,
pp. 34–47

(32) July 21, 1835. E.C.
> *Sketches of London No. XVII.* THE STREETS — MORNING
> Reprinted as "The Streets by Morning" in Second Series, Dec. 1836, pp. 3–16

(33) July 28, 1835. E.C.
> *Sketches of London No. XVIII.* OUR PARISH
> Reprinted as "The Broker's Man" in First Series, Vol. 1, Feb. 1836, pp. 48–66

(34) Aug. 11, 1835. E.C.
> *Sketches of London No. XIX.* PRIVATE THEATRES
> Reprinted in First Series, Vol. 2, Feb. 1836, pp. 196–208

(35) Aug. 20, 1835. E.C.
> *Sketches of London No. XX.* OUR PARISH
> Reprinted as "The Ladies' Societies" in First Series, Vol. 1, Feb. 1836, pp. 67–78

(36) Sept. 27, 1835. B.L.
> *Scenes and Characters No. I.* SEVEN DIALS
> Reprinted in Second Series, Dec. 1836, pp. 145–156

(37) Oct. 4, 1835. B.L.
> *Scenes and Characters No. II.* MISS EVANS AND "THE EAGLE"
> Reprinted in First Series, Vol. 1, Feb. 1836, pp. 79–87

(38) Oct. 11, 1835. B.L.
> *Scenes and Characters No. III.* THE DANCING ACADEMY
> Reprinted in First Series, Vol. 2, Feb. 1836, pp. 158–170

(39) Oct. 18, 1835. B.L.
> *Scenes and Characters No. IV.* MAKING A NIGHT OF IT
> Reprinted in Second Series, Dec. 1836, pp. 35–48

(40) Oct. 25, 1835. B.L.
> *Scenes and Characters No. V.* LOVE AND OYSTERS
> Reprinted as "Misplaced Attachment of Mr. John Dounce" in Second Series, Dec. 1836, pp. 193–208

(41) Nov. 1, 1835. B.L.
> *Scenes and Characters No. VI.* SOME ACCOUNT OF AN OMNIBUS CAD
> Reprinted (with additions and extensive changes) as "The Last Cab-Driver, and the First Omnibus Cad," in Second Series, Dec. 1836, pp. 285–308

(42) Nov. 22, 1835. B.L.
> *Scenes and Characters No. VII.* THE VOCAL DRESS-MAKER
> Reprinted as "The Mistaken Milliner — A Tale of Ambition," in Second Series, Dec. 1836, pp. 159–174

(43) Nov. 29, 1835. B.L.
> *Scenes and Characters No. VIII.* THE PRISONERS' VAN
> Reprinted in First Series, Vol. 1, Feb. 1836, pp. 331–337

(44) Dec. 13, 1835. B.L.
Scenes and Characters No. IX. THE PARLOUR
Reprinted as "The Parlour Orator" in Second Series, Dec. 1836, pp.
311–323

(45) Dec. 27, 1835. B.L.
Scenes and Characters No. X. CHRISTMAS FESTIVITIES
Reprinted as "A Christmas Dinner" in First Series, Vol. 1, Feb. 1836, pp.
338–348

(46) Jan 3, 1836. B.L.
Scenes and Characters No. XI. THE NEW YEAR
Reprinted in Second Series, Dec. 1836, pp. 79–92

(47) Jan. 17, 1836. B.L.
Scenes and Characters No. XII. THE STREETS AT NIGHT
Reprinted as "The Streets by Night" in Second Series, Dec. 1836, pp.
19–32

(48) Feb. 1836
A Visit to Newgate. First published in First Series, Vol. 1, pp. 107–135

(49) Feb. 1836
The Black Veil. First published in First Series, Vol. 2, pp. 77–100

(50) Feb. 1836
The Great Winglebury Duel. First published in First Series, Vol. 2, pp.
209–243

(51) Apr. 1836 L.F.
The Tuggs's at Ramsgate. Part 1, pp. 1–18

(52) June 1836 L.F.
A Little Talk about Spring, and the Sweeps. Part 3; pp. 113–119.
Reprinted as "The First of May" in Second Series, Dec. 1836, pp. 327–346

(53) Aug. 6, 1836. C.C.
The Hospital Patient
Written in the first person.
Reprinted (in the third person) in Second Series, Dec. 1836, pp. 133–142

(54) Sept. 24, 1836. M.C.
Sketches by Boz. (New Series) No. I. MEDITATIONS IN MONMOUTH-STREET
Reprinted in The Evening Chronicle, Sept. 26, 1836.
Reprinted in Second Series, Dec. 1836, pp. 95–112.

(55) Oct. 4, 1836. M.C.
Sketches by Boz. No. II. (New Series) SCOTLAND-YARD
Reprinted in Second Series, Dec. 1836, pp. 65–76.

(56) Oct. 11, 1836. M.C.
Sketches by Boz. No. III. (New Series) DOCTORS' COMMONS
Reprinted in Second Series, Dec. 1836, pp. 177–190

(57) Oct. 26, 1836. M.C.
    Sketches by Boz. No. IV. (New Series) VAUXHALL-GARDENS BY DAY.
      Reprinted in Second Series, Dec. 1836, pp. 211–224

(58) Dec. 1836
    Our Next-Door Neighbours. First published in Second Series, pp. 115–131
(59) Dec. 1836
    The Drunkard's Death. First published in Second Series, pp. 349–377

The purchase of the copyright by John Macrone led to the collection of all the separate articles, which, with a few deletions and minor alterations of text, as well as a change in some few titles, were published for the first time in book form, as a First Series in two volumes, February, 1836; and a Second Series in one volume in December of the same year, although the latter volume was dated 1837.

Any reader of the collected *Sketches by Boz* would have noticed a certain redundancy of character, theme, and subject in the papers in their gathered form; some of this has been commented on in the preceding chapters. While a catalog of such recurrences would itself be of interest, and some scholarship has been performed in this area,[6] it is perhaps more to our purpose to point to the discretion with which Dickens handled some of his recurrent themes. Thus, though three of Dickens' first four stories contain digressions on public conveyances ("A Dinner at Poplar Walk," "Horatio Sparkins," and "The Bloomsbury Christening"), the original readers of the stories, encountering them with at least a month's interval in publications of the *Monthly Magazine*, would not have experienced the sense of repetitiousness that bothers the reader of the collected papers. Moreover, Dickens was free to restate and expand some of his views on public transportation in his first sketch for the *Morning Chronicle*, "Omnibuses," because he could assume a different audience, just as he could when he again takes up the subject in his first sketch for the *Evening Chronicle* ("Hackney Coach Stands" Item 8). Many of the same ideas about transportation emerge again in the *"Bell's Life"* paper "Some Account of an Omnibus Cad" (Item 41), and these ideas find their final form in the revised and expanded version of the same paper, "The Last Cab-Driver and the First Omnibus Cad," published in the second series of *Sketches by Boz* (Item 41). Thus we see that because the original papers were published in widely varying places and at different times they were not nearly so repetitious as are the gathered papers.

---

6. Ernest Boll, "The *Sketches by Boz*," traces some of the elements in *Sketches by Boz* which occur later in Dickens' novels.

Even more importantly, though all of the transportation papers enumerated above are to some degree critical of public transportation services, a close examination of the attitudes expressed shows an evolution that parallels precisely the shift in attitude that dominates the stories and sketches. Dickens moves from a sardonic enumeration of all the frustrations that Mr. Minns must suffer in "A Dinner at Poplar Walk," to a genial celebration of the eccentric and colorful ways of an omnibus driver. This particular shift will be discussed in some detail in a later section of this chapter.

It would be unrealistic to expect, in a group of papers that ranges so widely in subject, a consistent evolution of such attitudes on all topics; in some topics the chronology suggests a coming full circle, a complete revolution of attitude, with the last paper bringing us back to a position much like the first. Such is the case with Dickens' comments on actors and acting; he begins with the smug burlesque denigration of the totally incompetent actors in his second short story, "Mrs. Joseph Porter. . . ." (Item 2) and then goes on to an equally derisive aside on the vanity and fatuousness of actors whose cast-off illusions bedeck "Brokers' and Marine Store Shops" in the form of used costumes (Item 13). But by the time Dickens discusses Richardson's theatre at "Greenwich Fair" (Item 24), he seems anxious to praise the stylized and ponderous postures of the actors. Similarly, his account of "Astley's" abounds in nostalgic and genial appreciation of the vaudevillians there (Item 26). But with the final paper on the subject of actors and the theatre, "Private Theatres" (Item 34), Dickens has come full circle, derisively satirizing the narcissistic actors who buy their parts in private theatres.

Yet from another perspective, the chronological reading of Dickens' various papers on actors shows that he was experimenting with various levels of abstraction, expanding and contracting his ideas in different papers. Thus, his early glancing derision of the "stage-struck" errand boys and chandler's-shop-keepers' sons becomes the basis for the full-blown and highly detailed satire on their delusory acting ambitions in "Private Theatres." In other papers, Dickens presents an elaborate character sketch of a particular archetype such as the wayward son, the long-suffering mother, or the swaggering clerk, and thereafter the archetype is alluded to rather quickly, in passing, almost as if Dickens had come to terms with that particular piece of reality and could be satisfied with a phrase alluding to his earlier work.[7]

---

7. Such recurrences are familiar to any reader of the *Sketches by Boz*. Our interest here is in noting the process, rather than recording each individual instance of it.

The chronology also helps us to see that during the writing of various periodical papers, there were periods when Dickens restricted himself to one tone, apparently either as an exercise in the craft of his writing, or perhaps as an expression of a particular mood that dominated him then. For instance, during the period from February 1836 when he published the "First Series" of the *Sketches by Boz*, through December 1836, when the "Second Series" was printed, almost all of the *new material* Dickens published was either highly melodramatic or rigorously critical of his society. The concentration here seems more than accidental.

The chronology also reveals that sometimes it took Dickens several papers to work up to a particular subject, or to achieve a new tone he was working towards. Thus though we have earlier suggested that the sketch called "The Old Bailey" is a landmark in Dickens' career because for the first time we see him focusing on institutions and working with a variety of tones, the chronology reveals that some of the accomplishment of "The Old Bailey" probably flows from Dickens' previous paper "Shops and Their Tenants." "Shops . . . ." begins to have some of the more serious appeals of the paper that succeeds it, experimenting with melancholy and pathos, the plight of the poor. Similarly the chronology suggests that "Love and Oysters" (the "mythic" story of John Dounce discussed at length in Chapter III) is really a re-telling on a more concrete, fictive level of the paper that immediately preceded it, "Making a Night of It." The earlier paper treats the genus of old bachelors who debauch themselves periodically with food, drink, and entertainment, while "Love and Oysters" focuses on a fictive presentation of one such man.

ii Original periodical groups of Sketches by Boz

Although the chronology is valuable for its completeness, and it allows us to see the history of a given paper from its original publication through its first appearance in book form, because of a density of detail the chronology obscures the equally interesting character of the groups of papers as they appeared in the various periodicals. The following list is useful because it demonstrates the clear separation of Dickens' fictional tales from the more essayistic sketches. For almost a year, Dickens discretely separated the two forms. It is important to have access to the titles in a given series, since inevitably each series would have had a separate audience and, as we have argued, Dickens as a novice author was obviously taking advantage of the opportunities for experimentation provided by his different publishing outlets.

PERIODICAL GROUPS OF THE *SKETCHES BY BOZ*
(As abstracted from the preceding corrected Chronology)

The Monthly Magazine, Dec. 1833–Feb. 1835

(1)*	Dec. 1833	A Dinner at Poplar Walk
(2)	Jan. 1834	Mrs. Joseph Porter "over the way"
(3)	Feb. 1834	Horatio Sparkins
(4)	Apr. 1834	The Bloomsbury Christening
(5)	May, 1834	The Boarding House
(7)	Aug. 1834	The Boarding House, No. II
(9)	Oct. 1834	The Steam Excursion
(14)	Jan. 1835	Passage in the Life of Mr. Watkins Tottle
(16)	Feb. 1835	Passage in the Life of Mr. Watkins Tottle, Chapter the Second

Bell's Weekly Magazine, June 1834

(6)	June 7, 1834	*Original Papers* ["Sentiments"]

The Morning Chronicle

Street Sketches

(8)	Sept. 26, 1834	No. I.	Omnibuses
(10)	Oct. 10, 1834	II.	Shops and their Tenants
(11)	Oct. 23, 1834	III.	The Old Bailey
(12)	Nov. 5, 1834	IV.	Shabby-Genteel People
(13)	Dec. 15, 1834	V.	Brokers' and Marine Store Shops

Sketches by Boz, New Series

(54)	Sept. 24, 1836	I.	Meditations in Monmouth Street
(55)	Oct. 4, 1836	II.	Scotland Yard
(56)	Oct. 11, 1836	III.	Doctors' Commons
(57)	Oct. 26, 1836	IV.	Vauxhall Gardens by Day

The Evening Chronicle, Jan. 31, 1835 – Aug. 20, 1835

Sketches of London

(15)	Jan. 31, 1835	No. I.	Hackney-Coach Stands
(17)	Feb. 7, 1835	II.	Gin Shops
(18)	Feb. 19, 1835	III.	Early Coaches
(19)	Feb. 28, 1835	IV.	The Parish
(20)	Mar. 7, 1835	V.	The House
(21)	Mar. 17, 1835	VI.	London Recreations
(22)	Apr. 7, 1835	VII.	Public Dinners
(23)	Apr. 8, 1835	VIII.	Bellamy's
(24)	Apr. 16, 1835	IX.	Greenwich Fair
(25)	Apr. 23, 1835	X.	Thoughts About People

*Chronological number

(26)	May 9, 1835	XI.	Astley's
(27)	May 19, 1835	XII.	Our Parish
(28)	June 6, 1835	XIII.	The River
(29)	June 18, 1835	XIV.	Our Parish
(30)	June 30, 1835	XV.	The Pawnbroker's Shop
(31)	July 14, 1835	XVI.	Our Parish
(32)	July 21, 1835	XVII.	The Streets — Morning
(33)	July 28, 1835	XVIII.	Our Parish
(34)	Aug. 11, 1835	XIX.	Private Theatres
(35)	Aug. 20, 1835	XX.	Our Parish

Bell's Life in London and Sporting Chronicle, Sept. 27, 1835–Jan. 17, 1836

Scenes and Characters

(36)	Sept. 27, 1835	I.	Seven Dials
(37)	Oct. 4, 1835	II.	Miss Evans and "The Eagle"
(38)	Oct. 11, 1835	III.	The Dancing Academy
(39)	Oct. 18, 1835	IV.	Making a Night of It
(40)	Oct. 25, 1835	V.	Love and Oysters
(41)	Nov. 1, 1835	VI.	Some Account of an Omnibus Cad
(42)	Nov. 22, 1835	VII.	The Vocal Dress-Maker
(43)	Nov. 29, 1835	VIII.	The Prisoners' Van
(44)	Dec. 13, 1835	IX.	The Parlour
(45)	Dec. 27, 1835	X.	Christmas Festivities
(46)	Jan. 3, 1836	XI.	The New Year
(47)	Jan. 17, 1836	XII.	The Streets at Night

Sketches by Boz, First Series, Feb. 1836 (the new sketches included)

(48)	A Visit to Newgate
(49)	The Black Veil
(50)	The Great Winglebury Duel

The Library of Fiction or Family Story-Teller, 1836

(51)	April 1836	The Tuggs's at Ramsgate, Part 1
(52)	June 1836	A Little Talk about Spring, and the Sweeps, Part 3

The Carlton Chronicle, Aug. 6, 1836

(53)	The Hospital Patient

Sketches by Boz, Second Series, 1837 (actually published Dec. 1836; the following are the new sketches included)

(58)	Our Next-Door Neighbours
(59)	The Drunkard's Death

While the preceding list of the periodical groupings of the original Boz papers documents Dickens' initial separation of the works by periodical and genre, a consideration of the third large group of papers, the *Evening Chronicle* series, reveals a gradual synthesis of these distinctions. In terms of our previous argument, this third periodical group suggests that neither the vision of the short stories — simple, mythic, negative — nor the vision of the early sketches — complex, pseudo-empirical, affirmative — created the precise tone that Dickens eventually wanted for his early writing.

By the time that Dickens began this longest of the periodical series, the twenty "Sketches of London," he was apparently anxious to begin experimenting again. Scattered throughout this series was a group of six papers in which Dickens assumed a stance quite different from those in either the stories or sketches published previously. In the six papers called "The Parish" he established a new form in his writing. "The Parish" combines the compassionate, apologetic, and affirmative narrator of the sketches with the detached, supercilious and ironic narrator of the stories. Moreover, the matter of "The Parish" hovers half-way between the diminished fictive involvements of the early story characters — idiosyncratic, trivial, and absurd — and the more generous reportorial omniscience of the sketches. In the Parish papers (as we shall attempt to demonstrate in the next sub-section of this chapter) Dickens appears to want to reconcile the divergent moods and attitudes that he established in the earlier periodical groups. Actually, the remaining history of the *Sketches by Boz* can be interpreted as an attempt to effect such a reconciliation.

A perusal of the titles in the remaining large group of periodical papers, the series published in *Bell's Life in London*, suggests that this was the least innovative of the work Dickens had published thus far. None of the *Bell's Life* pieces extends by much either the ideas or the techniques already developed; rather they appear to be variations on themes and characters Dickens had used in the earlier publications. The lack of innovation in the *Bell's Life* series probably stems from the fact that throughout their publication Dickens was working on new sketches, in a more serious and melodramatic tone, to be included in his first published book, the *Sketches by Boz, First Series*.

iii Sketches by Boz, First Series

The success of the periodical sketches led to their publication in book form by John Macrone as the *Sketches by Boz, First Series*, in two volumes, early in 1836; these were Dickens' first bound books. Revision, selection, ordering, and omission of certain sketches provide clues to the kind of book Dickens wished to submit to the public; additionally the listing reveals the specific contents that he assembled for his first work and allows us to note which materials were deliberately excluded from it.

Dickens' correspondence for the years 1835–1836 reveals considerable concern about the make-up and reception of his first books. The arrangement of the periodical papers into the first series, as reproduced below, shows that Dickens used "The Parish" to establish a kind of keynote for the book.

SKETCHES BY BOZ, FIRST SERIES.

London (Macrone), 1836 (as per the title page)

Volume One   *The Parish*:

(19)	E.C.*	Chap. I. The Beadle — The Parish Engine — The Schoolmaster
(27)	E.C.	Chap. II. The Curate — The Old Lady — The Captain
(29)	E.C.	Chap. III. The Four Sisters
(31)	E.C.	Chap. IV. The Election for Beadle
(33)	E.C.	Chap. V. The Broker's Man
(35)	E.C.	Chap. VI. The Ladies' Societies
(37)	B.L.	Miss Evans and "The Eagle"
(10)	M.C.	Shops and their Tenants
(25)	E.C.	Thoughts about People
(48)	1st Ser.	A Visit to Newgate
(21)	M.C.	London Recreations
(5)	M.M.	The Boarding House: Chapter I
(7)	M.M.	The Boarding House: Chapter II
(15)	M.C.	Hackney-Coach Stands
(13)	M.C.	Brokers' and Marine Store Shops
(4)	M.M.	The Bloomsbury Christening
(17)	M.C.	Gin Shops
(22)	E.C.	Public Dinners
(26)	E.C.	Astley's
(24)	E.C.	Greenwich Fair
(43)	B.L.	The Prisoners' Van
(45)	B.L.	A Christmas Dinner

Volume Two

(14)	M.M.	Passage in the Life of Mr. Watkins Tottle: Chapter I
(16)	M.M.	Passage in the Life of Mr. Watkins Tottle: Chapter II
(49)	1st ser.	The Black Veil
(12)	M.C.	Shabby-Genteel People
(3)	M.M.	Horatio Sparkins
(30)	E.C.	The Pawnbroker's Shop
(38)	B.L.	The Dancing Academy
(18)	E.C.	Early Coaches
(28)	E.C.	The River
(34)	E.C.	Private Theatres
(50)	1st ser.	The Great Winglebury Duel
(8)	M.C.	Omnibuses
(2)	M.M.	Mrs. Joseph Porter
(9)	M.M.	The Steam Excursion
(6)	B.W.	Sentiment

*publication where originally published. See key to abbreviations on page 87.

The prominence of "The Parish" in the contents of the *Sketches by Boz*, *First Series*, is most noteworthy. As we have suggested previously, "The Parish" sets up a balance between the conflicting tones and attitudes Dickens had created in his earlier papers. While "The Parish" does present portraits of characters who are much like those in the early stories, it is delivered from the entirely negative and ironic tone of those stories by the compassionate and affirming presence of the narrator, who opens this set of papers in the following manner:

> How much is conveyed in those two short words — the parish;* and with how many tales of distress and misery: of broken fortune and ruined hopes — too often of unrelieved wretchedness and successful knavery — are they associated! A poor man, with small earnings and a large family, just manages to live on from hand to mouth, and to procure food from day to day: he has barely enough for the present, and can take no heed of the future; his taxes are in arrear; quarter-day passes by; another quarter-day arrives — he can procure no more quarter for himself, and is summoned by — the parish. His goods are destrained; his very bed is taken from under him; his children are crying with cold and hunger, and his wife is both figuratively and literally *speaking in the straw.*** What can he do? To whom is he to apply for relief? To private charity? To benevolent individuals? Certainly not; *hasn't he*** — the parish? There's the parish vestry, the parish infirmary, the parish surgeon, the parish officers, the parish beadle. Excellent institutions, and gentle, kind-hearted men. The woman dies — she is buried by the parish. The man first neglects, and afterwards cannot obtain, work — he is relieved by the parish; and when distress and drunkenness have done their work upon him, he is maintained a harmless babbling idiot in the parish asylum. (*Sketches*, p. 1; *changes in punctuation throughout; **phrase omitted in later editions)

Here we see the typical ambivalence that marks the collected *Sketches by Boz*. On the one hand the narrator seems to deprecate *the parish* and the whole parochial structure; it conjures up "tales of distress and misery . . . broken fortune and ruined hopes." On the other hand the narrator is quite literal in his praise of parochial institutions; they are, after all, the only relief available to the average man. With a rather subdued irony — certainly nothing like the irony of the early short stories — the opening paragraph of "The Parish" is toying with a paradox, the terms of which are: 1) our modern society needs locally responsive charitable institutions; 2)

. such institutions must be supported by taxes; 3) sometimes the need to pay such taxes bankrupts a poor man, turns him into a charity case; 4) isn't it wonderful that the man who has become a charity case because he must pay taxes to support charities ultimately has access to the benign workings of our charities. But the curious thing about Dickens' presentation of these ideas is that, though his paragraph harbors such sardonic absurdities, the reader does not experience them as such. Instead, because connections are not made (there are no explicit agents in the man's tragedy; all is recorded in the passive voice) the reader is left with the impression of "The Parish" as the deliverer *from* but not the perpetrator *of* the man's tragedy.

The rest of the sketch and the other sketches that make up "The Parish" have a similar kind of ambiguity. Dickens continues with sketches of the parish Beadle, workhouse master, and schoolmaster, and though each of these characters has an affinity with the idiosyncratic characters of the early stories, the characters in "The Parish" finally come to support a much more affirmative view of the world. Thus though the Beadle is bumptious and officious, he is not malevolent; though the workhouse master is tyrannical and fawningly obsequious, it is a "good world" that has given him a sinecure and improved his condition; though the schoolmaster has a comic zealousness, he also has a reciprocal dedication.

In all, the characters Dickens presents in "The Parish" are significantly different from his story characters. First of all, they exist more completely within the affirmative context of the narrator's consciousness; their involvements and preoccupations are not formulary as they are in the stories; though they have their foibles and shortcomings, the characters are not created only to be overturned and exposed as are the characters in the early stories. Here Dickens is not writing-off the world; instead he seems to be "taking-it-on" as an apologist, seeing in it the comic limitations of human character, but at the same time endorsing the benignity of the system he is describing.

Significantly, though there is some evidence that the actual setting, characters, and events represented in "The Parish" are biographical reminiscences from Dickens' early years in Chatham,[8] he presents these papers as though he were writing about *a parish* in London. It is precisely the qualities of village-like intimacy and pastoral innocence that make "The Parish" a perfect keynote for a book that sets out to humanize the city, to reduce it to an archetypal and knowable world.

After opening with "The Parish," Dickens apparently organized the

---

8. Cf. Edgar Johnson, *Charles Dickens: His Tragedy and Triumph*, I, pp. 11–26.

rest of the work with an eye to variety; but the peculiar thing here is the number of kinds of variety that are operative in the *First Series*. First, with the exception of consecutive chapters of short stories, Dickens rarely places together papers that had originally appeared in the same periodical. Thus readers of any single periodical in which the papers were originally published were sure to find familiar pieces always in the presence of new ones. Secondly, in cases where papers from the same periodical do appear together, the subjects are usually very different from each other, and the techniques of handling the subjects reinforce their differences. Third, as a perusal of the chronology shows, the original order of the papers is thoroughly obscured in their gathering. (The parenthetical numbers in the listing refer to the original chronology.) The juxtaposition of chronologically separated papers guaranteed that the reader of the first series of *Sketches by Boz* would experience the author's amplitude and diversity rather than his growth and development; only by rereading the papers chronologically do we begin to have access to the latter. Fourth, the *First Series* is arranged to insure a diversity of tones; short stories are backed to sketches, serious pieces to farcical ones, generally producing a display of virtuosity — a fluid variety at the expense of a sustained point of view that might alienate some readers.

In order to issue the *First Series*, Dickens undertook extensive revision of the original periodical papers. Kathleen Tillotson has commented on these in detail;[9] basically, the revisions can be divided into two categories, mechanical and editorial. The mechanical revisions include those changes that were necessary to adapt the newspaper and magazine pieces to book form: removal of series headings, re-paragraphing, provision of new titles where necessary, and the elimination of some opening and closing paragraphs, many of which were relative only to periodical publication; the elimination of others was apparently dictated by space considerations.

The more important *editorial* revisions generally validate the thesis we have pursued thus far. That is, Dickens was attempting to reconcile divergent attitudes of his stories and sketches, to transform himself from the sardonic promulgator of an absurdist view into the mythic apologist for his own society. Thus he edited these first volumes in the following ways: he eliminates partisan commentary; he softens social criticism; he removes incidental topicalities; and he withdraws political allusions.

His exclusions from the *First Series* of pieces already published in periodical form also validates our thesis. Though some of the exclusions

---

9. Butt and Tillotson, p. 42 ff.

appear arbitrary, it is quite clear that others must have been deliberate.[10] As Kathleen Tillotson has noted, the "sketches containing specifically 'political' allusions — 'The House,' 'Bellamy's,' and 'The Parlour'" were all excluded. The readily identifiable portraits of political figures in "The House" and "Bellamy's," and the explicit condemnation of political partisanship in "The Parlour" were probably deemed too controversial by the fledgeling author.

> Dickens was alert to remove incidental topicalities in other sketches. The Irish orator from Exeter Hall, mentioned at the end of "The Ladies' Societies" (Our Parish VI) was presented to the *Evening Chronicle* readers of 1835 as "Mr. Somebody Something, a celebrated Catholic renegade and Protestant bigot"; in the first edition of 1836 he became "Mr. Mortimer O'Silly-one," later "a celebrated oratorical pedlar," and in the monthly parts edition "a celebrated orator . . . an Irishman." (Butt and Tillotson, p. 47)

The increasing gentility and anonymity evidenced in the evolution of the Dickens' references to the Reverend Mortimer O'Sullivan above are typical of the general softening that the sketches underwent in book versions.

Thus the revisions, selections, and editing Dickens undertook with the previously published periodical papers suggest that he was quite anxious to suppress some of his more radical views and political commentary. In effect, Dickens appears to have adjusted the tonality of the work in the direction of a greater consistency, a more even rhetoric. With the recognition that his widely scattered publications would soon be read in book form, he was careful to see that the sketches rather than the short stories presided over and shaped the tone of his first collection. Dickens gave more careful attention to the revisions of the sketches than to the short stories. His revisions of the short stories entail, for the most part, minor stylistic changes, and for good reason. Since the ironic tone of the short stories was so much a part of their substance, it could not be eliminated through revision. Therefore Dickens seems to have used the revised sketches to soften and diffuse the tone of the stories. The *First Series* of *Sketches by Boz* is an even more benign and harmonious vision of British society than Dickens had presented in the original sketches.

---

10. Cf. Ibid., p. 46. The entire list of pieces excluded from the first series includes: (1) "A Dinner at Poplar Walk," (6) "Original Papers" (i.e., "Sentiment"), (11) "The Old Bailey," (20) "The House," (32) "The Streets — Morning," (36) "Seven Dials," (39) "Making a Night of It," (40) "Love and Oysters," (41) "Some Account of an Omnibus Cad," (42) "The Vocal Dressmaker," (44) "The Parlour."

iv Sketches by Boz, Second Series

The *Second Series* of *Sketches by Boz*, one volume, published by Macrone in December, 1836 (the title page reads 1837), gathered the remaining periodical papers and added several pieces not previously published. The inclusion, here, of papers previously excluded from the *First Series*, suggests a greater confidence on the part of Dickens. Although Dickens did revise these sketches somewhat, eliminating some of the most incisive political caricature in "Bellamy's" and "The House," bowdlerizing "Love and Oysters," the volume as a whole is still more daring and less conservative than the preceding two volumes. Here again, the pursuit of amplitude and variety dominates and obscures the chronology of the papers. With the completion of the second series, Dickens had published all of the periodical papers in book form except for "The Tuggs's at Ramsgate," which (as Kathleen Tillotson suggests) may have been excluded for its length.

SKETCHES BY BOZ, SECOND SERIES
London (Macrone), 1837 (Dec. 1836) (as per title page)

(32)	E.C.	The Streets by Morning
(47)	E.C.	The Streets by Night
(39)	B.L.	Making a Night of It
(11)	M.C.	Criminal Courts
(55)	B.L.	Scotland Yard
(46)	B.L.	The New Year
(54)	M.C.	Meditations in Monmouth Street
(58)	2nd ser.	Our Next-Door Neighbours
(53)	C.C.	The Hospital Patient
(36)	E.C.	Seven Dials
(42)	B.L.	The Mistaken Milliner — A Tale of Ambition
(56)	M.C.	Doctors' Commons
(40)	B.L.	Misplaced Attachment of Mr. John Dounce
(57)	M.C.	Vauxhall Gardens by Day
(20) & (23)	E.C.	A Parliamentary Sketch — With a Few Portraits
(1)	M.M.	Mr. Minns and His Cousin
(41)	B.L.	The Last Cab-Driver, and the First Omnibus Cad
(44)	B.L.	The Parlour Orator
(52)	L.F.	The First of May
(59)	2nd ser.	The Drunkard's Death

One of the pieces passed over in publishing the *First Series* of *Sketches by Boz* but doubled in length for inclusion in the *Second Series*, perfectly illustrates the two styles of writing that Dickens apparently wanted to synthesize in publishing his first books. In its first publication the *Bell's*

Life piece, originally called "Some Account of an Omnibus Cad," opened in the following manner:

> Mr. William Barker was born; — but why need we recount *where* Mr. William Barker was born, or when? Why scrutinize the entries in parochial ledgers; why penetrate into the Luxinian mysteries of lying-in hospitals? Mr. William Barker *was* born, or he had never been. There was a father — there is a son. There was a cause — there is an effect. Surely this is sufficient information for the most Fatima-like curiosity; and, if it be not, we regret our inability to supply any further evidence on the point. Can there be a more satisfactory, or more strictly parliamentary course? Impossible.
>
> We at once avow a similar inability to record at what precise period, or by what particular process, this gentleman's patronymic, of William Barker, became corrupted into "Bill Boorker." (*Bell's Life*, Sunday, Nov. 1, 1835)

Here we have a good example of the voice of the ironic narrator, much like the voice in the earliest short stories. The tone is arch and condescending. The narrator diminishes his subject through sarcasm and inflation. In the first paragraph his over-concern for Bill Barker's percentage may be an oblique but discreet way of suggesting that Barker was your average fatherless bastard. But even allowing that such elaborate circumlocutions are justifiable, the classical allusions "Luxinian mysteries" and "Fatima-like curiosity" as well as others that run through the sketch, only add to the superiority of the narrator over his subject; they widen the gulf between the narrator's high-handed locutions and the subject's paltry background. The rest of the piece sketches out Barker's biography, his criminal pursuits that lead to seven years "transportation," his finding a place as the first omnibus cad; and finally the ironic praise of his genius at inventing all the frustrations and inconveniences of being an omnibus passenger. All is presented with a graceful sarcasm, insuring a more rigorous condemnation of the subject than a straightforward presentation would effect.

Yet when this piece was revised, primarily through expansion, for inclusion in the *Second Series*, it opens in a very different tone:

> Of all the cabriolet-drivers whom we have ever had the honour and gratification of knowing by sight — and our acquaintance in this way has been most extensive — there is one who made an impression on our mind which can never be effaced, and who awakened in our bosom a feeling of admiration and respect,

which we entertain a fatal presentiment will never be called forth
again by any human being. He was a man of most simple and
prepossessing appearance. He was a brown-whiskered, white-
hatted, no-coated cabman; his nose was generally red, and his
bright blue eye not unfrequently stood out in bold relief against a
black border of artificial workmanship; . . . In summer he carried
in his mouth a flower; in winter, a straw — slight, but to a
contemplative mind, certain indications of a love of nature, and a
taste for botany. (*Sketches*, p. 142)

Though the excerpt goes on to describe a man very much like the Bill
Barker of the original sketch, the striking thing here is the vast difference
in attitude towards the two drivers. The narrator in the revised sketch finds
it a "gratification" to see the cabman; he professes a quite genuine "admiration and respect" for him; he praises his "pre-possessing appearance," and
"love of nature." Curiously this second driver is guilty of the same offenses
against the community that the narrator in the original sketch had roundly
condemned with his false praise. Here the driver's many accidents, his
scrapes with the law for reckless driving, his eventual imprisonment and
subsequent solitary confinement for refusal to work in the House of Correc-
tion, where he "lies on his back on the floor, and sings comic songs all
day!" (*Sketches*, p. 146) are all presented as the rather harmless eccentricities
of an original.

The revised sketch opens with the portrait of the cabman; in the way
of transition Dickens suggests that the cabman was probably a cousin to
Bill Barker, whose history now makes up the second half of the revised
sketch. But seen in its bibliographical context, the transition does not
really come off. Just as in some of the earlier sketches, in his revision of
"Some Account of an Omnibus Cad" Dickens is still trying to reconcile
very ambivalent feelings about his subject, to affirm and negate at the same
time.

v Sketches by Boz, *periodical numbers*

With the transfer of the copyright of *Sketches* to Chapman and Hall
in 1837, the *Sketches* were issued in periodical numbers. Dickens once
again undertook some revisions, and his rearrangement of the papers reveals
a differing conception of them. The textual changes here are insignificant in
comparison to the new arrangement of the pieces, the arrangement which
survives into modern additions.

Although the division in "Scenes," "Characters," and "Tales," was
not officially included until the one-volume Chapman and Hall edition

(1839), the periodical numbers, as described below, follow the same order. (The categories of the one-volume edition are bracketed in the list of periodical numbers below.)

THE PERIODICAL NUMBERS OF *SKETCHES BY BOZ*

Twenty monthly parts, November, 1837, to June, 1839

Sketches by Boz, one volume complete, Chapman and Hall, London, 1839

(corrected from Hatton and Cleaver)[11]

[*Seven Sketches from Our Parish*]

Part 1, Nov. 1837

(19)	E.C.	The Beadle — The Parish Engine — The Schoolmaster, pp. 3–8
(27)	E.C.	The Curate — The Old Lady — The Half-Pay Captain, pp. 9–14
(29)	E.C.	The Four Sisters, pp. 15–20
(31)	E.C.	The Election for Beadle (continued to Part 2), pp. 21–24

Part 2, Dec. 1837

(31)	E.C.	The Election for Beadle (concluded), pp. 25–28
(33)	E.C.	The Broker's Man, pp. 29–38
(58)	2nd ser.	Our Next-Door Neighbours (continued to Part 3), pp. 45–48

Part 3, Jan. 1838

(58)	2nd ser.	Our Next-Door Neighbours (concluded), pp. 49–52

[*Scenes*]

(32)	E.C.	The Streets — Morning, pp. 55–60
(47)	E.C.	The Streets — Night, pp. 61–66
(10)	M.C.	Shops and their Tenants, pp. 67–71
(55)	M.C.	Scotland Yard (continued to Part 4), p. 72

Part 4, Feb. 1838

(55)	M.C.	Scotland Yard (concluded), pp. 73–76
(36)	E.C.	Seven Dials, pp. 77–81
(54)	M.C.	Meditations in Monmouth Street, pp. 82–88
(15)	M.C.	Hackney-Coach Stands, pp. 89–93
(56)	M.C.	Doctors' Commons (continued to Part 5), pp. 94–96

Part 5, Mar. 1838

(56)	M.C.	Doctors' Commons (concluded), pp. 97–99
(21)	E.C.	London Recreations, pp. 100–105
(28)	E.C.	The River, pp. 106–112
(26)	E.C.	Astley's, pp. 113–119
(24)	E.C.	Greenwich Fair (continued to Part 6), p. 120

Part 6, Apr. 1838

(24)	E.C.	Greenwich Fair (concluded), pp. 121–128
(34)	E.C.	Private Theatres, pp. 129–135

11. See note 2 above.

Part 14, Dec. 1838

(5)	M.M.	The Boarding-House Chapter the First (concluded), p. 313
(7)	M.M.	The Boarding-House Chapter the Second, pp. 314–333
(1)	M.M.	Mr. Minns and his Cousin (continued to Part 15), pp. 335–336

Part 15, Jan. 1839

(1)	M.M.	Mr. Minns and his Cousin (concluded), pp. 337–345
(6)	B.W.	Sentiment, pp. 346–357
(51)	L.F.	The Tuggs's at Ramsgate (continued to Part 16), pp. 358–360

Part 16, Feb. 1839

(51)	L.F.	The Tuggs's at Ramsgate (concluded), pp. 361–378
(3)	M.M.	Horatio Sparkins (continued to Part 17), pp. 379–384

Part 17, Mar. 1839

(3)	M.M.	Horatio Sparkins (concluded), pp. 385–395
(49)	1st ser.	The Black Veil, pp. 396–407
(9)	M.M.	The Steam Excursion (continued to Part 18), p. 408

Part 18, Apr. 1839

(9)	M.M.	The Steam Excursion (concluded), pp. 409–430
(50)	1st ser.	The Great Winglebury Duel (continued to Part 19), pp. 431–432

Part 19, May, 1839

(50)	1st ser.	The Great Winglebury Duel (concluded), pp. 433–488
(2)	M.M.	Mrs. Joseph Porter, pp. 449–459
(14 & 16)	M.M.	Passage in the Life of Mr. Watkins Tottle (continued to Part 20), pp. 460–488

Part 20, June, 1839

(14 & 16)	M.M.	Passage in the Life of Mr. Watkins Tottle (concluded), pp. 489–497
(4)	M.M.	The Bloomsbury Christening, pp. 498–514
(59)	2nd ser.	The Drunkard's Death, pp. 516–525

Dickens imposed on this version a form more conscious and coherent than the form in the previous Macrone editions. Surprisingly, no one has previously pointed out how rigorously structured is at least the first half of the *Sketches by Boz*, in this their final arrangement. The new arrangement again opens with "The Parish," seven papers which establish the pastoral tone and village-like intimacy of Boz's supposed corner of London. They graduate to a more general view of the city, a survey of its daily rhythm as it were, in "The Streets — Morning," and "The Streets — Night," the first of what were later called "Scenes."

The next two pieces, though widely separated as original papers (9 and 55 chronologically) are complementary and also treat the rhythm of the city, only in this case Dickens is concerned with the broader rhythm of time and its effects. "Shops and their Tenants" shows a large, respectable house with middle-class shops below it, degenerating gradually into split apartments and poor little shops with several tenants, literally becoming, and symbolically representing, the squalor and decay that time wreaks on the city. But the succeeding piece "Scotland Yard" completes the cycle, showing the regeneration of a poor and squalid neighborhood into a clean and respectable one.

In this final organization of Boz, the four pieces following "The Parish" are a highly unified and perfectly symmetrical unit. The reciprocity of morning and night, closing with the downbeat tonality of "night," is complemented and inverted in the upbeat tonality of degeneration and regeneration in "Shops . . ." and "Scotland Yard."

Although the possibilities of sustaining continuity with such disparate occasional pieces seem highly remote, Dickens, in this final organization, attempted to continue his exploration of the city with those essays describing other neighborhoods. "Seven Dials" and ". . . Monmouth Street" are an easy and natural transition from the preceding neighborhood sketch "Scotland Yard." Even though the paper on "Hackney-Coach Stands" (Part 4) breaks the focus on city neighborhoods — perhaps it was intended as a change of pace — the grouping here continues to be far more logical than previously. The six papers on London recreations give way to the papers on transportation (Part 7): "Early Coaches," "Omnibuses," and "The Last Cab-Driver, and the First Omnibus Cad."

Elsewhere, faced with a diversity of subjects, Dickens sustains continuity by shifting to tonality as an organizing principle. In Part 9 the first three "shop sketches" are probably joined to the two prison pieces because each of the five culminates in a somber, sentimental, and polemic statement critical of society.

In the second half of the periodical parts, the division into what were later called "Characters" and "Tales" seems rather arbitrary, with no clear-cut separation of the two readily distinguishable. Once again, we see the papers organized apparently for variety as in the previous first and second series. Dickens is careful to make sure that no single monthly part is composed of papers originally close together in chronology. The apparent indifference to sustained organization in the second half of the periodical parts may be traceable to Dickens' involvement in other literary projects — *Bentley's Miscellaney*, *Oliver Twist*, and *Nicholas Nickleby* were vying for his time.

vi On the Cruikshank illustrations to the Sketches by Boz

All of the gathered versions of the *Sketches by Boz* (starting with the two Macrone series and continuing through the periodical parts and their subsequent publication in various book forms) have profited from the inclusion of the Cruikshank illustrations. The artist was already firmly established as one of the finest cartoonists of his day. His willingness to illustrate the writings of a novice author surely added immeasurably to the favorable reception of Dickens' first books. While the illustrations are interesting for their own sake, they also help illuminate some of the basic difficulties of meaning in the *Sketches by Boz*.

That old saying about the relative "worth" of words and pictures is only partially true. Perhaps it is truest in cases where all the words are aimed at establishing a single perspective on a given scene. But when the words fall into the complex patterns and shifting perspectives so characteristic of Dickens' writing, any artist would be hard put to capture the subtleties. The Cruikshank illustrations are superb. They have subtleties of their own which make them as fine as the illustrations in almost any book one can name. But to expect that the genius of the illustrator be totally submissive to the genius of the author in effecting a one-to-one correspondence between the words and pictures would be unrealistic.

There are times when Dickens at his best happily coincides with Cruikshank at his best. For instance, there is the illustration for "Public Dinners" (frontispiece). Here the artist parades the awkward children with a pomp more appropriate to a coronation than a charity dinner; their marching is shown to be orderly, but only a partial attainment of the regimentation they appear to be striving for; the children's faces are drawn perfectly, revealing willful, controlled expressions of vacancy that are their solemn and eager concessions to the supposed grandeur of the event, but simultaneously, their admission of bewilderment at the meaning of it all. The figures of the first pair of stewards with their self-satisfied and patronizing expressions (possibly the figures of Chapman and Hall) are emphatically underscoring the ceremonial nature of the occasion with sweeping gestures. Meanwhile, the figure of Dickens, in the second pair of stewards, takes on an expression of casual but genial bemusement, and his partner, Cruikshank, shows a truly solemn dignity. One of the remaining stewards completes the "action" in self-importantly whispering to Cruikshank. In all, the illustration is a fine representation of a "public dinner" though actually it pictures only a few phrases in the original text:

> The stewards (looking more important than ever) leave the room, and presently return, heading a procession of indigent orphans, boys and girls, who walk around the room, curtseying and bowing, and treading on each other's heels, and looking very much as

if they would like a glass of wine apiece, to the high gratification of the company generally, and especially of the lady patronesses in the gallery. (*Sketches*, p. 167)

That the illustration could go so far in capturing the general tone of Dickens' sketch shows the common ground on which these artists met. A highlight of both Dickens' and Cruikshank's way of seeing things is an uncanny appreciation of the child's view of the world. Frequently Cruikshank takes the mere mention of children in a sketch as an opportunity to show his understanding. The illustration of "The Parish Engine" for instance (see p. 128) shows a gaggle of little urchins excitedly squabbling over positions of highest honor, i.e., those closest to the fire engine itself, while the winded Beadle, with a preposturous officiousness, knocks-up the inhabitants of the burning house. Here as in other sketches, the children are drawn with particular attention to detail, bestowing on each a whimsical yet revealing sense of individuality.

Generally speaking, Dickens the satirist and Cruikshank the satirist are entirely at home together. Sharp, penetrating, and incisive details, verbal and visual, achieve a complementary fullness in the relationship of satiric word to satiric picture. But this shared satiric excellence creates one of the limitations on the overall faithfulness of Cruikshank's illustrations to Dickens' writings. Cruikshank pushes Dickens' writings in the direction of pure satire. The drawings reduce our awareness of the feeling and compassionate sensibility that Dickens so deliberately created in some of the original pieces. Significantly, none of Cruikshank's drawings direct themselves to the truly serious moments in Dickens' writings. Dickens undoubtedly cooperated in the imposition of this limitation. The creation of a deliberately merry tone is in keeping with all of the revisions that Dickens imposed on the original writings. Perhaps he recognized that his *forte* resided in the comic and satiric, that the illustrations to the book versions of his writings could create a coherence and cohesiveness, a more unified tone, in addressing themselves exclusively to the comic and satiric moments. Whatever the reasons, it is clear that the illustrations have avoided the purely sentimental moments in the original writings. Occasionally Cruikshank seems to have gone out of his way to find the comic, for instance in the illustration of "The Hospital Patient" (*Sketches*, p. 239). Here he chooses to show the peripheral incident of a pickpocket being hauled away in a wheelbarrow rather than the central event of a badly beaten woman refusing to name her assailant upon her deathbed. He shows Dickens' readers none of the politically charged moments such as the somnolent and indifferent judges of "Doctors' Commons" or "The Criminal Courts." The almost libelously accurate descriptions of the politicians in "A Parliamentary Sketch" are avoided. Instead, Cruikshank furthers the illusion that a merry, inconsequential, bemusedly ironic vision is the essence of the *Sketches By Boz.*

An inevitable limitation on the Cruikshank illustrations lies in the impossibility of representing with a single picture all of the ground covered by a narrative. Thus, in illustrating various stories Cruikshank was forced to choose a "typical" moment. This he does quite well as in "Horatio Sparkins" or "Mr. Sempronius Gattleton as Othello" (Ibid., pp. 361 and 425). In these illustrations Cruikshank always chooses the climactic moment, the point towards which the story was driving, the ironic unmasking in "Horatio Sparkins" or the abortive private theatrical performance in "Mrs. Joseph Porter . . ." As a visual embodiment of the content of a *story* (as opposed to a sketch) Cruikshank's focus on the climactic moment is appropriate. Generally speaking, because of the uniformly ironic tone of the stories, Cruikshank's illustrations are a faithful complement to the narratives.

But Dickens and Cruikshank part company in those *sketch* pieces which aim at being something more than simply satiric. The more serious sketches suffer a significant reduction and contraction of tone and scope, perhaps inevitably, in the process of being illustrated. First, many of the sketches impose on a would-be illustrator the difficulty of a very mixed tone. They require at once that the subject be rendered with a penetrating and incisive irony, but also with a soft and forgiving affirmative tone. Thus an illustration like the one to "Greenwich Fair" (see p. 57) is totally faithful to the phrases it chooses to represent, a description of the general confusion of the ballroom dancers and their "scrambling, falling, and embracing, and knocking up against the other couples" (Ibid., p. 118). But the illustration cannot be said to be faithful to the sketch as a whole. Cruikshank's drawing eliminates the complexity of Dickens' narrative stance. It cannot cover the scope of the narrator's vision; it cannot show simultaneously the nostalgic, apologetic seer of the patterns of human frivolousness and the detached ironic commentator on those same events. Cruikshank's drawings, so excellent in their own right, are finally reductive to the scope of Dickens' sketches.

A similar difficulty can be seen in the illustration of "Our Parish" entitled "Our Next-door Neighbour" (see p. 84). The subject of the drawing is absolutely faithful to Dickens' account of the awakening of a parish resident by some tipsy carousers, but again the drawing misses the tone.

That sense of the village-like intimacy in "The Parish," the erratic comings and goings, the quirky idosyncracies that coalesce into an overall sense of harmony, are not suggested by Cruikshank's otherwise delightful depiction of the mischievous revellers.

The reductive imposition of a uniformly comic-satiric tone prevails in most of Cruikshank's illustrations of Dickens' *Sketches*. But in the illustration for "The Pawnbroker's Shop," (see p. 120) one does find, perhaps uniquely, an example of Cruikshank's ability to read a Dickens sketch very closely and to illustrate the content with a complexity that is true to its source. "The Pawnbroker's Shop" is one of those sketches in which Dickens uses a range of different tones in describing the relationship of several different people to the subject at hand.

The sketch opens with the familiar device of Dickens discriminating between the various classes of the object under discussion, i.e., pawnshops, and then going on to focus on the class of the "more humble money-lender" (*Sketches*, p. 189). Continuing in a typical manner, Dickens then proceeds to describe the customers of the shop, announcing a different attitude toward the three distinct classes of customers.

Cruikshank's illustration follows Dickens precisely. He captures the vulgar lower-class characters with exactly the kind of offhand, slightly derisive tone that Dickens had used in his sketch. Here both artists show their appreciation of the grotesque. The characters are described, and subsequently drawn as: 1) an "old sallow-looking woman . . . with both arms on the counter"; 2) "an unshaven, dirty, sottish-looking fellow whose tarnished paper-cap, stuck negligently over one eye, communicates an additionally repulsive expression to his very uninviting countenance"; and 3) a "ragged urchin . . . unable to bring his face on a level with the counter" (Ibid., pp. 190–191). Cruikshank's drawings echo the blend of detached, condescending bemusement with which Dickens describes this first class of characters.

But both artists shift attitudes in presenting the other two classes of character. First, there is the clearly "fallen woman" whom Dickens describes in "attire miserably poor but extremely gaudy, wretchedly cold but extravagantly fine" (Ibid., p. 194). Cruikshank follows suit by giving her a tawdry feathered bonnet as a frame to her peculiarly sharp features; her face is drawn in a clearer, cleaner line without the shading which in the faces of the "vulgar poor" creates a sense of caricature. She is seen as the embodiment of a lamentable social tragedy — somewhat more clearly in Dickens than in Cruikshank.

Both artists reserve the greatest sense of contrast for the third class of character, an ostensibly genteel young woman and her mother who have fallen on hard times. Cruikshank draws the young woman's face with a delicacy and refinement — eyes cast down, a look of slightly pouting humiliation — unlike anything else in his drawing. The somber shadowed presence of her mother behind her and the "fallen woman's" expression of attentive recognition complete the pathos of the illustration. In all it is a masterful drawing which juxtaposes the comicly grotesque plight of the poor with the "falling" and "fallen" women, all framed by the cavalierly indifferent postures of the pawn clerks. It embodies Dickens' sense of different social strata and the responses that are appropriate to each. Moreover, Cruikshank's drawing of "The Pawnbroker's Shop" illustrates the mixing of tones and attitudes so typical of the *Sketches by Boz* as a whole. That there are not more such perfect illustrations is in part traceable to the fact that Dickens rarely conjoins such a range of characters in a single setting at a single moment.

Only a very few of Cruikshank's illustrations seem to miss the point of a Dickens piece entirely. For instance there is the picture of the "Poor Clerk" in "Thoughts About People" (see p. 168). Dickens bemoans this figure as exemplary of a class of "poor, harmless creatures . . . contented but not happy; broken-spirited and humbled" (*Sketches*, p. 217). But Cruikshank's portrait of the man, animatedly engrossed in reading a newspaper at dinner, conveys no sense of the pathos that Dickens sees in the figure. Similarly, the illustration called "Private Theatres" does not begin to suggest the ludicrously mistaken pretentions that Dickens finds in the narcissistic would-be actors (see p. xvi). Or again, the illustration to "The Gin Shop" conveys neither the breadth of detail in Dicken's descriptions of the temptingly fine and glittering appointments, nor does it convey his sense of indignation at the desperation that drives the poor to such places; instead the drawing focuses on the garrulous celebratory confusion of the barroom. There is only a slight hint of the ominousness that Dickens reports, here represented in the heavily-shadowed, gnarled, figure of an old man standing next to a child at the bar (see p. 209). But certainly inaccuracies are the exception rather than the rule in Cruikshank's illustrations.

Generally speaking, Cruikshank adheres to a faithful representation of the moment, if not the overall spirit of the original. He is perhaps even more than Dickens a child of the eighteenth century, a lover of satire and irony. Each of his drawings shows a truly sophisticated sense of symmetry and balance. (The left side of the drawing is frequently more heavily weighted than the right, as it should be for the print-trained eye which moves instinctively from left to right.) The drawings reveal a clear sense of an artist who knows his own mind just as he knows the audience he has won for it.

In all, Cruikshank's drawings were an inestimable boon to the first published books of the young writer. If they are not entirely perfect, given the difficulty of illustrating such diverse works, they are as perfect as could be expected: perceptive, clever, witty, they contribute an additional way of meaning to the *Sketches by Boz.*

vii Reception of the Sketches by Boz

Dickens' editing of his own works demonstrates his intuitive skill at controlling public response from the very beginning of his career. His correspondence for February 1836 shows the impatience and anxiety with which he awaited publication of his first book; once published, we see Dickens maneuvering to insure his recognition by the critics.[12] As the following pages will show, the critical response to Dickens' first book obviated the necessity of much maneuvering thereafter. The critics saw and reported exactly what Dickens wanted them to see and report.

The successive contemporary reissue of the Boz papers, outlined above, belies the position of relative obscurity that twentieth-century criticism has assigned to them. In 1836, the first gathering and publication of Boz's work received considerable acclaim from the critics. One need only look at the reviews published that year in response to the *First Series* to see that Dickens' contemporary audience recognized his first book as a genuine literary event. Dickens' careful selection, editing and rearrangement of the periodical pieces quite clearly paid off; the general assessment of Dickens' first reviewers was as highly affirmative as any novice author could hope for.[13] The reviewer for *The Sun* (Feb. 15) recognized Boz's distinction in saying: "Two more amusing volumes in their way have not appeared this season;" the reviewer in the *Court Journal* (Feb. 20) was equally enthusiastic in calling the volumes "the merriest of the season. We have seldom read two more agreeable volumes than these." Both *The Satirist* (Feb. 13) and the *Morning Post* (Mar. 12) assessed (and perhaps presented Dickens with the adjective he was later to use as his own epithet: "inimitable," an attitude reiterated in the *Sunday Herald's* "inimitably accurate" (Feb. 28). Perhaps the general contentment with Boz is best summed up by the

---

12. Dickens, *Letters,* I, House and Storey, pp. 102, 126, 144.
13. "The Reception of Dickens's First Book," *Dickensian,* 32 (1936), pp. 43–50. The following citations are all quoted in this anonymous article.

Metropolitan Magazine's redundant insistence: "It is hardly possible to conceive a more pleasantly reading book . . . rarely met a work that has pleased us more" (March).

Though a twentieth-century reader might find *Sketches by Boz* occasionally tedious, Dickens' contemporaries obviously felt the *First Series* revealed a major literary talent who had somehow penetrated the ubiquitous, and therefore, invisible patterns of the contemporary experience. There is a striking unanimity of response. Boz was praised as an "acute observer," a "good observer," and a "close and accurate observer;" for his "great correct observation," and his "great powers of observation." While several critics felt obliged to point out that Boz's humour was "broad," there seemed to be a general satisfaction with the "fidelity" of his presentation. The papers were said to have "their principle merit in their matter of factness, and the strict and literal way they adhere to nature," "evincing a shrewd and quizzical insight into ordinary character."[14]

A genuine excitement about Boz's accomplishment as a kind of sociologist marks many of the reviews. He was praised as "a kind of Boswell to society . . . and the middle ranks especially." "The succession of portraits does not reach higher than the best of the middle classes, but descends with startling fidelity to the lowest of the low." Boz's depiction of the middle classes was seized on as having a textbook veracity: "We strongly recommend this facetious work to the Americans. It will save them the trouble of reading some hundred dull-written tomes on England, as it is a perfect picture of the morals, manners and habits of a great portion of English society." Boz was suggested as appropriate reading for "country readers," and "provincial readers," as well as inhabitants of the "great Wen" who were anxious to see contemporary mores faithfully described. The reviews were confident that Boz would provide "instruction" to all of his readers.[15]

Quite obviously, Boz's first audience took his writings far more seriously than successive generations have. His "pathos," his "intense feeling," his "tone of high and moral feeling," his ability to "display a feeling far

---

14. Newspapers in 1836 responding with the above comments were as follows, respectively: *The Morning Chronicle*, Feb. 6; John Forster, "The Literary Examiner," in *The Examiner*, Feb.; *The Atlas*, Feb. 21; Ibid; *The Sun*, Feb. 15; *The Court Journal*, Feb. 20; *The Sunday Herald*, Feb. 28; *Atlas*, Feb. 21; *The Mirror*, Apr. 16; *Sun* (Feb. 15), *Metropolitan Magazine* (Mar.), and *The Literary Gazette* (Feb. 13) with the word "fidelity"; *Sun*, Feb. 15; and *Court Journal*, Feb. 20.

15. Quoted, respectively, from (1836): *Court Journal*, Feb. 20; *Metropolitan*, Mar.; Ibid.; *Sun*, Feb. 15; *The Morning Post*, Mar. 12; Ibid.; *Sun*, Feb. 15; *Metropolitan*, Mar.; *Mirror*, Apr. 16; *The Weekly Dispatch*, Feb. 28.

deeper than the professed character of the work" were all evidence of the overriding seriousness that readers found in the *Sketches*. Yet, the seriousness of the *Sketches* was felt to be adequately counter-balanced by Boz's "perception of the ludicrous," his ability to see the "follies and absurdities of human nature," its "pungent absurdities." [16]

Not surprisingly, the preceding quotations suggest Dickens' contemporaries' awareness of the divergent voices of Boz, much like the divergence we have discussed throughout this study: Boz's curious blend of the absurd and the pathetic. As we might imagine, Dickens' contemporaries saw that he had created an harmonious vision of the world in which narrative sensibility controls and contains all subjects within an aura of benevolence: "His disposition . . . evidently leads him to look on the bright and sunny side of things; and a kindly and benevolent spirit tempers the severity of his ridicule, and softens the gloom of his descriptions of vice." [17]

Forster's biography assures us that the original periodical sketches "were much . . . talked of outside as well as in the world of newspapers," [18] and a number of the reviewers testify to their prior familiarity with them in periodical form. [19] While there was some sense that Dickens' powers far exceeded some of his trivial subjects, [20] there was considerable satisfaction that the papers had been rescued from the obscurity of newspapers.

---

16. Sources, respectively (1836): Forster, *Examiner*, Feb.; *Morning Post*, Mar. 12; *Morning Chronicle*, Feb. 6; *Sunday Herald*, Feb. 28; Forster, *Examiner*, Feb.; *Morning Chronicle*, Feb. 6; and *Sunday Herald*, Feb. 28.

17. *Morning Chronicle*, Feb. 6.

18. John Forster, *Life of Charles Dickens* (London 1927; rpt. London: J. M. Dent, 1948), I, p. 60.

19. Specifically (1836), *Court Journal*, Feb. 20; *Morning Post*, Mar. 12; *Sunday Herald*, Feb. 28; *Morning Chronicle*, Feb. 6; Forster, *Examiner*, Feb.

20. Forster, *Examiner*, Feb., and *The Athenaeum*, Feb. 15, 1836.

PART TWO

The Pawnbroker's Shop

CHAPTER SIX
ON TO THE NOVELS

i Summary and transition

ANY READER of Dickens can immediately recognize the relevance to the novels of much we have seen in the short stories and sketches. Dickens' first story sets middle-class, contemporary Britishness as the topic that was to engage him for almost forty years. His use of a formulary story approach centered around idosyncratic characters, his gradual evolution towards a reliance on dramatic situations and a proliferation of characters, his world that culminates in comic catastrophe, are all obviously important elements in the novels. Within the first year of his career we have seen Dickens developing techniques he used throughout his novelistic endeavors.

The clarity, simplicity, the objectification of human personality and motivation that we have seen in the early short stories are also conspicuous in the novels. The mythic way of seeing things, with its indifference to empirical time, and its simplistic notions of causality, continues to shape much of Dickens' vision. And though the absurd, sardonic, and solipsistic limitations of Dickens' early story characters never control a Dickens novel, such people continue to populate the Dickens world.

We have tried to demonstrate that the development and evolution of Dickens' first published writings reveals his desire to submit and subordinate his earliest narrative posture and vision — supercilious, condescending and negative — to the much more genial and affirmative omniscience that shapes the sketches.

Dickens never really resolves the problem created by the ambivalence of his sensibility and vision; instead he learns to accommodate it. His progress towards the mature novels is essentially an exercise in the rhetoric of paradox. The questions become: "How can I write a novel endorsing heroism, dignity, a benign and harmonious world, when all I see seems trivial, arbitrary, and if planned at all, malevolent? How can I fabricate a life-affirming myth in a world incapable of generating a mythic action?" In order to resolve the paradox Dickens ends by creating two worlds in each of his novels: first of all, he gives us the ideal world in which the hero and heroine achieve a mythic dignity; secondly, he mounts that world in a rhetorical framework that undermines and collapses it. The second half of this study will be concerned with describing the rhetorical complexity which allows Dickens to have it both ways. My focus shall be briefly on *Pickwick Papers* and then on three early novels, *Nicholas Nickleby, The Old Curiosity Shop*, and *Martin Chuzzlewit*. Rather than a belabored application of the apparatus of the first half of this study, I shall attempt to pursue the conclusion we reached there: that Dickens' stories and sketches, both in their inception and his later treatment of them, reveal conflicting attitudes toward the world. Dickens' novels are all attempts at resolving the conflict.

ii *Boz and* Pickwick

In the year 1836 "Boz" became a household word. Though clearly the publication of *Sketches by Boz* was the fuse for the explosion that became *Pickwick*, the explosion was not an immediate one. Something was initially wrong with the conception of *Pickwick*, and the *Sketches by Boz* suggest what it was.

We have seen how Dickens recast the tonality and overall effect of the original Boz papers in gathering and editing them for collections. His change of mind in editing *Sketches by Boz* is reiterated in his writing of *Pickwick Papers.*

The first chapters of *Pickwick* have a double narrative frame; they are being told by a narrator who is recounting the narrative of the Secretary of the Pickwick Club, as recorded in the "posthumous papers." The effect of these first chapters is very different from the effects of the later chapters where the double narrative frame is dropped.

To begin with, in the opening chapters Mr. Pickwick and the Pick-wickians generally are presented to the reader as blatant, middle-class fools. They belong to an inane organization given over to useless abstruse scholarly speculations. The narrative suggests that the Pickwickians are as hopelessly irrelevant, but nowhere near as imaginative, as Swift's model speculators the Laputans. Dickens' satire here is both heavy-handed and explicit. If the reader fails to see the inanity in the Pickwickians' "unmingled satisfaction, and unqualified approval" of the primary topic of the treatise Mr. Pickwick reads to the membership, "Speculations on the

Source of the Hampstead Ponds," his secondary topic "some Observations on the Theory of Tittle-bats," cannot possibly miss its satiric mark.[1]

A comparable satiric contempt shapes much of the opening of the book. For instance, the first chapter closes after recounting the debate sparked by Mr. Pickwick's announcement of his intended peregrinations. Mr. Blotton pronounces a singular "No!" midst the chorus of cheers that greets Pickwick's travel plans, and bestows the epithet of "Humbug!" on Pickwick. Pickwick proceeds to inquire if the word Humbug has been used in its "common sense," to which Blotton replies: "he had used the word in its Pickwickian sense . . . he had merely considered him humbug in a Pickwickian point of view" (I, p. 5). Of course the reader really has no way of penetrating this nonsense — what is the difference between the common and Pickwickian senses of the word "Humbug"? Fools making foolish distinctions. Typically, Dickens' narrator steps in and closes the chapter with a further transparently sarcastic denigration of the Pickwickians: "Here the entry terminates, as we have no doubt the debate did also, after arriving at such a highly satisfactory and intelligible point."

Dickens is of course asserting that such goings-on are as inanely trivial as they are unintelligible. But the reading public's response at being offered such high-handed smartness, at a shilling a number, is entirely intelligible: only 400 of the first number sold; of the second through fifth numbers the provincial booksellers returned an average of 1450 out of the 1500 they had received.[2] Before *Pickwick* could succeed Dickens had to abandon his self-conscious irony; he had to eliminate the double-frame narrative.

Dickens' subsequent change in narrative technique is more than a simplification of a cumbersome writing situation as previous commentators have assumed. In effect, the removal of one of the narrative frames alters the tonality of *Pickwick* radically. The rhetorical effect of the opening chapters of *Pickwick* is similar to the effect that presides in the earliest short stories by Boz. In both situations the tone is negatively satirical, condescending and aloof. With the removal of one of the frames the tone of *Pickwick* becomes more sympathetic and affirmative. Another way to describe the revised tone of *Pickwick* is to say that it moves in the direction of becoming more like the tone of Boz's sketches.

Of course, Dickens himself recognized the limitations of his opening

---

1. Charles Dickens, *Pickwick Papers* (London: Oxford University Press, 1948), p. 1. Subsequent references are to the Oxford edition and are parenthesized with chapter and page within the text.

2. Edgar Johnson, *Charles Dickens: His Tragedy and Triumph*, I, p. 135.

chapters. In the Preface of the 1837 first edition of *Pickwick Papers*, writing of himself in the third person, Dickens points to the machinery of the club as the culprit.

> Deferring to the judgment of others in the outset, he adopted the machinery of the club . . . but finding that it tended to his embarrassment than otherwise, he gradually abandoned it, considering it a matter of very little importance to the work whether strictly epic justice were awarded to the club or not.

Similarly Dickens offers the same excuse in the Preface to the first Cheap Edition, published ten years later: ". . . the machinery of the club, proving cumbrous in the management, was gradually abandoned."[3]

Yet even a cursory reading of *Pickwick Papers* suggests its problems go beyond the purely mechanical, the club machinery. The reader must be made to feel that Pickwick the buffoon of the opening chapters is really a quixotic man of good feeling who transcends both the banality and the philosophical seriousness of his episodic encounter with the world.

The transformation of Pickwick is so obvious that Dickens felt obliged to apologize for it in the Preface to the first Cheap Edition:

> It has been observed of Mr. Pickwick, that there is a decided change in his character, as these pages proceed, and that he becomes more good and more sensible. I do not think that this change will appear forced or unnatural to my readers, if they will reflect that in real life the peculiarities and oddities of a man who has anything whimsical about him, generally impress us first, and that it is not until we are better acquainted with him that we usually begin to look below these superficial traits, and to know the better part of him. (*Pickwick*, xii)

In some respects Dickens' apology is both straightforward and accurate as a description of Pickwick's change. If the change does not seem "unnatural or forced" as Dickens claims, it is because the change represents a shift in Dickens' attitude towards Pickwick rather than a preconceived change in the quality or content of his character's dramatic life. Pickwick does not really become "more good and more sensible." Thus, we cannot point to a specific locus in the book, or a specific incident, in which there is a radical shift in Pickwick's character simply because it is not Pickwick who

---

3. *Pickwick Papers*, p. x.

changes, but Dickens. Pickwick the character undergoes a rhetorical transformation, not a conceptual one. In eliminating one of the narrative frames, Dickens lightens the overloaded rhetoric of the opening chapters where the reader is asked against his better judgment to concede that Pickwick's foibles make him an heroic character. Eventually, Pickwick becomes a transcendent anti-hero, a man whose good nature triumphs over his bumptiousness and short-sightedness, a man whose very limitations spell out the essence of the human fallibility that enshrouds most mortal aspirations to heroism.

But before the reader could experience Pickwick's power, Dickens himself had to acquire a belief in it. Dickens had to relinquish his search for bathetic effects; he had to abandon the sarcasm of the self-aggrandizing tone that he used in most of the short stories by Boz.

For instance, consider the following passage from the fourth chapter of *Pickwick* where the club members feel threatened by the field-day maneuvers of the army:

> It was in this trying situation, exposed to a galling fire of blank cartridges, and harassed by the operations of the military . . . that Mr. Pickwick displayed that perfect coolness and self-possession, which are the indispensable accompaniments of a great mind. He seized Mr. Winkle by the arm, and placing himself between that gentleman and Mr. Snodgrass, earnestly besought them to remember that beyond the possibility of being rendered deaf by the noise, there was no immediate danger to be apprehended from the firing. (IV, p. 48)

Here Dickens is being highly ironic. Our belief in the "perfect coolness and self-possession" of Pickwick's "great mind" is undercut by the narrator's pointing to Pickwick's instinctive cowardice, his perhaps unconscious self-protective action; for as a preliminary to his assuring his companions of their safety, he doubly insures his own safety by using their bodies as shields. This is not an act of hypocritic meanness on the part of Pickwick; rather we see demonstrated a kind of prudential heroism, an unconscious revelation of Pickwick's sense of his own vulnerability that estranges him from The Heroic. But at the same time, Pickwick's actions render ironically irrelevant the narrator's extended praises. In the same episode, the narrator insists that though Pickwick's "lips might quiver, and his cheek might blanch, no expression of fear or concern escaped the lips of that immortal man." Once again the reader sees primarily the contradiction between Pickwick's entirely understandable human fears and the narrator's self-consciously superior sarcasm towards them. We are forced to acknowledge that heroism and bravery are states of mind far from Pickwick's tentatively stiff upper lip and his decorous masculine obstinacy; that at best these are the conventional costume of a far more universal cowardice. The narrator forces us to see that Pickwick is truly neither brave nor heroic; but eventually we understand that Pickwick is truly human, limited, fragile, well-meaning but fallible. The reader comes to this realization only after Dickens' narrative technique halves the irony of his presentation.

The narrative voice in *Pickwick* is really a combination of two conflicting narrative intelligences. The dominant intelligence is an *internal* quasi-omniscient narrator who follows the dramatic action in *Pickwick*. His intelligence eventually presides and shapes the reader's rhetorical responses to the book. He accompanies the club members on their journeys; through his repeated insistence on the sublime status of Pickwick, "the immortal Pickwick," the reader comes to recognize the non-ironic implications of his statements: Pickwick is immortal by virtue of his humble mortality. Because the *internal* narrator records and points to all of Pickwick's foibles, and yet still insists on his grandeur as a man, the reader eventually transcends the surface irony of the narrator's praise and sees through to the truth beyond the irony. Pickwick becomes an heroic Everyman.

But before the internal dramatic narrator could have this effect, Dickens had to abandon his external narrative intelligence, the narrator who reminds us he is reconstructing the history of the Pickwickians from "posthumous papers" in records, letters, and notes. As long as the external narrator remains on the scene, Pickwick has little possibility of coming to life, of transcending his limitations. The external narrator is entirely too arch, or stupid, or both. His effusions on Pickwick simply do not work; they reveal a psyche either entirely lacking in judgment or so self-consciously condescending in its irony that rhetorically Pickwick is arrested in a bathetic low. The external narrator's praise is too effusive and general; he has too vague an understanding of the Pickwickians to effect the transcendence of irony. He cannot move the reader's responses beyond the awareness that Pickwick's life is mundane, trivial, and fatuous. When he asserts that the Pickwickians had arrived at an "intelligible" point in their discussion, the reader has no way around the irony of the manifest unintelligibility of the discussion.

The internal dramatic narrator is close enough to Pickwick's adventures to convince us that Pickwick is worthy of our admiration. We see through to the man beneath the narrator's heroic costuming. But when the reader is switched to the limited external narrator, Pickwick's transcendent humanity falls flat. We find such a switch at the end of the first interpolated tale, "The Stroller's Tale" in chapter three:

> It would afford us the highest gratification to be enabled to record Mr. Pickwick's opinion of the foregoing anecdote. We have little doubt that we should have been enabled to present it to our readers, but for a most unfortunate occurrence.
>
> Mr. Pickwick had replaced on the table the glass which, during the last few sentences of the tale, he had retained in his hand, and had just made up his mind to speak — indeed, we have the authority of Mr. Snodgrass's note-book for stating, that he had actually opened his mouth — when the waiter entered the room, and said —
>
> "Some gentlemen, sir."
>
> It has been conjectured that Mr. Pickwick was on the point of delivering some remarks which would have enlightened the world, if not the Thames, when he was thus interrupted. (III, pp. 40–41)

As long as Pickwick's life depended on such highly contrived and condescending smugness — "the Thames," "the world —" the purchasers of shilling numbers were willing to forego whatever illumination might be in store for them. But with the publication of the fourth number of *Pickwick* in July 1836, the *Posthumous Papers* soared immensely in popularity. One explanation of the change in the public's attitude attributes it to a fascination with the new content, the introduction of Samuel Weller. While the ingenious creation of that character was undoubtedly a sufficient enticement for many readers, neither Sam Weller, nor his mentor Pickwick, would have had much of a chance of surviving had not their world undergone an equally significant change in its form. Dickens dropped his second narrative frame, simplified his rhetorical posture, and Pickwick has endured.

In all, Dickens' various revisions and arrangements of these earliest works, his success at eliciting a favorable response from the reading public, and his changes in the rhetorical shape of *Pickwick*, suggest a pattern. Both consciously and perhaps unconsciously Dickens was moving away from the negative, satirical, and aloof posture of his earliest writing. While he was never able to abandon totally the penetrating satirical — even absurdist — vision of his earliest stories, much of his later writing can be seen as an attempt to subordinate it to the more affirmative vision of the novels.

The Parish Engine

CHAPTER SEVEN

SAYING
IT BOTH WAYS

i Nickleby *as the earliest "Dickensian" novel*

THOUGH MUCH neglected in our own century, *Nicholas Nickleby* is in many ways the first typically Dickensian novel. Neither the sporadic episodic brilliance of *Pickwick*, nor the sustained melodramatic flare of *Oliver Twist* are ultimately as typical of much that is most typical of Dickens. Those first two novels are in many respects complementary. In *Oliver Twist* Dickens quite consciously set out to demonstrate that he could write a novel as polemically serious in its treatment of society as *Pickwick* was thought to be comically non-consequential. Though a study of any of Dickens' novels would undoubtedly yield considerable information that is relevant to our purposes, in light of the relative freshness of the material, *Nicholas Nickleby* seems far more deserving of our detailed attention here. Moreover, *Nicholas Nickleby* is Dickens' first book originally conceived of as a *novel* to attain the typical length of most of his major works. As such, it is the first of his novels that could be said to carry the "orchestration" as well as the "melody" of the Dickensian novel.

Nicholas Nickleby combines the comic nonchalance of *Pickwick* with the polemic seriousness of *Oliver Twist*. Its polemic burdens are various: implicitly it attempts an evaluation of country life versus city life, an opposition that runs throughout the novel; explicitly it condemns the economic network of exploitation that seems to threaten the very possibilities of humanness in the contemporary scene; and finally it generally affirms the viability of the world it depicts as a way to the good life and happiness. That the novel should at once seek to condemn and affirm the same objects is by virtue of all we have said in this study thus far, characteristically Dickensian.

Moreover, because Dickens, in *Nicholas Nickleby*, confronts so many problems for the first time, the resultant limitations on its success as a novel also reveal much about *what* Dickens was trying to do. Our discussion of *Nicholas Nickleby*, therefore, will begin with a consideration of some of the general problems that arise in the novel: Dickens' use of the conventional hero, the relationship of the hero to the other characters in the novel, and the notion of characterization generally, as seen in *Nicholas Nickleby*.

Nicholas Nickleby, a *bildungsroman*, is Dickens' first attempt at a novel with a conventional adult hero. In its broad outlines the novel undertakes to move Nicholas Nickleby from a pastoral innocence, relatively in harmony with nature, through a number of trials in which he is deprived of that basic innocence and harmony, finally bringing him to rest as a man of experience, capable of controlling his destiny and his world. In order to achieve this state Dickens has to give Nickleby all the conventional traits of the hero: he must be good, kind, generous, strong, industrious, modest, honest, courageous and so on. Though previously Pickwick had been made to possess similar virtues, the problem of instilling them in Nicholas Nickleby is considerably more complex. Pickwick, like the characters in the short stories by Boz, exercises his virtues in a world that refuses to cooperate with him, that usually frustrates his intentions. Pickwick is a transcendant anti-hero whose steadfastness and earnestness eventually deliver him from his bumptiousness. Though he is victimized by the world, he represents an affirmative advancement over the early story characters in that he emerges unscathed. Nicholas Nickleby, however, as a conventional hero, is obliged to undertake a program of positive action in which his will dominates the way of the world.

With Nicholas, for the first time, Dickens is trying to dramatize the moral and intellectual superiority of a character by investing him with traits that previously had been the exclusive property of the narrator of his sketches. There, a humane, compassionate, knowledgeable and generous sensibility triumphs over the world primarily by seeing through it and responding to it in a kindly fashion. The narrator of the sketches attains a kind of heroism through his intelligence, vision and simultaneous sympathy and detachment. But there are no dramatic heroes or heroines in either Dickens' stories or sketches. Those earliest works show that Dickens' impulse, except for the shaping of his own persona, is anti-heroic. Though Dickens does not believe in the possibility of heroism, throughout his career as a novelist he tries to transcend his anti-heroic vision. His writing ultimately shows that though it is possible to look at the world through heroic eyes, creating legs that will walk and hands that will grasp in the manner of a hero is a very different problem.

Though Nicholas achieves a satisfying level of swashbuckling, rhetorically he cannot fulfill all of his obligations. The success of Nicholas' undertakings would be difficult to present convincingly even in a form that restricted itself to pure, non-dramatic narrative; but since so much of this novel (as in most Dickens' novels) is given over to the dramatic technique of dialogue, the language that Dickens gives Nicholas to speak becomes a rhetorical encumbrance. It floats above the rest of the novel as an almost parodistic example of heroic speech:

> "Forgive me," said Nicholas, with respectful earnestness, "if I seem to say too much, or to presume upon the confidence which has been entrusted to me. But I could not leave you as if my interest and sympathy expired with the commission of the day. I am your faithful servant, humbly devoted . . . in strict truth and honour to him who sent me here, and in pure integrity of heart, and distant respect for you. If I meant more or less than this, I should be unworthy his regard, and false to the nature that prompts the honest words I utter." [1]

The chief difficulty in the cited paragraph (Nicholas' first interview with Madeline Bray) is that not atypically, Dickens attempts to validate Nicholas' heroism by making him speak a piece on abstract virtues. Nicholas presents himself as a vessel of "confidence," "entrusted" by the Cheerybles, a "faithful servant," "humbly devoted." His diction is little more than a self-bestowal of honorifics, an assertion of his heroism tempered only by an equally heroic modesty and self-effacement: "truth," "honour," "integrity," "respect" and "honest words." Here and elsewhere, the reader is presented with the form but not the substance of heroism.

The way that Nicholas speaks is undermined even further by the prevailing attitudes towards communication, human expression and speech in the novel. In contrast to the modes of communication that are established elsewhere in the novel, Nicholas' heroic set-pieces acquire the ring of pious oratory. Nicholas and most of Dickens' aspirants to heroic eloquence are at odds with the attitudes towards language that prevail in the *Sketches*

---

1. Charles Dickens, *Nicholas Nickleby* (1839: rpt. London, Oxford University Press, 1960), Ch. XLVI, p. 608. Subsequent references are to the Oxford edition and are parenthesized in the text.

by Boz. Both Dickens' stories and sketches show us characters who frequently use speech as a façade for fending off the world, for masking themselves against the incursions of others: Mr. Minns as well as his cousin, the Gattletons, Maldertons, and all the characters in the "Boarding House" are among those in whom we have seen this characteristic. Moreover, both the condescending, supercilious narrator of the stories, and the compassionate, sympathetic narrator of the sketches show us their abilities in seeing beyond language in order to understand the world. The story narrator ironically reconstructs the meaning of his characters' locutions, while the sketch narrator surveys and reports the patterns of the world, omnisciently dispensing with the precedence of language as the primary way for understanding the meaning of events that surround him; the sketch narrator frequently reads the habits, attitudes, and fates of the characters he presents without the need of their speaking a single word.

In keeping with the superfluousness of language that is demonstrated throughout the *Sketches by Boz*, in *Nicholas Nickleby* Dickens demonstrates both the complete adequacy and even primacy of gesture as a way of communication. Nods, winks, smiles, expressions — non-verbal communication — acquire for almost all the characters a significance that presides over language. Thus, Nicholas himself overrides Miss La Creevy's insistence that he "not . . . repeat the impertinence" of kissing her, by doing just the opposite (XX, p. 247); or, in a related manner, Newman Noggs' nervous gesture of cracking his knuckles becomes an idiosyncratic expression of his happiness that needs no articulation (XI, p. 132). Mrs. Witterly, who tries to live the bad novels she reads, communicates primarily through a "pantomime of graceful attitudes" (XXVIII, p. 361).

In fact, as long as the characters in a given situation occupy the same moral hemisphere (i.e., either both good or both bad morally), language seems to be entirely superfluous. Thus, Ralph Nickleby and Sir Mulberry Hawk embark on the attempted seduction of Kate Nickleby through an agreement established by Nickleby's "curious look" and Hawk's responding "careless smile" (XXVI, p. 334). Comparably, the Mantalinis can dispense with ordinary language entirely, communicating through inversion:

> "Is my life and soul there?"
> "No," replied his wife. . . .
> "May its poppet come in and talk?"
> "Certainly not," replied Madame . . . [He enters and kisses her]
> "Oh! I can't bear you," replied his wife. (XXI, p. 258)

Even more comically, Mr. Knag and his sister convey meanings with repeated "Ah's" and "hem's" respectively (XVIII, p. 221).

In fact, the morally suspect characters frequently use language to mask and distort what should be the unmistakably clear language of gesture. Accordingly on the basis of "looks" and "smiles" Miss Squeers very early becomes convinced that she is almost engaged to Nickleby (IX, p. 104). Or when jealous Mr. Lillyvick protests his wife's molestation by the drunken advances and winks of Snevelicci, Mrs. Lillyvick who vainly enjoys such low-grade compliments tries to establish her suitor's innocence by insisting on the primacy of language over gesture:

> "Lor, what nonsense he talks!" exclaimed Mrs. Lillyvick in answer to the inquiring look of Nicholas. "Nobody has *said* anything to me." (XXX, p. 394, my italics)

In a manner that demonstrates her corruption, here Mrs. Lillyvick insists, quite incorrectly, that she can only be compromised through an exchange of language. Similarly, when John Browdie strikes Mr. Squeers because Squeers has succeeded in recapturing Smike, Squeers forces the gesture to accommodate to his own distorted view of the world:

> . . . Squeers, staggering in his chair under the congratulatory blow on the chest which the stout Yorkshireman dealt him; "thankee. Don't do it again. You mean it kindly, I know, but it hurts rather." (XXXIX, p. 506)

Squeers has either falsely or mistakenly interpreted the meaning of Browdie's action. An inability to interpret gesture correctly, or an excessive reliance on language become keys to a corrupt moral stature. So in Mrs. Witterly's mistaken view,

> coarseness became humour, vulgarity softened itself down into the most charming eccentricity; insolence took the guise of an easy absence of reserve. (XXVIII, pp. 364–65)

Thus the novel abounds in characters who use language perversely, or inversely or not at all. Though Dickens probably intended that the clarity and directness of his hero's (and heroine's) language would place them at the top of a moral-linguistic hierarchy, in many ways he undermines the distinction.

ii Problems in characterization

A second and related problem in Dickens' attempt to create a conventional hero arises from his manner of characterization. The Boz of the *Sketches*, and *Pickwick*, had shown his skill in using idiosyncrasy as a base for character. But since in those works the reduction of character to idiosyncratic traits frequently sets up an opposition between diminished characters and the exalted intelligence that reports character, Dickens avoided giving his hero any idiosyncrasy that would limit him in the way that other characters are limited. The result is that there is little that makes Nicholas, the embodiment of "heroic youth," into *an heroic youth*. Ideally, in the course of the novel, the Dickensian hero should acquire a knowledge, intelligence and taste comparable to those in the sensibility that presides over the *Sketches by Boz*; but in retaining such an *open* characterization, Dickens only succeeds in creating a flat conventional character. Most of the cast of *Nicholas Nickleby* have individuating idiosyncrasies which, juxtaposed to the character of Nicholas, only make him appear more wooden by comparison.

Previously we have seen that in the earliest fiction, the short stories by Boz, the idiosyncratic characters are all enmeshed in a world that conspires to frustrate their idiosyncrasies. Perhaps because the short stories are only incidentally rather than overtly concerned with making moral distinctions, they end by treating all idiosyncrasies alike in awarding them repeated frustration and exposure. But in *Nicholas Nickleby* and subsequent novels, frustration and exposure become an instrument of poetic justice necessary only for the morally culpable. Thus here, the portrait artist Miss La Creevy can continue her search for noses, Magog can continue his grotesque courting with vegetables, the Cheerybles can continue their bland benignity; but Squeers' hypocritic cruelty, Ralph Nickleby's necro-obsessional greed, and even Snevelicci's oleaginous courtliness must all have their comeuppance.

Moreover, the kinds of changes that characters undergo in *Nicholas Nickleby* are reminiscent of the changes we have seen in the short stories by Boz. Though none of the characters in *Nicholas Nickleby* undergo radical metamorphoses, those characters who change at all do so with a plasticity that we have heretofore called characteristic of mythic thinking. That is, rather than conceiving of changes in character empirically, whereby a man has certain traits and abilities which allow us to understand his personality and accomplishments, the characters here are made to change *ad hoc*, in order to fit situations. For instance, Nicholas, about whose education the reader is never informed, automatically becomes a tutor; later, he just as easily becomes an actor, a language teacher, and a business manager. Other characters undergo different but related kinds of changes. For instance, the reader's first introduction to John Browdie (IX) very firmly fixes his image as a blunt, crude man who laughs at the starvation diet at Dotheboys Hall and bullies his fiancée. But when we next see Browdie, he is championing Nicholas' victory over the Hall; by some mysterious agency he has been transformed into a rustic man of humanitarian feelings. Similarly, though Lord Verisopht's name phonetically anticipates his later display of principle, no explanation intercedes between his identification with the decadent aristocrats of the Hawk circle and his subsequent moral superiority to them. As in all of Dickens' work, people simply change, and the reader is left with the burden of understanding why. Of course, one way of explaining away this puzzling technique of Dickens' is to suggest that such changes are a way of presenting different facets of a character's personality. But the problem of course is that the character thus remains so-many disconnected facets; the reader has no way of putting them all together.

Though this brief discussion of the hero, his characterization, and characterization generally begins to suggest ways that *Nicholas Nickleby* is like the *Sketches by Boz*, the comparable similarities in structure, and the meaning generated by that structure, are much more complex. The first half of this study has attempted to show that Dickens' earliest writings reveal an ambivalence on his part, a desire both to affirm and negate, condemn and praise, incense and pacify, frequently encouraging these conflicting emotions toward the same object. Though it is much more skillfully masked, an identical ambivalence runs all through *Nicholas Nickleby*. Let us therefore consider *Nicholas Nickleby* in terms of its structure, with an end to showing how it culminates in the peculiarly ambivalent and paradoxical statement we have previously characterized as the essence of Dickensian art.[2] In order to demonstrate our point, we shall need to consider both the advances and the withdrawals within the novel, both the affirmative and optimistic direction that the novel pursues, and the negative and pessimistic rhetorical devices that collapse the surface of the novel.

iii The first movement of Nickleby

Basically the novel is divided into three large movements, each of

---

2. Edgar Johnson, in "The Paradox of Dickens," *Dickensian*, 51 (1955), pp. 237–41, claims that Dickens' personality is the essential paradox; the divergences and contradictions that occur between works are testimonies to Dickens' amplitude.

which corresponds to stages in Nickleby's spiritual enlightenment; each part also presents Nickleby's allegorical encounter with metaphysical forces arranged in a moral hierarchy ascending upward — evil or hell as represented in Squeers' school, the mixed state of the world as seen in the Crummles' theatre, and absolute good or heaven as seen in the corporate benignity of the Cheerybles. This section of the study will begin by presenting an analysis of these three movements, the affirmative directions of the novel. Subsequently we shall turn our attention to the rhetorical techniques by which that affirmative surface is undermined.[3]

The first part of *Nicholas Nickleby* is meant to be a condemnation and satire of the conspiratorial network of collusion that has transformed agrarian England into a toy for speculators, a plaything for *business*. The first chapter traces the spread of this phenomenon, showing how it eventually comes to burden the hero. We begin in the fourth generation preceding the hero with the death of the first Ralph Nickleby and the transfer of his 5000 pounds to his nephew Godfrey, the hero's grandfather; in turn we follow the passing of that money to the hero's father Nicholas and his uncle Ralph; we conclude with father-Nicholas' loss of his inheritance through speculation, his subsequent death, his heirs' loss of their estate, and their move to the city to seek shelter and livelihood. Thus the genealogy shows four generations of Nicklebys who typify the increasing burdens that speculation has produced in England, and the impact it has had on forcing the urbanization of a pastoral country-people.

Dickens' sketches had already shown his awareness of the human impact implicit in new and on-going business practices in the city. He had denounced the veneer of dazzle and elegance currently being installed by London saloon-keepers in order to increase the allure of their "Gin Shops." He had aimed obliquely at the slum-lording that degrades neighborhoods by carving properties into smaller and smaller parcels in "Shops and their Tenants." He had described the ganglia of economic competitiveness that made for the chaos of "Seven Dials;" and he had bemoaned the crass exploitation and dramas of dehumanization regularly enacted in "Pawnbrokers' Shops." The sketches are filled with allusions to the tawdry and manipulative practices of business in London.

Thus, in *Nicholas Nickleby*, as the scene switches to London, Dickens suggests the pervasiveness of collusive economic forces by focusing on the

---

3. Jerome Meckier, "The Faint Image of Eden," refines the structure of the novel into a series of circles, rather than just three movements. Meckier shows that Nicholas and Kate go through a series of initiations in the various circles, and moreover, shows how the circles coincide with periodical publication.

"United Metropolitan Improved Hot Muffin and Crumpet Baking and Punctual Delivery Company," the enterprise alluded to in the subtitle of chapter two, "A Great Joint Stock Company of Vast National Importance." The repetition of exaggerated muffin company name becomes a leitmotif in the second chapter; the name is repeated five times and with each repetition Dickens intensifies his satire on capitalistic monopoly, investments, and speculations, showing how the investors finally succeed in having their fingers in every muffin-box in the country. Accordingly, when the third chapter moves the job-seeking young Nicholas into the orbit of Squeers, the reader who has been veritably dunned by the muffin-leitmotif immediately recognizes a similarity to it in Squeers' *refrain*, which he repeats four times within a few pages: "Squeer's Academy, Dotheboys Hall, at the delightful village of Dotheboys, Near Greta Bridge in Yorkshire" (III, p. 26ff). Squeers and the speculators use the same kind of inflated slogan language because, as Dickens wants us to see, they are part of the same conspiratorial network. Throughout the chapter, while Squeers is concerned with taking on new pupils he constantly refers to his "business;" and when one of the new pupils fails his first lesson by ingenuously substituting the phrase "Never perform business" for the "Never postpone business" he has been asked to parrot after Squeers, the identification of Dotheboys Hall with the world of business and commerce is complete (IV, p. 37).

Nicholas' interlude at Dotheboys Hall is meant to be a kind of descent into the underworld, an encounter with the most clear-cut evil in the novel. Though the Hall represents both literally and symbolically the *under*, hidden side of the business world, as a place it is conceived of primarily in symbolic terms. With grotesque comedy Dickens has his devil-figure, Squeers, introduce us to the "domestic economy" of the Hall.

> They have the brimstone and treacle partly because if they hadn't something or other in the way of medicine they'd be always ailing and giving a world of trouble, and partly because it spoils their appetites and comes cheaper than breakfast and dinner. (VIII, p. 86)

Moreover, as the exposition continues we are given a powerful symbolic description of the conditions at the Hall in a Dantesque inferno scene.

> Pale and haggard faces, lank and bony figures, children with the countenances of old men, deformities with irons upon their limbs, boys of stunted growth, and others whose long meagre legs would hardly bear their stooping bodies, all crowded on the view

together; there were the bleared eye, the hare-lip, the crooked foot, and every ugliness or distortion that told of unnatural aversion conceived by parents for their offspring, or of young lives which, from the earliest dawn of infancy, had been one horrible endurance of cruelty and neglect. There were little faces which should have been handsome, darkened with the scowl of sullen, dogged suffering; there was childhood with the light of its eye quenched, its beauty gone, and its helplessness alone remaining . . . With every kindly sympathy and affection blasted in its birth, with every young and healthy feeling flogged and starved down, with every revengeful passion that can fester in swollen hearts eating its evil way to their core in silence, what an incipient Hell was breeding here! (VIII, p. 88)

The striking thing about the passage is the way that its symbolic equivalence with Hell dominates its literal existence as a schoolroom. The individual boys hardly exist at all; instead they are reduced to abstract deformities and mutilated body parts surreally blending into the embodiment of evil-magic from which the hero must eventually gain his independence. As in many of the sketches, the meaning of a given scene, its symbolic import, dominates our apprehension of it as an actual scene. The main impression is not that of an objective recording of reality, but a symbolic representation of it, in which the boys, like so many objects, are vessels of meaning.

Nicholas enters this scene gullible, innocent and obsequious. Once he understands the enormity of evil in the "business" he serves, as part of his moral education he is obliged to extricate himself from complicity. The starkness and absoluteness of the evil at the Hall is directly proportional to the simplicity and directness with which Nicholas removes himself from its influence. Incensed at Squeers' gratuitous cruelty to Smike, Nicholas gives Squeers a sound thrashing and immediately departs for the city (XIII, p. 155).

iv The second movement

With the second movement of the novel, Nicholas' return to the city, the situation becomes considerably more complex. At the Hall, Nicholas acted without sophistication, without subterfuge, with directness. But with his move to the city he is obliged to adapt his mode of action to his new self, that is, he must act with the knowledge of a young man who has had an encounter with absolute evil; secondly, he must adapt himself to the moral dimensions of the city itself — a much more subtle blend of good and evil. Frequently events in the city present a façade of moral neutrality, thereby masking their real moral implications. Accordingly Nicholas must learn to deal with façades. In order to cope with a world of appearance, one must know how to manipulate appearances. Thus, structurally the novel preserves a perfect symmetry; in the first part a simple moral righteousness overcomes an absolute evil; the second part requires that an expert at appearances conquer a world where appearances preside.

Much of the second movement of the novel is given over to variations on the theme of acting.[4] Although there is a transitional section in which Nicholas retains some of his old identity in working as a French tutor to the Keniwig children, and much of the focus shifts to sister Kate's activities here, the center of this section is really Nicholas' triumphant success in a literal and symbolic world of actors. Initially it appears that Dickens intends to use the notion of acting as a symbolic statement in condemnation of false appearances and deception.[5] Certainly the little plays that the Mantalinis perform for each other make it appear so (cf. XVII, where Mantalini plays a kind of male trollop to his wife, enticing her with spite). Nicholas' bewilderment at the transformations of the Crummles company also suggests that acting will become some kind of moral yardstick:

> Here all the people were so much changed, that he scarcely knew them. False hair, false colour, false calves, false muscles — they had become different beings. (XXIV, p. 302)

But the notion of falseness is subsumed into necessity as Dickens turns the novel to showing that the world is a stage, and living in it is a necessary performance.

During this part of the novel most of the major and minor characters seem to be giving their energies to some kind of performance. Mrs. Witterly who professes "such an interest in the drama" (XXVII, p. 352), lives in an "artificial bloom" and,

> by dint of lying on the same sofa for three years and a half, had got up a little pantomime of graceful attitudes, and now threw herself into the most striking of the series, to astonish the visitors. (XXVIII, p. 361)

The Lillyvick-Petowker wedding is conceived of as a drama, complete with props, scenery, and costumes:

---

4. J. Hillis Miller, *Charles Dickens: The World of His Novels*, pp. 89–90, discusses the extensive use of the theatre in the novel.
5. Bernard Bergonzi, "Nicholas Nickleby," points to the divergent meanings of theatricality in the novel, i.e., "showy and affected" and "deficient in reality."

The bridesmaids were quite covered with *artificial* flowers, and the phenomenon . . . was rendered almost invisible by the *portable arbour* in which she was enshrined. . . . The other ladies displayed several dazzling articles of *imitative* jewellery, almost equal to real. . . . Mr. Crummles . . . who *personated* the bride's father, had, in pursuance of a happy and original conception, *"made up"* for the part by arraying himself in a theatrical wig. . . . The better to support his assumed character he had determined to be greatly overcome, and, consequently, when they entered the church, the sobs of the affectionate parent were so heartrending that the pew-opener suggested the propriety of his retiring to the vestry. . . . (XXV, p. 326, my italics)

The rest of the scene is comparably "arranged and rehearsed," with Mrs. Crummles playing the mother of the bride with a "stage walk." Though the wedding act is innocent enough, and not so far removed from the extravaganzas of non-theatrical people to diminish its general satiric value, elsewhere the *staging* of human affairs takes on ominous overtones.

Pyke and Pluck, Sir Mulberry Hawk's henchmen in his designs on Kate Nickleby, prove to be very skillful actors. As Hawk's party leaves the theatre they cleverly manoeuvre the group so that Kate and Hawk are "left some little distance behind," accomplishing their work like superb actors, "without an appearance of effort or design" (XXVII, p. 354). When Kate recoils from Hawk's advances, Pyke and Pluck enter on "cue" and cover the scene by creating a diversion. In a second attempt on Kate, Pyke and Pluck put on a little play, using Mrs. Witterly's actress narcissism, her "appetite for adulation," as means of distracting her while Hawk pursues Kate (XXVII, p. 362).

Sir Mulberry himself is presented as an actor "ambitious for distinction and applause" in a "world peopled with profligates, and he *acted* accordingly" (XXVIII, p. 357, my italics). His several attempts at seduction of Kate consist of scenarios to which he has written the "plot" (XXVII, p. 355) and he mistakenly imagines that Kate is also an actress, only putting up a *"show* of displeasure" (XXVII, p. 354, my italics). Later for the benefit of Verisopht he stages a disinterest in Kate (XXVII, p. 356).

Newman Noggs is also an actor of a very complex kind. While he comforts Kate, who is distressed by the aggressive attentions of Hawk, Noggs is the classic embodiment of the cliché "Laughing on the outside, crying on the inside;" "Newman Noggs opened the door once again to nod cheerfully, and laugh — and shut it, to shake his head mournfully, and cry" (XXVIII, p. 372). But trapped as he is, forced to be an unwilling accomplice to machinations of Ralph Nickleby, he resorts to a pantomime of the righteous and heroic actions he would like to perform:

> As the usurer turned for consolation to his books and papers, a *performance* was going on outside his office-door . . . Newman Noggs was the sole *actor*. He stood at a little distance from the door, with his face towards it; and with the sleeves of his coat turned back at the wrists, was occupied in bestowing the most vigorous, scientific, and straightforward blows upon the empty air. (XXVIII, p. 373, my italics)

In another instance Noggs wears himself out with shadow-boxing of the same kind (XXXI, p. 405). Noggs even further complicates the meaning of acting in the novel. Which is his self? which his act? — his obsequious cooperation with a man he despises? or the subterfuge that he enters against him, and the pantomimes he performs outside his closed door?

Even Ralph Nickleby is presented as an actor when he visits Hawk, whose face has been scarred in an encounter with Nicholas:

> As he turned his face, Ralph recoiled a step or two, and making as though he were irresistibly impelled to express astonishment, but was determined not to do so, sat down with *well-acted* confusion. (XXXVIII, p. 491, my italics)

Dickens very confusingly describes both the good and the bad characters in the novel as actors.

The theatre, as a place, seems to retain a symbolic meaning synonymous with "a place of deception." It is at the theatre that Hawk arranges for his first assault on Kate (XXVII, p. 345). Similarly, in order to keep Nicholas from doing "something desperate" Noggs and La Creevy conspire to take Mrs. Nickleby to *the theatre*, thereby concealing Kate's whereabouts from her brother (XXXI, p. 407).

The Crummles and their troupe, as the only professional actors in the novel, partake of the mixed moral quality of the city itself. Superficially they seem kind, generous, and humane. But one of the mainstays of their troupe is their own daughter, "The Phenomenon," whose physical growth they have stunted by calculation. Upon finding out that the virtuoso is only ten, Nicholas responds "it's extraordinary!" The narrator continues:

> It was; for the infant phenomenon, though of short stature, had a comparatively aged countenance, and had moreover been precisely

the same age — not perhaps to the full extent of the memory of the oldest inhabitant, but certainly for five good years. But she had been kept up late every night, and put upon an unlimited allowance of gin-and-water from infancy, to prevent her growing tall, and perhaps this system of training had produced in the infant phenomenon these additional phenomena. (XXIII, p. 290)

Though the Crummles are not nearly so conspicuously evil as Squeers, their treatment of their daughter suggests an affinity with him. Squeers' starved pupils have comparable physical deformities and aged countenances. Similarly "The Phenomenon" whose age has been officially arrested echoes the situation of Smike, who has undergone a mental and spiritual retardation at the hands of Squeers, and who grotesquely wears the scraps of infant clothing in which he was delivered to Squeers; comparably "The Phenomenon" is always dressed with infantile coyness. Without over-emphasizing the point, Dickens makes it quite clear that the Crummles, in a much less exaggerated fashion than Squeers, are also in the "business" of exploiting children. And once again Nicholas is working for the exploiters.[6]

In all, the way in which acting is used in the second movement of the novel creates a typically Dickensian problem of meaning. On the one hand the reader is tempted on the symbolic level to equate "acting" with a moral flaw. But on the other hand, it is the hero who is the most superb actor in the novel. While the novel frequently repudiates the notion of acting, at the same time it asserts the necessity of being an actor in order to control the world. That Nicholas acquires the necessary skills is shown in his treatment of Mr. Lenville, shortly before Nicholas leaves the Crummles troupe. Mr. Lenville has expressed again his bizarre desire to pull Nicholas' nose. Nicholas responds in a parody of nonchalant heroics:

> "Come," said Nicholas, nodding his head, "apologise for the insolent note you wrote to me last night, and waste no more time in talking."
> "Never!" cried Mr. Lenville.
> . . . The weak husband . . . relents. "I apologise."
> "Humbly and submissively?" said Nicholas.
> "Humbly and submissively," returned the tragedian. (XXIX, p. 380–381)

---

6. J. A. Carter, "The World of Squeers and the World of Crummles," rather sees Crummles (because he is a teacher of young actors, particularly in chapter XXII) as a reflection of Squeers. The sham and violence of the theatre echoes the real violence of Dotheboys Hall, and Smike connects the two.

At this point, when Nicholas can exact the "humble and submissive" tone of the apology he demands, he has acquired the manipulative skill which seems to reside at the center of what Dickens means by "acting."

But the problem here is that having gone so far in setting up moral connotations for acting in the other characters, Dickens undercuts his hero's heroism by making him the best of actors in a novel that demonstrates that acting is both reprehensible and necessary. Dickens' ambivalence here, in the symbolic use of actors and acting, is really only an amplification of the ambivalence towards the same subjects he had shown in both his stories and sketches: denigrating the comic incompetence of the actors in "Mrs. Joseph Porter . . . ," deriding the fatuousness of actors in "Brokers' and Marine Store Shops," praising the ponderous majesty of actors at "Greenwich Fair," applauding the actors' illusion-making power at "Astley's," and then derisively satirizing the performers in "Private Theatres."

The coincidence of Dickens' ambivalence towards the subject of the theatre and acting, both in his literal descriptions in *Sketches by Boz*, and his use of those ideas symbolically in *Nicholas Nickleby*, is undoubtedly worth noting for its own sake; but more important than the coincidence itself is the sense of conflict and ambivalence that develops when we try to focus on Dickens' ideas. As we have seen in the *Sketches by Boz*, Dickens frequently pronounces conflicting attitudes towards his subjects: the court that is both censored for its expeditiousness and commended for its patiences in "The Old Bailey;" the derelicts who are condemned for their slovenliness and pitied for their destitution in "The Shabby-Genteel;" the cab-driver who is both the most charming and ingratiating original and the despicable public nuisance in the revised "The Last Cab-Driver. . . ." This presence of illusive, shifting, and conflicting attitudes towards the same subjects shapes Dickens' rhetoric as a novelist. As the following pages will show, Dickens — consciously or unconsciously — fills his novels with devices that allow him to maintain conflicting attitudes while promoting the illusion of clarity and simplicity.

Nicholas' superiority as an actor is evidence of his moral superiority. He has acquired an ability to control his fate and manipulate appearances in the world. He closes this stage of his life with one melodramatic, almost operatic gesture. Overhearing Hawk speak of his sister, and unable to force him to identify himself, a fight ensues in which Nicholas opens a gash in Hawk's face using Hawk's own whip (XXXII, p. 417–418). Here Nicholas is at the apex of his swashbuckling. His defeat of Hawk echoes his defeat of Squeers, but is different from it in two important ways: First, there is the melodrama of the encounter itself, a kind of set-piece for the world as stage. Second, in a world of appearances, Nicholas achieves only the appearance of a moral victory, since Hawk's machinations continue to dog him throughout the novel; significantly in such a world Nicholas leaves a scar on Hawk's face, a blemish in *appearance*.

v The third movement

The third movement of the novel treats Nickleby's moral maturation. Here Nicholas abdicates his theatrical ways and adopts those of his new mentors and employers, the Cheerybles. These jolly brothers and businessmen are peculiarly similar in appearance:

> What was the amazement of Nicholas when his conductor advanced, and exchanged a warm greeting with another old gentleman, the very type and model of himself — the same face, the same figure, the same coat, waistcoat, and neckcloth, the same breeches and gaiters — nay, there was the very same white hat hanging against the wall! (XXXV, p. 453)

The two men, veritably indistinguishable from each other, do everything in concert. In contrast to the fragmented half-people who populate the novel, the Cheerybles achieve a wholeness in their unified pursuit of Christian benevolence.

Though Dickens' imagination seems to fail him somewhat in providing any kind of concrete business for the Cheerybles, other than their perpetual do-goodery, he makes it quite clear that they represent the polar opposite of the evil businesses of Squeers and Ralph Nickleby. In keeping with their identity as businessmen, they are presented as conspirators, only naturally their conspiracies center around principles of charity, goodness, generosity, a mirror image of the other businessmen.

The Cheerybles occupy a pregnantly symbolic house in the pregnantly symbolic landscape of City Square, the chief qualities of which are a sense of naturalness and celestial somnolence that presides there. No false and artificial pompousness is to be seen:

> The City Square has no enclosure, save the lamp-post in the middle; and has no grass but the weeds which spring up round its base. It is a quiet, little-frequented, retired spot, favourable to melancholy and contemplation, and appointments of long-waiting; and up and down its every side the Appointed saunters idly by the hour together, waking the echoes with the monotonous sound of his footsteps on the smooth worn stones. . . . It is so

quiet, that you can almost hear the ticking of your own watch when you stop to cool in its refreshing atmosphere. (XXXVII, pp. 468–69)

The other quality that presides in the Cheerybles' world is neatness, emblematic of the moral order of their domain. Their ultrafastidiousness is maintained by Tim Linkinwater:

> The old clerk performed the minutest actions of the day, and arranged the minutest articles in the little room, in a precise and regular order, which could not have been exceeded. . . . All had their accustomed inches of space. Except the clock, there was not such an accurate and unimpeachable instrument in existence, as the little thermometer which hung behind the door. There was not a bird of such methodical and business-like habits in all the world, as the blind blackbird, who dreamed and dozed away his days in a large snug cage, and had lost his voice, from old age. (XXXVII, pp. 469–70)

In contrast to the jumbled confusion of Dotheboys Hall, and the noisy garrulity of the Crummles, Nicholas enters the spiritually quieting balm (and embalm) of the Cheerybles' house. Though their meaning is clear enough, perhaps too clear, the Cheerybles represent a naive vision of the good that never transcends the compulsively neat workshop of twin Santa Clauses who come every day.

Yet it is under the tutelage of the Cheerybles that Nicholas will attain his ultimate moral refinement. Primarily we see the changes in Nicholas' conduct as an imitation of the idealized modesty and self-effacement of the Cheerybles. Many of the changes emerge as Nicholas pursues his love for Madeline Bray. Typically, he contemplates his affection with Cheeryblian self-denial:

> What if I do love and reverence this good and lovely creature. Should I not appear a most arrogant and shallow coxcomb if I gravely represented that there was any danger of her falling in love with me? Besides, have I no confidence in myself? Am I not now bound in honour to repress these thoughts? Has not this excellent man a right to my best and heartiest services, and should any considerations of self deter me from rendering them? (XLVI, pp. 602–3)

Nicholas becomes plagued by a sense of "double-duty," to the Cheerybles and Madeline (XLVIII, p. 625). Sworn to silence as the agent of the

Cheerybles' charitable dealings with Madeline, Nicholas' loyalty to his employers becomes so exaggerated that he cannot "betray the confidence reposed" in him, even to save his love from a forced marriage with Gride (LII, p. 680).

Nicholas' experience of first love while under the shadow of the Cheerybles' philanthropy turns yesterday's swashbuckling actor into today's moral philosopher. Nicholas' new social conscience is part of what happens to him when his "hot enthusiasm [is] subdued, and cool calm reason substituted in its stead; doubt and misgiving revive" (LIII, p. 693). Thus,

> everything appeared to yield him some new occasion for despond-
> ency. . . . But when he thought how . . . youth and beauty died,
> and ugly griping age lived tottering on; how crafty avarice grew
> rich, and manly honest hearts were poor and sad; how few they
> were who tenanted the stately houses, and how many those who
> lay in noisome pens, or rose each day and laid them down each
> night, and lived and died, father and son, mother and child, race
> upon race, generation upon generation, without a home to shelter
> them or the energies of one single man directed to their aid. (LIII,
> p. 693)

In the final state of Nicholas' evolution he hears the "still, sad music of humanity;" the passage quoted above is only one-fourth of the whole attack of *weltschmerz* Nicholas suffers at this point.

Of course Nicholas' experience as an actor has not gone to waste. It is an ineradicable part of his education. Eventually Nicholas marshals his ability to control the world and with the fury of an avenging angel delivers Madeline from the impending forced marriage with Gride, upsets the plots against her inheritance, and rebuffs the curses of his uncle with the news that much of his fortune has dissolved in "one great crash" (LIV, p. 720). Later Ralph Nickleby bitterly and jealously acknowledges that Nicholas has played an "angel" to his dying son (LXII, p. 803).

Much of the ending of the novel is given over to painful convolutions of self-deprecation and unworthiness that both Nicholas and Kate suffer before surrendering to the natural inevitabilities of their marriages. Having been schooled by the Cheerybles' Christian meekness, they take their steps gingerly, above all seeking to avoid any air of presumption. The novel ends with happy marriages established all around, and with Nicholas a partner in the Cheerybles' still unspecified business, and with Nicholas once again in possession of the estate his father had lost though speculation.

Thus the three movements of *Nicholas Nickleby* present the hero's spiritual evolution from innocence and naiveté, through his three major encounters with moral forces: with the absolute evil of business, with the mixed morality of the world-as-a-stage, and finally with the absolute good of the Cheerybles, to whose benevolence he brings his other experiences, enabling him ultimately to become a full-fledged partner in their goodness enterprise.

Philosophically *Nicholas Nickleby* is certainly the most ambitious work Dickens had undertaken thus far. It moves beyond the blithe nonconsequence of *Pickwick*, or the purely-magic, guardian-angel vision of *Oliver Twist*. Instead, *Nicholas Nickleby* attempts to present a portrait of the moral extremes operative in the broad economic framework of contemporary England.

Read in isolation, the depiction of evil as represented in Squeers' school, the conspiring aristocrats, and the speculators is undoubtedly the most forceful part of the novel. In contrast the depiction of goodness in the Cheerybles appears to be an attempt on Dickens' part to deliver the novel from an irredeemable pessimism by subscribing to a Manichean vision.[7] Where *Pickwick* never really confronts evil directly, and *Oliver Twist* only eludes its grasp through the intervention of almost magical circumstance, *Nickleby* attempts to sustain an argument for the actual existence of a counter-balancing good. In the Preface to the first edition of *Nickleby*, undoubtedly responding to criticism of the Cheerybles, Dickens goes so far as to claim that the impossible goodness of the Cheerybles is drawn from real life:

> Those who take an interest in this tale, will be glad to learn that the BROTHERS CHEERYBLE live; that their liberal charity, their singleness of heart, their noble nature, and their unbounded benevolence, are no creations of the Author's brain; but are prompting every day (and oftenest by stealth) some munificent and generous deed in that town of which they are the pride and honour. (xviii–xix)[8]

---

7. Meckier, p. 145, suggests that the novel reflects the "Manichean paradox." The good triumph as the world remains evil. Graham Greene in "The Young Dickens," p. 56, discusses the use of the Manichean system in *Oliver Twist*.

8. For an interesting note on the impact that Dickens' announcement of the actuality of the Cheerybles had on the lives of the Grant Brothers, see Arthur A. Adrian, "The Cheeryble Brothers: A Further Note:" Dickens later announced the death of the Grants, though one was still alive, probably to save the survivor from the flood of charitable applications Dickens had occasioned.

Here Dickens seems to be begging the question, relying on his actual acquaintance with stealthy do-gooders to validate his failure at depicting the good. Further, Dickens' failure with the Cheerybles returns us to our primary observation about *Sketches by Boz*. Dickens' vision of the world entails conflicting impulses. On the one hand his stories culminate in a negative and sardonic vision that repudiates, rather than affirms, the society they depict. On the other hand, his sketches are generally consolatory and approving of society. In *Nicholas Nickleby*, these conflicting impulses emerge most clearly in the Manichean system that Dickens tries to sustain.[9]

Moreover, the rhetorical failure of the hero as well as the Cheerybles stems from Dickens' inability to resolve the paradox which lies at the center of his vision. While the main story moves Nicholas towards a resolution with the benign Cheerybles, a resolution that subscribes to a conventional and pietistic morality — all's right with the world — other structures move towards a dissolution and confusion of the problem.

One such structure is Dickens' use of the metaphor of acting in *Nicholas Nickleby*. Were it not that Dickens so heavily imbues the notion of acting with negative moral connotations, Nicholas' accomplishment as the best actor in the novel might stand as evidence of his superiority to other characters in the novel. But within the context that Dickens establishes, Nicholas' acting ability becomes a rhetorical liability which his much-protested heroism cannot entirely displace. Though the reader can find a solution to the conflict that Dickens sets up, rhetorically the conflict undermines the hero's heroism. The rest of this chapter will be given to a discussion of other techniques and structures which undermine the optimism that surrounds the hero in *Nicholas Nickleby*.

vi Conflicts and paradox

First, there is a problem created by the general mimetic process by which Dickens works. Is there *a reality* which he attempts to imitate? If so, what is it? The third chapter of this study argues that Dickens' way of representing reality in his short stories has much in common with myth; that in his conception of character, change, time, and causality, Dickens works within a mythic framework. Without repeating that argument here,

---

9. A. O. J. Cockshut finds a related kind of conflict in the "two dreary poles" of Dickens' humor. "One is reached when he feebly attacks the contempt for common things which nevertheless forms an undercurrent of his own writing, and the other when the objects of satire are facitious bogies denied human status and moral choice" (*The Imagination of Charles Dickens*, p. 94).

it seems quite obvious that many of Dickens' minor characters continue to be characters like those in the world of myth.

Nicholas' crypto-cousin Smike is a good example. As a character Smike has the kind of concreteness and total objectivity of personality that we associate with the world of myth; he is more of an animistic object than a person. Smike exists entirely within the *post hoc, ergo propter hoc* context that is so common to mythic thinking. With Smike, as with the object in the mythic world, "thing and signification are undifferentiated, they merge, grow together, concresce into an immediate unity";[10] thus every detail of Smike's character is symbolic: he is a retarded nineteen-year-old, so he wears infant's clothing, including a tattered child's frill around his neck (VII, p. 79); he has been maltreated by Squeers, so he walks with a limp. Smike is a concrete repository for the collusive evil of Squeers, Ralph, and the world of business. Though his diminished humanness is meant to be emblematic of the dehumanization and brutality he has suffered at the hands of Squeers, his character with respect to Nicholas is conceived along the lines of a pathetically faithful dog:[11]

> Smike, since the night Nicholas had spoken kindly to him in the school-room, had followed him to and fro, with an ever restless desire to serve or help him; anticipating such little wants as his humble ability could supply, and content only to be near him. He would sit beside him for hours, looking patiently into his face; and a word would brighten up his careworn visage, and call into it a passing gleam, even of happiness. (XII, p. 143)

With respect to the action of the novel, Smike has a function, but not a life.[12] Smike is a symbol of Nicholas' loss of innocence in his encounter with the evil of Dotheboys Hall. Appropriately, when Nicholas leaves the Hall, Smike goes with him. Moreover, as Nicholas moves towards a firm alignment with the absolute good of the Cheerybles, Smike begins to grow ill. The logic of his symbolic role requires that he die once Nicholas has

---

10. Ernst Cassirer, *Mythical Thought*, p. 24.

11. In contrast to my insistence that Smike is a shadowy symbolic figure, see Roy A. Ball, "The Development of Smike," who argues for the "complexity of Smike's personality developing through self-realisation." He applauds Smike as evidence of Dickens' "craftsmanship." My own feeling is that Ball is applauding the complexity of the social moral issues represented in Smike, rather than the character as presented.

12. A. Coppock's "Smike" also seems to promote the excellence of Smike as a character, primarily because he embodies Dickens' early humanitarianism and his feelings that promote a benign social welfarism.

finally overcome the evil forces that have created creatures such as Smike. And Smike's own father's suicide stems from his recognition of the evil he has created and sustained as embodied in the deformity of his son.

Though Smike's function in the meaning of the novel is quite clear, his effect on its texture is very disturbing. In apprehending Smike, the reader intuitively recognizes that the fictive dimensions of his existence have been contracted into something like a grotesque cartoon. Though the conception of the hero is stylized, it is stylized in a different way. Smike exists almost entirely within a different mimetic system from the one that is used for his idol and deliverer, Nicholas; it is a system that has a different density from the one in which Nicholas exists. Smike is drawn broadly and symbolically without details beyond his symbolic meaning. He exists on a level of reality in which his whereabouts and activities need not be accounted for in the same way that the hero's are. Thus though Smike is supposedly with Nicholas throughout the interlude with the Crummles, weeks go by without his appearing once. He dines (XXIII, p. 297), he carries Nicholas' bag (XXIII, p. 299), and he tries to learn to play the "apothecary" in *Romeo and Juliet* (XXVI), but his conception does not entail the same kind of continuity and accountability for elapsed time as does Nicholas'. He appears and disappears, something in the manner of Nicholas' coin purse or pocket watch.

The juxtaposition of two mimetic systems with varying densities in effect creates two different kinds of reality within the novel. Moreover, when we consider the tonal circumstances that surround various characters, it appears that there are many different kinds of reality co-existing within the novel. For instance, though "The Phenomenon" is just as much, even more, of a cartoon character as is Smike, our manner of apprehending her is controlled by the sprightly and witty syntax from which she always springs:

> But she had been kept up late every night, and put upon an unlimited allowance of gin-and-water from infancy, to prevent her growing tall, and perhaps this system of training had produced in the infant phenomenon these additional phenomena. (XXIII, p. 290)

Here we seem to be in the presence of the narrator of the early short stories. It is a world in which syntax and wit dominate sentiment and morality; a world in which the consequence of any situation is never allowed to be more than the chuckle to which the narrator directs us. Even the linguistic playfulness of the passage, "phenomenon — phenomena," is reminiscent of the early stories.

The two exploited, deliberately retarded children, Smike and "The Phenomenon," are kept on different rhetorical levels throughout the novel.[13] The morose and melancholy voice that shapes our responses to Smike entirely disappears when the novel focuses on "The Phenomenon." Thus the structure of *Nicholas Nickleby* is made complex by Dickens' inter-weaving of different levels of reality with varying degrees of mimetic density and differing affective appeal. Moreover, the structure of the novel becomes an amplified version of the kind of structure that we have observed in some of the *Sketches*. There we have seen how the sketches go beyond the peculiar flatness and limited affective appeal of the short stories by generating a multilayered vision of their subjects, where each layer may have an affective appeal different from and in conflict with the appeal of the preceding layer.

A comparable kind of layering exists in many of Dickens' novels. Thus in *Nicholas Nickleby* the portentous and swashbuckling world of Nicholas, which advances along conventional heroic lines, drags in its wake the heavily symbolic world of Smike which struggles under a burden of melancholy polemics; and Smike's world, in turn, is left to sustain itself in opposition to its reflection in the comically non-consequential world of "The Phenomenon." In a sense, what we have here is a combination of Dickens' early story narrator, sardonic and detached, the voice that presents "The Phenomenon," added to Dickens' sketch narrator, compassionate and concerned, the voice that presents Smike. Neither of these voices is synonymous with the voice that shapes our apprehension of the hero, nor do any of the voices assert precisely the same values. Just as with the coherence of many of Dickens' sketches, the coherence of the novel depends on his ability to keep the several voices, the several value systems from colliding. Just as in his sketches, the discrete, unsynthesized, conflicting attitudes that inhere in the various mimetic levels allow Dickens to mask a paradox, to announce his detachment and his compassion simultaneously. Many of the devices within *Nicholas Nickleby* and the later novels culminate in comparable paradoxical effects.

vii Echoes and parodies

Throughout the novel Dickens shows a remarkable skill in making minor characters and incidents both anticipate and echo the problems and

---

13. Bergonzi, p. 75, also points to the similarity between Crummles and Squeers and their respective abused children, but Bergonzi believes it is the Keniwigs who are the closer reflection of Squeers.

configurations of the more important characters. Some of this is done very subtly and as such deepens and fortifies the point Dickens is making. For instance, as Nicholas in all innocence embarks on his coach trip to Dotheboys Hall, the main narrative line appears to stop when the coach passengers begin to tell stories. One of the stories we read is a sweet and sentimental story of loving devotion, the story of Alice, in the "Five Sisters of York" (VI, pp. 57–64). Though the story is somewhat saccharine, the reader is left with a very clear statement about an idealized Christian way of dying, the Sisters' loving solicitude for each other, and the beautiful shrine that is established at York Cathedral as a cherished monument to the girls. But the function of this story does not become clear until Nicholas arrives at the desolation of Dotheboys Hall. As Nicholas gradually comes to understand the "economy" of the Hall, Smike recounts the story of the death of a Dotheboys student, and his own fears of death:

> "I was with him at night, and when it was all silent he cried no more for friends he wished to come and sit with him, but began to see faces round his bed that came from home; he said they smiled, and talked to him; and he died at last lifting his head to kiss them. . . . "What faces will smile on me when I die!" cried [Smike], shivering. "Who will talk to me in those long nights! They cannot come from home." (VIII, p. 97)

With Smike's recounting of the ignominy of the boy's death, neglected and alone at Squeers' school, the loving death scene of Alice comes into focus. Alice's death stands as an ironic anticipation and accusation of the depraved state of things at the Hall, as well as suggesting the degeneration of human responsibility since her time. In this instance, Dickens' use of a parallel situation strengthens the thrust of his main story line. But there are two stories told in the coach.

Though the second story that the travellers tell also anticipates the situation at Squeers' school, its relationship to those events is neither direct nor simple. The story of the "Baron of Grogswig" is a rather grotesque and surreal comic tale (VI, pp. 66–75). It tells of a heavy-drinking Baron and the band of followers with whom he hunts; out of boredom the Baron begins to abuse his followers; he takes a wife who turns out to be a shrew who bears him thirteen children; the unhappiness of his situation leads him to contemplate suicide; an interview with the "genius of Suicide" dissuades him from his rash action. Ultimately the baron lives happily into an old age.

This story is the very last thing that the novel gives us before plunging Nicholas into the degradation of Squeers' school, but placed as it is, it has a very peculiar effect on our responses to the situation at Dotheboys Hall. Curiously, analogues to the various situations in the Baron's story are scattered throughout the opening account of the Squeers' school. This process begins immediately by presenting Squeers in a comic echo of the Baron's habitual drunkenness:

> Mr. Squeers . . . ran into the tavern and went through the leg-stretching process at the bar. After some minutes, he returned, with his legs thoroughly stretched, if the hue of his nose and a short hiccup afforded any criterion. (VII, p. 76)

Besides the Baron's drunkenness, his gratuitous cruelty to his followers, farcical in his story, is echoed in the much more serious mistreatment of Squeers' students. The Baron's shrewish wife and thirteen children of course have analogues in Mrs. Squeers and the pupils. But, whereas it is the Baron who finds his situation intolerable and contemplates suicide, though up to now the Baron has been identified with the Squeers, suddenly it is Nicholas who echoes that detail of the Baron's story:

> Nicholas sat down, so depressed and self-degraded by the consciousness of his position, that if death could have come upon him at that time he would have been almost happy to meet it. (VIII, p. 95)

Read in isolation, Dickens' description of Squeers' school is powerful and affecting. But read under the shadow of the farcical tale that precedes the description, the whole situation acquires a tinge of irony that makes Squeers' school and Nicholas' responses to it seem both more highly stylized and less ponderous. The rhetorical effect of Nicholas' death-thought is undercut by echoic relationship to the farcical tale.[14]

A comparable echoing of the main characters persists throughout the novel. Mr. Lillyvick, the collector of the "water rate" (XIV, p. 163), and his impoverished nephew and niece, the Keniwigs, are a comic version of the relationship between Ralph Nickleby and his brother's children Nicholas and Kate. Lillyvick, like Ralph, is a domineering Uncle who uses his position in "business" to manipulate and terrorize the Keniwigs:

---

14. Ann Roulet, "A Comparative Study of *Nicholas Nickleby* and *Bleak House*," is typical of the prevailing attitudes towards these stories. She describes them as "fill elements," typical of Dickens' early "episodic form and picaresque models."

Here was an untoward event! The collector had sat swelling and fuming in offended dignity for some minutes, and had now fairly burst out. The great man — the rich relation — the unmarried uncle — who had it in his power to make Morleena an heiress, and the very baby a legatee — was offended. Gracious Powers, where was this to end! (XV, p. 178)

Though the Keniwigs are much more ambitous towards the Uncle's wealth than are Nicholas and Kate, still they are meant as a foil to the main characters. Both uncles repudiate their nephews' kindnesses. Where Ralph becomes incensed at Nicholas' humaneness in overturning Squeers, Lillyvick becomes incensed at his nephew's profligate generosity in offering Newman Noggs a second glass of punch:

> Quadruped lions are said to be savage, only when they are hungry; biped lions are rarely sulky longer than when their appetite for distinction remains unappeased. Mr. Lillyvick stood higher than ever; for he had shown his power; hinted at his property and testamentary intentions; gained great credit for disinterestedness and virtue; and, in addition to all, was finally accommodated with a much larger tumbler of punch than that which Newman Noggs had so feloniously made off with. (XV, p. 179)

Lillyvick's indignation is a parody of Ralph Nickleby's.

Further, the Lillyvick-Petowker marriage, the triumph of staging already discussed, is a comically symbolic merger of the conspiratorial forces that Dickens has stressed so heavily in the first part of the novel; the world of business and the world of acting are comically joined in Lillyvick-Petowker. Of course, because of its falseness the marriage is doomed to failure. But on a more serious level, the marriage and its failure are again echoed very precisely in the secret marriage of Ralph Nickleby that is disclosed at the end of the novel. The parallelism here is very explicit. We learn that Ralph Nickleby's wife is also an "actress" of sorts; though his marriage is said to have lasted for some time, throughout its duration both parties *pretended* that they were single (LXI). Moreover, the situations are brought even closer together in that both marriages end with the wife's elopement with a younger man (XXII, LXI).[15]

---

15. In a different vein, see G. D. Wing, "A Part to Tear a Cat In," for a discussion of the psychological complexity of the portrait of Ralph Nickleby; Wing opposes the more conventional claims of shallowness attributed to the portrait of the usurer.

Curiously, in a manner that is entirely typical of the technique of the novel, the situations of both Ralph Nickleby and Lillyvick have a third, even more comic and grotesque echo in Mrs. Nickleby's neighbor. His hilarious insanity is explained in a manner that identifies him immediately with Ralph Nickleby: "He went mad at last, through evil tempers, and covetousness and selfishness" (XLII, p. 539). But now, in the confusions of his madness, he courts Mrs. Nickleby in a manner that identifies him with the Lillyvick circle; Lillyvick's niece is forever awestruck by her Uncle's immense stature as the "collector of the water rate." This in turn is parodied by the madman's exaggerated obsequiousness in one of his approaches to Mrs. Nickleby: "Forgive me if I am wrong, but I was told you were a niece to the Commissioners of Paving" (XLII, p. 535).

Thus the concern on the primary level of the novel for the manipulation and greed of Ralph Nickleby is parodied on a second level by Lillyvick-Petowker; and both of these levels are parodied on the level of the mad Magog. Significantly, as we move away from the primary level the consequences of greed, manipulation, and madness diminish; moral concerns evaporate. The three levels here do not exist within the same moral framework. Sandwiched in between the seriously melodramatic level of Ralph Nickleby and the surreally grotesque comedy of Magog, we find the sardonic nonconsequence of Lillyvick-Petowker, a story which by itself is very much like an early story by Boz. (In fact, the basic relationship of Lillyvick to the Keniwigs is really just a retelling of Boz's *fourth* published story, "The Bloomsbury Christening;" a sardonic, prosperous, bachelor-uncle exploits his nephew's family and their testamentary expectations by lording it, grumpily, over their pathetic attempts at a social life.)

The rhetorical effects of the minor characters, with their constant echoing of the more important characters, become very important when we attempt to make statements about the meaning of the novel. The portentous events and concerns of the main characters are ironically diminished by the imitations of their actions that occur on different strata of the novel. Even the shadowy and melodramatic symbol-figure of Smike has his comic echo, as we have seen, in "The Phenomenon." Moreover, as Smike moves towards the inevitability of his demise, called for by the logic of his symbolic role, Dickens introduces another Smike-figure in the form of "a little deformed child, sitting apart from other children, who are active and merry, watching the games he is denied the power to share in" (XL, p. 514). Tim Linkinwater reports on his long acquaintance with the "double-wallflower in the back-attic window, at No. 6, in the courtyard" (XL, p. 514). The boy grows flowers "in old blacking bottles," and as he languishes into his death, the reader immediately recognizes that the crippled boy, his deformity and pathetic milieu, are all meant to signal and fortify the pathos of the approaching death of Smike. But when Smike, already a melodramatic symbol-figure, generates an additional level of symbolic melodrama, richness becomes overripeness, pathos becomes parody.[16]

Perhaps the most flagrant and successful instance of Dickens' setting-up ironic parodies of his main characters' lives comes in the juxtaposition of Nicholas' courting of Madeline to Magog's courting of his mother. Both are overwhelming instances of love at first sight. In a manner that highlights the arbitrariness of Nicholas' attack of love fever, Dickens ensnares him in an episode of secret-rendezvous turned mistaken-identity, and Nicholas makes it into the wrong girl's kitchen (cf. XL), recalling the kind of ironic and farcical endings so familiar in Boz's stories. Immediately following Nicholas' embarrassing episode with the wrong girl, Dickens presents a chapter on Mrs. Nickleby's bizarre love affair with the mad neighbor. Mrs. Nickleby has become a coquette, grooming and preening for her suitor. But the reasons she gives for her sudden coquetry reflect back on Nicholas' own conduct; she is preening to prove that the manifest insanity of her neighbor is rational, nothing more than the lover's doldrums suffered by a man ravaged by passion. She says:

> "If Nicholas knew what his poor dear papa suffered before we were engaged . . . he would have a little more feeling." (XLI, p. 529)

Thus, when Nicholas himself becomes the "dull and abstracted" lover (XLVIII, p. 626) the reader apprehends him not only in the light of the conventional courtly lover, but also in the light of the hilarious madness that has preceded him. That Nicholas faces much danger in his courting of Madeline is mocked by his mother's insistence that she believes *her* courtier "to be sincere" when she finds him "placing himself in such dreadful situations" (XLIX, p. 647) on her account. The pallid and conventional courtliness of Nicholas — straight out of a fairy tale — cannot sustain itself in conjunction with the dazzling fractured-fairy tale that surrounds it. Mrs. Nickleby's courtier has a mind much like her own, broken loose from its moorings:

---

16. Steven Marcus, *Dickens: From Pickwick to Dombey*, p. 127, points to the presence of other parodic elements in the novel, but he feels they testify to the progress of Dickens' imagination "toward liberation and self-command."

He . . . demanded a thunder sandwich. This article not being forthcoming either, he requested to be served with a fricasee of boot-tops and goldfish sauce. . . . "She is come!" said the old gentleman, laying his hand upon his heart. "Cormoran and Blunderbore! She is come! All the wealth I have is hers if she will take me for her slave. Where are grace, beauty, and blandishments, like those? In the Empress of Madagascar? No. In the Queen of Diamonds? No. In Mrs. Rowland, who every morning bathes in Kalydor for nothing? No. Melt all these down into one, with the three Graces, the nine Muses, the fourteen biscuit-baker's daughters from Oxford-Street and make a woman half as lovely. Pho! I defy you. (XLIX, pp. 648–49)

Against such a barrage of words, added to the barrage of vegetable marrows which Magog continuously heaves over the fence as tokens of his love, Nicholas' conventional posturings simply fail to be convincing. Even Gride's attempt to play January to Madeline's May acquires some of the irony of the mad lover when Gride, in anticipation of his victory over Madeline, sings comic songs that echo the mad Magog (cf. LI, p. 667).

viii Parodying the protagonists

Not only does Dickens rhetorically undermine the events of his main characters' lives by producing ironic parallels in the other strata of the novel, but he also creates characters on the same strata as his hero and heroine who are their exact replicas. This process seems to arise by extension of his techniques in the short stories. There we noted Dickens' early tendency toward repetition: the earliest stories generally show Dickens' inventiveness in having the characters enact the same idiosyncrasy in a surprising number of ways. Mr. Minns and his cousin repeat the same action over and over again. Later we noted that Dickens replaces the simplistic redundancy with the introduction of new characters into the story. Though *Nicholas Nickleby* also relies on the introduction of new characters as a way of sustaining the action, curiously in the second half of the novel Dickens introduces two new characters who are so much like Kate and Nicholas Nickleby as to be downright disturbing to the reader. That Madeline Bray and Frank Cheeryble should share the same genteel speech and conventional virtuousness as their eventual mates, Nicholas and Kate, is understandable enough. But Dickens doesn't stop there; he places both sets of young people in precisely the same situations. Kate and Madeline are both perfect young ladies thrown on their own resources, to earn their way in the world, as the result of improvident fathers, Kate as a seamstress and

Madeline as drawer of pretty pictures. Both girls undergo identical crises in nearly being sold by patriarchal figures to lecherous men much older than they are. Ralph Nickleby is a party to both transactions. Nicholas Nickleby is significant in delivering both girls from their predators. Similarly, Nicholas and Frank are both young men out to make their fortune. Both come to reside under the patriarchal benevolence of the Cheerybles. Both Nicholas and Frank at different times have quarrels with strangers in public rooms, because the strangers have mentioned cavalierly the name of a lady that each is obliged to protect (Frank, XLIII; Nicholas, XXXII). Both men encounter Madeline Bray for the first time by accident, and both lose sight of her immediately afterwards.

The number and specificity of such coincidences among the two couples is truly perplexing. In one sense, the parallel events seem to be one way of Dickens' dealing with his early tendency towards redundant action. The action repeats itself but the actors have taken on new identities. But if we consider the coincidences from the point of view of their meaning in the novel, they acquire considerable importance. Dickens is trying to imbue his stereotypes with archetypal meaning, to use the events in the lives of his principles as the model for situations that confront youths who must make their way in the modern England. In such a context the maidens' escapes from their predators and the young men's defenses of the maidens take on almost ritualistic significance.

Further, the notion of coincidence itself had considerable importance in the *affirmative* thrust of Dickens' novels which we have acknowledged heretofore as one side of the ambivalent impulse that lies behind his writings. Dickens wants us to be aware of the operation of coincidence in the novel, and goes out of his way to point to it in having Tim Linkinwater comment on the coincidence of Nicholas and Frank meeting for the first time:

> "That those two young men should have met last night in that manner is, I say, a coincidence, a remarkable coincidence. Why, I don't believe now," added Tim, taking off his spectacles, and smiling as with gentle pride, "that there's such a place in all the world for coincidence as London is!" (XLIII, p. 561)

Coincidence is supposed to operate as a humanizing element in the great heartless city that swirls through the novel; it is meant to preserve part of the profound mystery of human events through the interlacing of characters in a manner that defies the deterministic operation of forces so graphically depicted elsewhere. But the Linkinwater speech quoted above only points to the superficial coincidence of Frank and Nicholas meeting; the reader is much more aware of the amplitude of the coincidence, that they should meet in a scene that so clearly echoes Nicholas' barroom encounter with Mulberry Hawk. Thus, even though Dickens may have intended that coincidences would help to sustain the *mythos* of the novel, rhetorically they seem to overload it, to create even with this technique the parodistic effects that undermine so much of the novel.

ix A more stable evaluative system

Yet it would be inaccurate to insist that the whole of *Nicholas Nickleby* has the rhetorical ambivalence we have stressed thus far. Actually, there are several axes of value operating simultaneously. The parallel configurations, echoic effects, and parodistic devices ultimately do dominate our response to the novel. But running alongside of them, Dickens creates a much more stable evaluative axis which, though modified by them, is not negated. This stable evaluative axis operates through pure symbol, a situation where meaning and value inhere entirely in objects, much in the manner of myth. Accordingly, a person's eyes and the quality of his sight becomes an entirely stable index to his moral stature.

Thus, Mr. Squeers having "but one eye" (IV, p. 30) and that a "malevolent" one (XLII, p. 547), and his daughter having "a remarkable expression of the right eye, something akin to having none at all" (IX, p. 98), become symbolic of a congenital deformity with highly important moral connotations. Similarly Nicholas' "beautiful dark eyes" (IX, p. 101) and his sister's "bright eyes" (XLIX, p. 644) are explicit symbols of their goodness. Ralph Nickleby's "trick of almost concealing his eyes under their thick and protruding brows" (X, p. 117) certainly aligns him with the deficiencies of vision we see in the Squeers. Sir Mulberry settles his immoral plans with his "eyes" (XIX, p. 238) and frequently allows his "glass" to distort his vision of the world. Mrs. Witterly maintains her corrupt pantomime of life by speaking with her eyes "shut" (XXI, p. 266). Crummles' exploitation of his daughter is called a "blinding" (XXIII, p. 291) of his own interest. Naturally, Mr. Cheeryble's absolute goodness is born out by the "old gentleman's eye — never was such a clear, twinkling, honest, merry, happy eye, as that" (XXXV, p. 448). Mrs. Nickleby, who for the most part of the novel exists in a kind of moral confusion, admits that her "eyes are not very good," she has been "short-sighted from a child" (XXXVII, p. 485). And even Mr. Bray's decadence is clearly seen in the "old fire" in his large "sunken eye" (XLVII). And there are many more such references.

Elsewhere, obliquely and comically, Dickens sets up a similar moral-symbolic hierarchy with his references to legs, limbs, and feet. Miss Squeers' love for Nicholas arises partly from her feeling that she "never saw such legs" in all her life (IX, p. 103). Her father suffers from cramped legs which leads him to "stretch" them (by tippling) constantly (VII, XIII). Nicholas' resounding defeat of Squeers leads Miss Squeers to be doubtful whether her "pa" will ever "recuvver the use of his legs which prevents his holding a pen" (XV, p. 175). Miss Knag's essential meanness of character is revealed in the fact that her Uncle

> "had such small feet, that they were no bigger than those which are usually joined to wooden legs. . . . They must have had something the appearance of club feet." (XVII, p. 210)

Despite the grotesque comedy here, Dickens' use of limbs and feet has serious moral connotations.

x The paradox of Mrs. Nickleby

But finally, the other structures in the novel outbalance the stability of Dickens' symbols. We are faced with a novel that *says* and then *un-says* almost everything it has said. The one remaining most clear example of the kind of ambivalence which is at the heart of *Nicholas Nickleby* is the way that Mrs. Nickleby is made to function in the novel. From the very beginning, she operates as a kind of anti-value system; her problem is not so much one of moral culpability, but rather, foolishness and stupidity. It is Mrs. Nickleby's nagging of her husband to speculate that catapults the family into financial disaster (I). The reader comes to see that Mrs. Nickleby's judgments of situations are reliably wrong. While Ralph Nickleby plots to sell Kate to Hawk, Mrs. Nickleby blithely misconstrues his interest in her daughter as "extraordinary good fortune" (XIX, p. 231). Her judgments of people are also flagrantly inverted. She interprets Hawk's attentions to Kate as a "triumph" (XXVII, p. 348) and later goes on extrolling him "to the skies . . . asserting . . . that he was precisely the individual whom she (Mrs. Nickleby) would have chosen for her son-in-law, if she had had the picking and choosing from all mankind" (XXVIII, p. 358). Her inability to understand the world leads her to be "quite in love" (XXVII, p. 348) with Hawk's reprehensible and scheming toady Pluck; Pluck's equally scheming companion Pyke she finds "so like" Smike that it brings her to tears — obviously allowing the rhyme to override all moral distinctions (XXXV, p. 445).

Mrs. Nickleby's vision is consistent; while she imbues the villainous characters with virtues they do not have, she mistakenly censors several of the good ones. The Browdies, who have clearly become Nicholas' friends and allies, she treats with condescension (cf. XLV). Equally wrong is her treatment of Miss La Creevy and Tim Linkinwater, two of the least morally culpable characters in the novel; nevertheless, Mrs. Nickleby

> conducted herself towards Miss La Creevy in a stately and distant manner, designed to mark her sense of the impropriety of her conduct, and to signify her extreme and cutting disapprobation of the misdemeanor she had so flagrantly committed. (LXIII, p. 818)

Throughout the novel Mrs. Nickleby shows an almost senile mentality, peculiar in its disruption of logical categories and dominated by an arbitrary association of events across time. After a long reminiscence in which she summons up all of her own and her late husband's responses to roast pig, she prattles on, parenthetically digressing in the manner of a mind that has lost its moorings:

> "I recollect dining once at Mrs. Bevan's in that broad street round the corner by the coachmaker's, where the tipsy man fell through the cellar-flap of an empty house nearly a week before the quarter-day, and wasn't found till the new tenant went in — and we had roast pig there. It must be that, I think, that reminds me of it, especially as there was a little bird in the room that would keep on singing all the time of dinner — at least, not a little bird, for it was a parrot, and he didn't sing exactly, for he talked and swore dreadfully; but I think it must be that. Indeed I am sure it must. Shouldn't you say so, my dear?" (XLI, p. 529–30)

Past, present, fact, error, and speculation are all spoken aloud, in an almost Joycean stream except that this is Mrs. Nickleby's speech, an unedited blending of the relevant and irrelevant, characteristic of the way that many people think, but very few people speak.

Mrs. Nickleby's mentality is peculiarly weak in its apprehension of time. Besides the associationist base of her mentality, whereby connections between events and across time are made absurdly and arbitrarily, she is incapable of grasping the human implications of time. Thus she sees nothing wrong in a possible match between her daughter and Mulberry Hawk, despite the fact that Hawk is old enough to be Kate's father. Similarly she draws on the fact that her own husband was "four years and a half older" (LV, p. 722) than she, as evidence for the propriety of Madeline marrying Gride. Both in her conversation and her understanding of the world, Mrs. Nickleby seizes on a single similarity between things, be it sound (Smike-Pyke, lob*sters*-oy*sters* [LV, p. 725]), or "older," or whatever, to establish a complete identity between things. She is incapable of making finer distinctions.

Though all of this is marvelously comic, Mrs. Nickleby creates problems for the novel. While generally she operates as an anti-value system, ultimately the novel validates her vision. It is Mrs. Nickleby who foresees "the fortunes of the family 'as good as made'."

> Without precisely explaining . . . she subsided, whenever she mentioned the subject, into such a mysterious and important state, and had such visions of wealth and dignity in perspective, that (vague and clouded though they were) she was, at such times, almost as happy as if she had really been permanently provided for, on a scale of great splendour. (LV, p. 723)

Even though the passage quoted above tempts the reader to believe that it is more of Mrs. Nickleby's false understanding in its "vague and clouded" vision, at the end of the novel we are forced to concede the accuracy of her prophecy:

> Before many years lapsed, the business began to be carried on in the names of "Cheeryble and Nickleby," so that Mrs. Nickleby's prophetic anticipations were realised at last. (LXV, p. 829)

We are faced with a situation where just about the least reliable character throughout the novel becomes the only one to accurately forecast and understand the way of the world. That Mrs. Nickleby should force upon us such a sudden and total inversion is, in the light of all that we have said, characteristically Dickensian.[17]

xi *Paradoxical polemics*

Even the most polemic aspects of the novel are marked by comparable ambivalences. Quite clearly the first part of the novel condemns the opera-

---

17. Leslie M. Thompson, "Mrs. Nickleby's Monologue," finds Mrs. Nickleby's role much more coherent and consistent; she "forms an undercurrent of hope that occasionally punctuates the grim realities of the novel and presages its final happy consummation." I agree that she "symbolizes a dream which Dickens could neither fully believe nor wholly abandon," but any assessment of her role must also acknowledge her foolishness, and the part it plays in shaping the reader's response.

tion of business, from the speculation that originally ruined the Nicklebys to the investments that dominate the muffin business; from the treatment of schoolboys like packaged commodities to the network of collusion that binds together the manipulative and exploitative interests at every level of society. Yet the novel also wants to say that business is not inherently bad, so it gives us the Cheerybles, businessmen of an unspecified nature, who exemplify — much too abstractly to be convincing — Dickens' counter-inclination towards the idea that business really can perform a humanizing function in society.

Similarly the novel wants to show us that the city is not only a treacherous jungle that ensnares the innocent, but is also a place where a young man like Nicholas can make his way. The Cheerybles represent the triumph of goodness in the city, and they speak nostalgically of the day when they "were two friendless lads and earned [their] first shilling in this great city" (XXXV, p. 454). Their employee Tim Linkinwater becomes the most explicit apologist for urbanism; he rejects the Cheerybles' offer to send him to the country where he "would grow young again in time" (XXXV, p. 454). He truly loves and endorses his corner of the city:

> "There an't such a square as this in the world . . . not one. For business or pleasure, in summer time or winter — I don't care which — there's nothing like it. There's not such a spring in England as the pump under the archway. There's not such a view in England as the view out of my window." (XXXV, p. 455–56)

Elsewhere, Tim even debates the merits of the city versus the country:

> "Pooh! pooh!" said Tim Linkinwater. "Don't tell me. Country!" . . . "Nonsense! What can you get in the country but new-laid eggs and flowers? I can buy new-laid eggs in Leadenhall Market, any morning before breakfast. And as to flowers, it's worth a run up-stairs to smell my mignonette, or to see the double-wallflower. (XL, p. 514)

Later Tim regrets that Nicholas has passed up the superior burial grounds of the city in favor of laying Smike to rest in the country. He wishes "we could have had him buried in town" (LXI, p. 797).

Yet despite the explicit and implicit apologetics for the city, this issue, like so much in the novel, finally turns back on itself. Though Nicholas himself never becomes a literal spokesman for the city, his whole action, and that of the novel, are given to a demonstration that one can make his way in the city, and that the city offers possibilities of humaneness and benignity. Once having formed an action in support of this thesis, Dickens characteristically and paradoxically concludes the action by rejecting his thesis. Nicholas and all return to the country:

> The first act of Nicholas, when he became a rich and prosperous merchant, was to buy his father's old house. As time crept on, and there came gradually about him a group of lovely children, it was altered and enlarged; but none of the old rooms were ever pulled down, no old tree was ever rooted up, nothing with which there was any association of bygone times was ever removed or changed. (LXV, p. 830)

The history of the Nickleby family has come full cycle. Nicholas has advanced into the urban mode of the contemporary world, only to retreat to his paternal homegrounds and establish a retrogressive and static pastoral domesticity.

xii A complexity other than empirical

Though the foregoing discussion demonstrates the increasing complexity of Dickens' art, significantly that complexity is still very different from the *empirical* or *rational* complexity we have seen in the art of George Eliot. (See Chapter III, section ii.) A review of the distinctions there and a comparison to the comparable situation in *Nicholas Nickleby* will clarify this. Eliot forces us to see that events within her novel have several meanings simultaneously. The love of Lydgate and Rosamond Vincy exists for the principals as a mutually understood passion that they need not discuss; yet, from an external point of view, the two young people appear rather dull and dispassionate in their relationship to each other. We are shown that their feelings have developed over time, that their love is a product of Lydgate's boredom, quest for amusement, and lack of attractive alternatives. While allowing for a genuine sincerity in her principals, Eliot forces us to acknowledge that Lydgate's love can also be seen as a combination of biological impulse, social convention, and self-deception, all prompted by the circumstances of his situation. The various causes, influences and attitudes towards Lydgate's love are presented as simultaneous, competing, and interrelated elements of an explanation. The reader is invited to balance Lydgate's sincerity against his lack of self-knowledge, his real attraction for Rosamond against "the way of all flesh." The reader understands simultaneously that Lydgate is both the hero of a love story and the antihero of his own self-deception.

The comparable situation in *Nicholas Nickleby* is very different. While our attitude towards the love story of Nicholas and Madeline is potentially as complex as our attitude towards Eliot's story, significantly, Dickens discourages us from apprehending the situation in its complexity. Only a very careful reading of *Nicholas Nickleby* redeems Dickens' treatment of love from the most banal, simplistic, and conventional interpretation that he allows to preside. On the surface Dickens subjects us to the collision of two *automata*, hero and heroine, and they fall in love. The novel begs that we take that love seriously. Yet at the same time, it ironically juxtaposes the central love affair to several other love situations which totally undermine the possibility of taking Nicholas and Madeline seriously: the farcical prelude of Nicholas in the wrong girl's kitchen, the parody of Mrs. Nickleby and the mad Magog, the curiously ironic coincidences of Frank Cheeryble, the cartoon presence of Lillyvick-Petowker. If we extrapolate from each of these situations the manner in which they reflect on Nicholas and Madeline, Dickens' discussion of love acquires considerable complexity. Together they dramatize the notions that young love is frequently automatic, fatuous, conventional, and filled with absurd self-deceit. But as a narrative, as a series of continuous and related comments which present and evaluate the action, the novel refuses to own up to such charges. The complexity of Dickens' attitude toward love sits in the novel as a series of unmade connections, unresolved and confusing. The presiding attitude towards Nicholas' love preserves a conventional sanctimoniousness, untouched and uninformed by the critical comments dramatized elsewhere. Where Eliot forces us to see that the disparate and conflicting interpretations of the Lydgate-Vincy relationship are all necessary to our "understanding" of the relationship, Dickens is content to allow the simple and conventional young-love affair to dominate the reader's awareness.

In all, *Nicholas Nickleby* rhetorically and stylistically sets the pattern for many of the subsequent Dickensian novels. It shows Dickens' unsuccessful attempt to create a hero out of the conventions of heroism, a hero with an eloquent wooden voice in a novel-world where eloquence is generally suspect. The novel shows Dickens' continuing reliance on idiosyncrasy as a base of character, though he fails to give his principal characters their own idiosyncrasies, thereby depriving them of the essence of Dickensian life. Character change remains an unexplained mystery, having no specific obligations to articulated causes. The most important settings in the novel continue to be symbolic rather than realistic.

Metaphysically, *Nicholas Nickleby* presents a Manichean vision which fails to balance out rhetorical liabilities arising from so many of Dickens' techniques. The unsynthesized blending of different modes of reality with varying mimetic densities and varying affective appeals, strains at the conventional optimism of the main story line. Grotesque and witty cartoons and echoic configurations ironically anticipate, mimic, and mock the main characters' lives. Parody, redundant action, coincidences overload the novel, ironically diminishing Dickens' attempts at stable and consistent statements of value. Ultimately, an accurate description of *Nicholas Nickleby* or any Dickens' novel must deal with the submerged complexities, the hidden paradoxes which undermine the blithely simple world that Dickens allows to preside over our responses.

Our discussion is not meant simply to document the failure of *Nicholas Nickleby*. Rather, most of what we have said can be used to suggest Dickens' success here, of another kind. For in *Nicholas Nickleby* Dickens uses both ideas and techniques that stem from his earliest writings; the techniques move him toward a much more complex restatement of the vision of the world he offers us in *Sketches by Boz*. If *Nicholas Nickleby* only attains a wooden heroism, it is partly because, as we have seen in Dickens' earliest short stories, Dickens does not believe in the possibility of heroism. If Nickleby's world culminates in an unconvincingly bland and benign vision of goodness, it is partly because that goodness is an *ex post facto* deliverance from a much more sardonic view, like the view that shaped Dickens' earliest fiction. If the landscapes of the novel have a symbolic pregnancy that dominates their literal existence, it is because Dickens apprehends the physical world with a mythic eye, where meaning and signification preside over a more neutral empirical view where the world has little inherent meaning. If the empirical categories of time,[18] space, cause and effect, are of diminished significance in *Nicholas Nickleby*, it is because those categories are being used with a plasticity characteristic of myth. Dickens wants to write myths that sustain and validate his culture and society. On the surface of his novels he does just that. But the totality of his response to the world will not finally allow him to subscribe to the simple optimism of the mythic view. Thus, intuitively his artistry leads him to techniques which deepen and complicate his vision at the same time they negate his conven-

---

18. John Henry Raleigh's "Dickens and the Sense of Time" discusses the problem of Dickens' several systems of time: time as "essential unity," as the "explosive force of change," and as an "inevitability." Though pointing in a different direction, Raleigh does agree that time is a complex, contradictory, and confusing element in the novels.

tional mythic optimism.[19] Dickens creates a world in which neither the heroic nor the anti-heroic posture is sufficiently complex; instead, *both* postures and *neither* posture coexist in a rhetorical framework that supports the ambivalent impulse behind Dickens' art.

---

19. John Holloway, "Dickens's Vision of Society," is typical of critics who argue for the wholeness of Dickens' social vision; the wholeness is usually found in putting together several novels, rather than in a single novel.

The Poor Clerk

CHAPTER EIGHT
THE PATTERN
IS SET

i Humanizing the hero

THE FIRST part of this chapter will be concerned with two of Dickens' other
remaining early works, with an end to showing how those novels solve
some of the problems that arose in *Nicholas Nickleby* while preserving the
ambivalence so fundamental to Dickens' vision. Here we shall treat broadly
Dickens' changing conception of the hero and heroine in *The Old Curiosity
Shop* and in *Martin Chuzzlewit*, proceeding to a more detailed analysis of
each of those novels, showing how each demonstrates qualities we have
called typically Dickensian.

From the point of view of our own century, Dickens does not advance
his ability to create a hero or heroine in *The Old Curiosity Shop*. How little
Nell succeeded in wringing the hearts of Dickens' contemporaries on both
sides of the Atlantic may remain a profound mystery. In truth, the problem
does seem, as George H. Ford has suggested, beyond the "limits of explanatory criticism."[1] Though it is presumptuous to dismiss the opinions of
the crowds that waited on American piers for the next periodical install-
ment of Nell,[2] perhaps our vantage point in time will allow us to say
without self-righteousness that relatively sophisticated readers of English
may never again be capable of believing in Nell with anything like the
fervor of her contemporaries. The Nell problem becomes part of a broader
historical one in which literary psychologists and sociologists reconstruct
the mentality which so strenuously celebrated the impossible perfection of

---

1. See George H. Ford, *Dickens and His Readers*.
2. Edgar Johnson, *Charles Dickens: His Tragedy and Triumph*, I, p. 304.

such a sentimental heroine, so pure and so innocent. That Nell succeeded does not make her a success.

Nell is obviously the female version of the kind of heroic perfection that Dickens had tried to instill in Nicholas Nickleby. Both Nicholas and Nell, like the narrator in the short stories by Boz, occupy moral spheres that are totally superior to those occupied by the other characters in their stories. Nell's maidenly perfection, Nicholas' heroic swashbuckling, and the story narrator's condescending superiority separate them from the characters in their respective worlds.

With Nell, Dickens aggravates the false direction he had pursued with Nicholas. She is even more perfect, more devoted, unselfish, self-effacing, guileless, loving — more impossibly virtuous — than any character Dickens had created thus far. But just as the reader tends to lose the hero Nicholas in his abstract swashbuckling, so we lose the heroine in the fragile bundle of martyrish virtues that is Nell Trent.

In a manner entirely typical of Dickens' heroes and heroines thus far, Nell has no recognizably human problems or foibles. The novel treats a would-be tragic crisis in her life, but maintains the view that she is entirely innocent of creating the crisis. She is a double victim: first, of her grandfather's gambling, which leads to his indebtedness to Quilp and the ensuing loss of the Curiosity Shop; second, she is a victim of Quilp's lechery and unbridled libidinous impulses. The novel insists that the surrendering of Nell's living perfection to this crisis is simply a matter of circumstance. Nell has no human or personal problems, only problems of *strategy*. How to preserve her grandfather from his mania and herself from Quilp? Her extended peregrinations cannot be directed to moral horizons; nor can she, in the manner of a picaresque heroine, acquire a greater sophistication in working her will on the world. Nell can only sustain herself *when and if* the external world can right itself, can make itself a proper vessel to contain such perfection.

The intensity of the pain Nell feels in her plight momentarily threatens to bring her to life, to make her very vulnerability a humanizing trait in an otherwise unhuman creature. Some of Nell's death-thoughts and dreams have an authenticity that she never attains as a waking being; but finally the stereotype of perfection even prevails over them.[3]

With the move to *Martin Chuzzlewit*, Dickens inaugurates a new kind

---

3. Many of Nell's twentieth-century defenders want to justify the aura of pathos that surrounds her. John W. Gibson, "The Old Curiosity Shop," insists that the pathos makes the characters "fabulous."

of hero for his novel. Till this point in his career, he had never chosen to create a hero or heroine with any faults beyond their innocence. Pickwick errs, but he does so with all good intentions and without any lasting consequences. Nicholas Nickleby has only to loose his innate virtue on the world to triumph over life. But Martin Chuzzlewit, from his first scene in the novel, is shown to be morally culpable and in need of instruction. We first meet him, selfishly warming himself before a fire excluding Tom Pinch, who has made a journey through the bitter cold in order to escort Martin to Pecksniff's. Dickens goes out of his way to make sure that we understand the import of such an apparently insignificant detail; he compounds Martin's fault by having him apologize to Pinch, thereby making clear that Martin's behavior was not an oversight, but a deliberate act of selfishness, undertaken with the supposed impunity of rudeness to a stranger he will never see again: "'And I have been keeping the fire from you all this while! I had no idea you were Mr. Pinch.'"[4] The inference of course is that Martin's sense of generosity and manners is entirely artificial and operative only in self-seeking situations.

Later we see Martin's selfishness compounded by his arrogance and condescension; his mistake here is set into relief by the far better judgment of Westlock, Pecksniff's old pupil:

> The old pupil could not do enough to show Tom how cordially he felt toward him, and his friendly regard seemed of a graver and more thoughtful kind than before. The new one, on the other hand, had no impulse but to laugh at the recollection of Tom's extreme absurdity; and mingled with his amusement there was something slighting and contemptuous, indicative, as it appeared, of his opinion that Mr. Pinch was much too far gone in simplicity to be admitted as the friend, on serious and equal terms, of any rational man. (XII, p. 203–4)

Martin persists in such faults throughout the first half of the novel. Embarked on a plan to make a fortune in Eden, Martin self-righteously bestows one-half of the forthcoming profits on his partner, Mark Tapley. He arrogantly considers the arrangement quite generous in view of their difference in station, even though Tapley has supplied two-thirds of the necessary capital. Accordingly the narrator points to Martin's self-deception:

---

4. Charles Dickens, *Martin Chuzzlewit* (London, 1844; rpt. London: Oxford University Press, 1959), Ch. V, p. 74; subsequent references are to the Oxford edition and are parenthesized in the text.

Poor Martin! Forever building castles in the air. Forever, in his selfishness, forgetful of all but his own teeming hopes and sanguine plans. Swelling, at that instant, with the consciousness of patronising and most munificently rewarding Mark! (XXI, p. 352)

Yet it is precisely through such diminutive details that Martin Chuzzlewit acquires some measure of *life* that was lacking in all of his predecessors, male and female.

Eventually, Martin goes through an extended purgation of his faults in his experience at Eden. He returns to England chastened and improved. The reader is finally presented with an exemplary young hero, much like Nickleby, with the exception that we have witnessed Martin's moral evolution. He has perfected his integrity within the novel, not prior to it. His final rather abstract conventionalism is modified by the faults he has overcome.

Dickens' earliest stories created a schism between narrative voice and the fictive events reported by that voice; the schism is carried over into the opposition between the moral perfection of the earliest novel heroes-heroines and the moral inferiority of the worlds they occupy. But with Martin Chuzzlewit, Dickens moves towards an integration of his central figure, morally culpable and in need of instruction, with the rest of his particular novel world.

ii Nell versus necro-comedy

Yet even with the achievement of a more complex and believable hero in Martin Chuzzlewit, both of the novels show Dickens' continuing use of techniques that undermine the surface of the novel. In its way, *The Old Curiosity Shop* is even more given over to rhetorical ambivalence than was the preceding novel, *Nicholas Nickleby*. Part of the ambivalence emerges in Dickens' handling of the death of little Nell. Does the novel set up a situation that really necessitates her death? According to Forster, Nell's death was an afterthought on Dickens' part, pursued at Forster's initiation and suggestion:

He had not thought of killing her, when, about half way through, I asked him to consider whether it did not necessarily belong even to his own conception, after taking so mere a child through such a tragedy of sorrow, to lift her also out of the commonplace of ordinary happy endings, so that the gentle pure little figure and form should never change to the fancy. All that I meant he seized at once, and never turned aside from it again.[5]

Thus it appears Dickens' original conscious intention was to write a tragicomedy of sorts. Yet elsewhere, Dickens claimed to have had the ending in mind from the book's inception:

> I never had the design and purpose of a story so distinctly marked in my mind from its commencement. All its quietness arose out of a deliberate purpose; the notion being to stamp upon it from the first, the shadow of early death.[6]

Yet we also have Dickens' letter to Forster which credits him with having made the suggestion.[7] But it is entirely in keeping with all we have said about Dickens to suggest that on the one hand he wanted and intended to write a story with a happy ending, and on the other he intuitively moved toward a much more pessimistic tale.

Dickens' confusion over whether or not Nell should die is an example on the plot level of the kind of confusion we have previously seen in Dickens' treatment of various themes in his earliest sketches. The questions that such confusion gives rise to are the same in both cases: What really are Dickens' feelings towards his world, its institutions, its possibilities? Does he understand those feelings? Is he willing, is he able, to take a single and sustained attitude for or against a given issue, or does he want it both ways? All evidence points to the latter.

Certainly long before he was "half-way through" the novel Dickens had established a concern with death that would have made Nell's demise appropriate to the novel. The allusions to death begin in the fourth paragraph of the novel, where the peripatetic narrator offers us some reflections on bridges:

> Then, the crowds for ever passing and repassing on the bridges . . . where some . . . pause with heavier loads than they, remem-

---

5. John Forster, *The Life of Charles Dickens*, ed., J. W. T. Ley (New York, 1928), p. 151.
6. Charles Dickens, *The Letters of Charles Dickens*, Nonesuch Edition, I, eds., Waugh, Walpole, Dexter, and Hatton, p. 300; quoted in Steven Marcus, *Dickens: From Pickwick to Dombey*, p. 132 n.
7. Ibid., I, p. 295.

bering to have heard or read in some old time that drowning was
not a hard death, but of all means of suicide the easiest and best.[8]

Shortly the narrator again introduces the possibility of death, subsequent to
visiting Nell in the Curiosity Shop:

> Yet I lingered about, and could not tear myself away: thinking of
> all possible harm that might happen to the child — of fires, and
> robberies, and even murder — and feeling as if some evil must
> ensue if I turned my back up on the place. (I, p. 11–12)

This is the first time that the possibility of Nell's death is suggested, and
within a few pages, Nell's grandfather begins suggesting the possibility of
his own death in commenting on Nell's brother:

> "This fellow will murder me one of these days. He would have
> done so, long ago, if he had dared." (II, p. 15)

And in turn, Fred Trent accuses his grandfather of homicidal impulses,
which the grandfather does not deny, as he calls on Nell's *dead* mother to
witness the disrespect of her son, and his grandson.

Very early in the novel, the narrator raises the question of Nell's fate
in the event of her grandfather's death. And shortly, Mrs. Quilp's neighbor
joins this chorus of death-speakers, in proposing murder disguised as
suicide as the best way of dealing with Quilp's tyranny (IV, 32). Mrs.
Jiniwin, Mrs. Quilp's mother, rejoins, "she daren't call her soul her own,
he makes her tremble with a word and even with a look, he frightens her to
death" (IV, p. 33).

As the novel progresses, both the significant and the incidental
characters demonstrate an almost pathologic concern with death. Nell's
grandfather says, "If it was not for the child [I] would wish to die" (VI, p.
50). Throughout the novel he feels that "ruin and self-murder are crowding
in every street." Additionally, as Stephen Marcus has remarked, "Nell's
itinerary seems to include every churchyard in which some mute inglorious
Milton lies buried."[9] In the course of her travels Nell meets a widow of
fifty-five years, who has had ample time to ruminate on the significance of

---

8. Charles Dickens, *The Old Curiosity Shop* (London, 1841; rpt. London: Oxford University Press, 1965), Ch. I, pp. 1–2. Subsequent references are to this edition and are
parenthesized in the text.
9. Marcus, p. 146.

her widowhood, coming to the conclusion that "Death doesn't change us more than life," and accordingly "prayed to die herself" (XVII, p. 129). Nell waits out the death of a country schoolmaster's favorite pupil, consoles the boy's grandfather who laments "my grandson's dying" (XXV, p. 191), and later philosophizes on the frequency of childrens' deaths. Much later in her travels she dreams of the boy's death (LII, p. 389). In an abortive attempt to gain sustenance from a roadside hovel, Nell's request is answered by a mute parent holding a dead child (XLV, p. 337). She visits a church which reputedly contains the vault of a "grey-haired lady who had been hanged and drawn and quartered" (LIV, p. 400).

Naturally as her own death approaches Nell develops an even more exaggerated preoccupation with death.[10] Her first reflections on the old church and melancholy setting where she finally does die are "thoughts of death" (LIII, p. 398). It is rumored that Nell "will be an Angel before the birds sing again" (LV, p. 411). Yet she still has enough time to discuss death extensively with the sexton (LIV, p. 403–4), and even give some of her dying energies to working on childrens' graves (LIV, p. 408).

Of course much of the landscape Nell traverses has a wasteland quality to it, a kind of living death, a

cheerless region . . . where not a bud put forth its promise in the spring, where nothing green could live but on the surface of stagnant pools, which here and there lay idly sweltering by the black roadside. (XLV, p. 335)

Occasionally, Dickens parodies the death concern in the novel by giving us an ironic echo. Against the sombre death-wish of Nell's grandfather, Dickens plays Dick Swiveller's wish for the grandfather's death, as well as his own aunt's death:

"Does the old man look like a long-liver?"
"He don't look like it," said Dick shaking his head, "but these old people — there's no trusting 'em Fred. There's an aunt of mine down in Dorsetshire that was going to die when I was eight years old, and hasn't kept her word yet. They're so aggravating, so unprincipled, so spiteful — unless there's apoplexy in the family, Fred, you can't calculate upon 'em, and even then they deceive you just as often as not." (VII, p. 56)

---

10. Michael Steig, "The Central Action of *Old Curiosity Shop*," agrees with Mark Spilka in seeing the increasing preoccupation of death as an "internalization of her sexuality"; Nell is a "fugitive from her sexuality."

In another scene Dickens has Swiveller parody Nell's constant visitation of graveyards in a moment of Shakespearean bantering with Mr. Chuckster:

> "Won't you come in?" said Dick. "All alone." Swiveller solus.
> "'Tis now the witching —'"
> "'Hour of Night!'"
> "'When churchyards yawn,'"
> "'And graves give up their dead.'"[11] (XLIX, p. 368)

Perhaps the most felicitous parody of death in the novel comes in Sampson Brass' inquest into the imagined death of Quilp. Quilp remains in hiding while his mother-in-law replies to a battery of legalistic questions aimed at establishing the description of the deceased, but finally he can stand it no more:

> "A question now arises, with relation to his nose."
> "Flat," said Mrs. Jiniwin.
> "Aquiline!" cried Quilp, thrusting in his head, and striking the feature with his fist. "Aquiline, you hag. Do you see it? Do you call this flat? Do you? Eh?"[12] (LVI, p. 415)

Elsewhere, incidental characters such as the schoolmaster's pupils speak of death very cavalierly: "Richard Evans . . . [wi]ll never die in his bed; he's always falling asleep in sermon-time" (LII, p. 392). In a novel where, for the most part, the theme of death is being treated so ponderously, even a sprinkling of such ironic allusions to death cannot but cut across the pervasive seriousness; we see again the Dickensian ambivalence, the tendency to undermine even his most serious postures.[13]

The melodramatic and ironic discussions of death are another instance of the clash, in this novel, of the two narrative postures that Dickens had developed in the early story and sketches. The early stories almost always take a sardonic attitude towards death, as we have seen in "The Boarding

---

11. Gabriel Pearson, "The Old Curiosity Shop," sees Swiveller's role as "neutralizing opposition to Nell's blank verse elegiacs" (p. 88).

12. Pearson, p. 83, asserts that Quilp's "resurrection scene almost parodies Nell's apotheosis."

13. For a diametrically opposed view of Quilp's effect, see James R. Kincaid, "Laughter and Pathos," p. 85. Kincaid feels that Quilp's "parody has lacked the freedom and detachment necessary for success. His humor ultimately *reinforces rather than undercuts the pathos of the main plot* . . . Our laughter at Quilp is contributory to our tears for Nell" (my italics). My view coincides more closely with Pearson's (p. 83) that the "lyrical blank verse of the Nell sequences cannot balance the theatrical vitality of Quilp's cackling monologues and ferocious practical jokes."

House," part one, and the story of Watkins Tottle's suicide. Other such instances occur in "The Boarding House," part two ("He felt ill after breakfast and died after supper,") as well as in the "Bloomsbury Christening" where Mr. Dumps gleefully exults in discussing the probability of the christening-child's death. But in Dickens' sketches, the subject of death is usually given very serious treatment. Frequently as in "The Hospital Patient," and "A Visit to Newgate," the narrator demonstrates his compassionate sensibility in reflecting on the ponderous significance of death. And the last of Dickens' sketches, "The Drunkard's Death," very precisely anticipates the kind of melodrama that surrounds the whole issue of Nell's death:

> It is a dreadful thing to wait and watch for the approach of death; to know that hope is gone, and recovery impossible; and to sit and count the dreary hours through long, long nights — such nights as only watchers by the bed of sickness know. It chills the blood to hear the dearest secrets of the heart — the pent-up, hidden secrets of many years — poured forth by the unconscious helpless being before you; and to think how little the reserve and cunning of a whole life will avail, when fever and delerium tear off the mask at last. (*Sketches*, p. 485)

Though the passage above goes on to reflect on the astounding quality of death-bed confessions, in its milking of the ponderous significance of death, in its appeal to pathos, it anticipates the treatment of Nell's death that was to follow in a few years. But it is totally characteristic of Dickens that Nell should be made to enact her melodrama amidst a chorus of comic voices.[14]

iii Contradictory Quilp

Though the serious concern for death far outweighs the effect of the ironic allusions here, and thus seems to validate Dickens insistence that the death of Little Nell was part of his initial conception of the novel, if we turn to a broader view of the structure, the focus on death becomes very diffuse. Part of the diffuseness arises from the rhetorical effects of Dickens' continuing efforts to write a novel within a Manichaean framework. Just as in *Nicholas Nickleby*, here the moral sphere has been polarized. On the one side we have the moral purity and perfection of Nell; on the other, the

---

14. Or, as O. J. Cockshut describes the contradiction: "Dickens' morbid temperament would naturally feast upon a little girl's suffering, while his moral sense told him he should feel only pity and grief," *The Imagination of Charles Dickens*, p. 94.

complete depravity and immorality of Quilp. Quilp creates problems for the novel in two ways. First of all there is a problem in Quilp's general conception and the effects arising from that conception. Dickens wants to present a portrait of a motiveless evil, an arbitrary force that has come to rest in a grotesque and malevolent dwarf. But in disconnecting Quilp's evil ways from more ordinary conceptions of motivation, he produces a grotesquely comic, arbitrary, and absurd depiction of evil.[15] Quilp's diet, a prime example of his comic side, is meant to represent the gross sensualist gone mad:

> He ate hard eggs, shell and all, devoured gigantic prawns with the heads and tails on, chewed tobacco and water-cresses at the same time and with extraordinary greediness, drank boiling tea without winking, bit his fork and spoon till they bent again, and in short performed so many horrifying and uncommon acts that the women were nearly frightened out of their wits and began to doubt if he were really a human creature. (V, p. 40)

While Quilp's menu is rather unusual, rhetorically it is far more amusing than it is terrifying. Such could be said of every aspect of Quilp's personality.

Quilp, lust incarnate, has a voluptuary's appreciation of Nell's beauty. But rhetorically, Quilp's lechery produces more laughter than tears. He is presented as a slapstick vice, whose viciousness cannot move us beyond a chuckle:

> "Ah," said the dwarf, smacking his lips, "what a nice kiss that was — just upon the rosy part. What a capital kiss! . . . Such a fresh, blooming, modest little bud," . . . said Quilp . . . making his eyes twinkle very much; "such a chubby, rosy, cosy, little Nell!" (IX, p. 72–73)

The lip-smacking lustfulness is even more comic in light of the fact that elsewhere Quilp appears as more of a misogynist than a womanizer. He threatens to *bite* his wife (IV, p. 37) and continually intimidates her with a sardonic witticism: "I'll have man-traps, cunningly altered and improved for catching women" (L, p. 377). Of his mother-in-law he says, "If I could

---

15. Though Robert S. Maclean, "Putting Quilp to Rest," shows convincingly that Quilp has his origins in the traditional figures of the "evil dwarf, devil, and stage comic devil," the Quilp problem still remains, as long as we look at his effect on both the rhetoric and meaning in the novel.

poison that dear lady's rum and water . . . I'd die happy" (XLIX, p. 366). His attempts on a chambermaid combine both his misogyny — "He first made faces" — and his lustfulness — "and then wanted to kiss her" (XLVIII, p. 356). Comparably, his proposal to Nell combines his lust with his sardonic assurance that his wife will not live more than five years (VI, p. 45).

In contrast to the pietistic and maudlin aura of death that surrounds Nell, Quilp is a macabre celebration of Malevolence: "Stand on your head again and I'll cut one of your feet off' he shouts at a boy (V, p. 42). We cannot help but laugh when Quilp laughs at a boy falling on his head (VI, p. 46), when Quilp wants to wring a bird's neck (XIII, p. 105), when Quilp tortures Kit in effigy by "screwing gimlets" into him, by "sticking forks in his eyes," cutting his "name on him," and finally intending "to burn him at last" (LXII, p. 462).

The problem is that most of Quilp's cruelty has no referent in the reader's experience. It does not exist within the dramatic conflict of the novel, but absurdly drops out of the air whenever Quilp is on stage. Moreover Dickens gives Quilp a marvelous sense of humor that cannot help but endear him to the reader. For instance, consider his response to the boy who says,

> "You see if ever I offer to strike anybody again because they say you're a uglier dwarf than can be seen anywhere for a penny, that's all." (VI, p. 47)

Quilp's rejoinder, "Do you mean to say, I'm not, you dog?" has an ineffable comic charm. Against such inverted pride, the reader has no defenses. Moreover in a novel that so laboriously parades virtue in its heroine, the reader's responses become very susceptible to inversion, and he is likely to transfer allegiance to a man like Quilp who openly proclaims he hates "your virtuous people!" (XLVIII, p. 360). Thus Dickens' attempt at a moral dichotomy is undermined by our rhetorical responses to his evil genius Quilp. In contrast to Nell's maudlin virtuousness, Quilp becomes a clown of chaos.

iv Conflicts in an aborted fairy tale

Just as in *Nicholas Nickleby*, *The Old Curiosity Shop* offers us several heterogeneous kinds of reality. There is virtually no way of integrating the ponderous seriousness of Nell's pilgrimage with the comic nonconsequence of Quilp's malevolence. Though their paths intersect, and though Quilp is presented as the cause of Nell's flight, his relationship to Nell's fate seems arbitrary and contrived. Neither syntax nor the moral spheres of the two coincide in a manner that will permit an interpenetration, a way of apprehending both characters from the same perspective. Instead the reader is constantly in the position of adjusting his orientation towards the novel, depending on who is at the center of a given scene.

Quilp is born of the spirit of early short stories, from a world that is sardonic, absurd, a world without important consequences that invites our laughter at every turn, at every event. Nell, on the other hand, derives from the world of Dickens' sketches where compassion, concern, a feeling sensibility surveys the world and engages our sympathies while assuring us of the frequently lamentable but coherent progress of events. Significantly, because Nell and her tormentor are products of such different mimetic and rhetorical impulses, the novel rarely allows them to speak to one another without the intervention of the narrator; the clash would be too great and the discontinuity overwhelming.[16]

Thus while Nell is obliged to enact a psychological melodrama, the rest of the characters hover on the brink of a fairy tale. Had Dickens pursued his original conscious impulse, which was apparently to give the novel a happy ending, *The Old Curiosity Shop* would probably have been a rather elaborately amplified fairy tale, focusing on the psychological plight of the heroine. But as it is, *The Old Curiosity Shop* excludes its heroine from the fairy-tale world that the other characters aspire to and occupy. For instance, Quilp, whose literary like is only found in fairy tales, both lives in a fairy-tale setting and frequently speaks a fairy-tale language. Our introduction to Quilp's home reads like the opening of a fairy tale, modified by anachronistic allusions to "business" which maintain the aura of irony that always surrounds Quilp:

> Mr. and Mrs. Quilp resided on Tower Hill; and in her bower on Tower Hill Mrs. Quilp was left to pine the absence of her lord, when he quitted her on the business which he has been already seen to transact. (IV, p. 29)

Elsewhere the Quilp's home is called an "ogre's castle." Moreover, Quilp is anxious to remake the world into a kind of fairy tale; on taking possession of Nell's home, he pronounces her room "quite a bower" (XI, p. 86); in his sarcastic deprecation of his wife, he draws on the language of fairy tale, ironically describing her as a fairy tale protagonist's prize:

---

16. Pearson, p. 85, also notes Dickens needs to keep the figures separate.

"She's such . . . such a jewel, such a diamond, such a pearl, such a ruby, such a golden casket set with gems of all sorts!"

Moreover, Quilp himself is frequently described with epithets from fairy tales; besides an "evil spirit" (XXIII, p. 173) he is called

> a dwarf . . . goblin, demon, imp, ogre, will o'the wisp, savage, African chief, Chinese idol, panting dog, monkey, salamander, moe, weasel, hedgehog, bluebottle.[17]

Thus Quilp is identified with a whole spirit bestiary reminiscent of the fairy-tale world.

Nell and her grandfather are banished from the Curiosity Shop, only to enter a world even more abounding in *curiosities*. Ironically, many of Nell's resting places in route to her death have a very oblique relationship to a normal physical world. She is sheltered by a variety of people, all of whom are given over to the production of fantasy, of importing into the ordinary world some aspect of the world of fairy tale. First off, she encounters the puppeteers practicing at Punch and Judy on the gravestones of a churchyard (XVI). Later she meets "Grinder's lot," stilt-walkers who create the illusion of gigantism (XVII). Subsequently, she encounters a group of magic dogs, dressed fantastically in spangled coats and hats (XVIII), and the dogs can play the organ (XVIII). Some of the characters Nell encounters have even lived in the world of fairy tales:

> "Why, I remember the time when old Maunders as had three-and-twenty [dwarfs] — I remember the time when old Maunders had in his cottage in Spa Fields in the winter time, when the season was over, eight male and female dwarfs setting down to dinner every day, who was waited on by eight old giants in green coats, red smalls, blue cotton stockings, and highlows: and there was one dwarf as had grown elderly and wicious who whenever his giant wasn't quick enough to please him, used to stick pins in his legs, not being able to reach up any higher." (XIX, p. 144)

Here, just as in *Nicholas Nickleby*, incidental characters ironically echo the main characters. The cruel dwarf in the paragraph above is an explicit allusion to Quilp; rhetorically, the allusion diminishes even further our abilities to respond to the arbitrary malevolence of Quilp.

---

17. Marcus, p. 155, lists these names.

Nell's progress is a search for a resting place within the fairy tale she has been excluded from. Ironically, Nell takes refuge with Mrs. Jarley's waxworks, only to find herself a refugee in a traveling show that commemorates other heroines like Nell who have been trapped in lives that abort their fairy tale inceptions. The irony increases as Mrs. Jarley narrates the history of two of her figures. First there is an Elizabethan version of Sleeping Beauty gone wrong:

> "an unfortunate Maid of Honour in the Time of Queen Elizabeth, who died from pricking her finger in consequence of working upon a Sunday. Observe the blood which is trickling from her finger; also the gold-eyed needle of the period, with which she is at work." (XXVIII, p. 214)

In the world that Nell is seeking, the pricked finger produces the sleep, from which the maid is delivered by Prince Charming. Mrs. Jarley's version of Bluebeard is just as disappointing:

> "Packlemerton of atrocious memory, who courted and married fourteen wives, and destroyed them all, by tickling the soles of their feet when they were sleeping in the consciousness of innocence and virtue. On being brought to the scaffold and asked if he was sorry for what he had done, he replied yes, he was sorry for having let 'em off so easy, and hoped all Christian husbands would pardon him the offence." (XXVIII, p. 214)

Here again, the details of the story echo both the gratuitous cruelty and sardonic comedy of Quilp's world. Packlemerton's wives, with their "innocence and virtue" seem deliberate parodies of Nell. Moreover, Quilp, who plans to dispose of his wife within five years (VI), and who speaks the same kind of ironically inverted platitudes, is both a diminished and amplified version of Packlemerton. Nell is obliged to learn verbatim the stories referred to above, ironically earning her keep first as a conductress, and later as an unofficial attraction in the waxworks, spokesman and artifact in a museum of wry fairy tales (XXIX).

Both of the wry fairy tales that Nell is forced to relate (but that we never hear her speaking) are given us in a tone and syntax that derive from the sardonic world of Dickens' short stories; as in the short stories, the preposterous juxtapositions of atrocity and piety, of portent and triviality occur within sentence patterns that explode into absurdity the consequences of what they relate.

Increasing the irony of Nell's exile from the fairy-tale world are the many allusions to fairy tales and fantasy literature which shape our responses to the other characters in the novel. Dick Swiveller's grandiose self-deception is really an attempt to live a fairy tale. The novel identifies him with the legend of Dick Whittington, "Lord Mayor of London" (L, p. 373). Later Dick plays at pygmallion, transforming an ignorant chamber maid, whose name is "nothing" (LI, p. 380), into a "Marchioness" of his imagination's making (LVII, p. 427); he suggests that they model the merriment of their future lives after "Old King Cole" (LVIII, p. 430). Much later Dick recovers from his severe illness, firm in the belief that his life has become a fairy tale:

> "It's an Arabian Night; that's what it is," said Richard. "I'm in Damascus or Grand Cairo. The Marchioness is a Genie, and having had a wager with another Genie about who is the handsomest young man alive, and the worthiest to be the husband of the Princess of China, has brought me away, room and all, to compare us together. . . . Arabian Night, certainly," thought Mr. Swiveller; "They always clap their hands instead of ringing the bell. Now for the two thousand black slaves, with jars of jewels on their heads!" (LXIV, p. 475–476)

Similarly, Kit Nubbles dreams of fairy tales as he goes about his hum-drum routines:

> . . . he was sitting upon the box thinking about giants' castles, and princesses tied up to pegs by the hair of their heads, and dragons bursting out from behind gates, and other incidents of the like nature, common in story books. (XXII, p. 169)

Even Quilp sees himself as a character out of fantasy literature in proclaiming that he has "got a country-house like Robinson Crusoe" (L, p. 372). Sampson Brass, the lawyer who supervises Nell's eviction from the Curiosity Shop, is described as a "curiosity," "the ugliest piece of goods in all the stock;" and his sister, with her red beard, and vampire-like headdress, is obviously a character in transit from a fairy tale (XXXIII, p. 245). At the end of the novel, Quilp's burial is described in terms reminiscent of the most grim fairy tales and horror stories; he was "left to be buried with a stake through his heart in the centre of four lonely roads" (Ch. Last, p. 549).

Though other characters enact snippets of fairy tale, Nell fails to escape an inexorable fate; her path leads her through a kind of nether world:

> In a large and lofty building, supported by pillars of iron, with great black apertures in the upper walls, open to the external air; echoing to the roof with the beating of hammers and roar of furnaces, mingled with the hissing of red-hot metal plunged in water, and a hundred strange unearthly noises never heard elsewhere; in this gloomy place, moving like demons among the flame and smoke, dimly and fitfully seen, flushed and tormented by the burning fires, and wielding great weapons, a faulty blow from any one of which must have crushed some workman's skull, a number of men laboured like giants. Others reposing upon heaps of coals or ashes, with their faces turned to the black vault above, slept or rested from their toil. Others . . . opening the white-hot furnace-doors. . . . Others drew forth, with clashing noise, upon the ground, great sheets of glowing steel, emitting an insupportable heat, and a dull deep light like that which reddens in the eyes of savage beasts. (XLIV, p. 329–30)

As Steven Marcus suggests, this is Nell's encounter with "Pandemonium, the Hall of the Mountain King, Vulcan's forge."[18] But unlike her counterparts in fairy tales, myths, and folk literature, Nell gains no strength or secret from the underworld which would allow her to triumph over life. She simply continues toward her inevitable doom.

Thus, thematic elements and the main movement of the plot produce the kind of ambivalence we have called characteristic of Dickens. He begins writing a story that was to have an affirmative, happy ending, only to recognize the implicit pessimism he had committed himself to — the necessity of Nell's death — at the half-point in his novel. Intuitively he had set the stage for her death, even while intending to deliver her from that fate. At the same time, however, he counterbalanced his pessimism by leaving his heroine to fend for herself against a rhetoric that celebrates the comedy of evil, in a world that ironically mocks her inability to achieve the fairy-tale status that colors most of the other characters.

v Parodies and problems

Moreover, just as in *Nicholas Nickleby*, Dickens loads the novel with parallels and echoes that subtly undermine its main directions. Overtly, the

---

18. Marcus, p. 157.

narrative insists on the unalloyed purity of Nell. But alongside this insistence Dickens plants suggestions that tentatively identify the purity of Nell with the depravity of Quilp. In any realistic sense, Nell's moral perfection exists at the expense of any carnal forces that are represented in Quilp. Yet symbolically, occasional details encourage the reader to align Nell and her grandfather with Quilp. There are several aspects of Nell's identification with Quilp. First of all, similarities between Nell's grandfather and Quilp establish a symbolic connection between the man Nell is trying to save and the man she is trying to save herself from. For instance, in the opening chapters of the novel, the narrator emphasizes the fact that Nell's grandfather's obsessive gambling keeps him up all night; it is the fact that the grandfather is out all night that causes the narrator's initial concern for Nell's well-being (I). Shortly thereafter we are told of Quilp's staying up all night, but we are never given any reason to explain his action.[19] The narrative seems to want to establish a connection between Quilp and Grandfather by this symbolic similarity (V). Much later in the novel we are presented with an even more striking similarity between Quilp and Nell's grandfather. Returning to Mrs. Jarley's caravan at night, Nell suddenly comes upon Quilp:

> There was an empty niche from which some old statue had fallen or been carried away hundreds of years ago, and she was thinking what strange people it must have looked down upon when it stood there, and how many hard struggles might have taken place, and how many murders might have been done, upon that silent spot, when there suddenly emerged from the black shade of the arch, a man. The instant he appeared, she recognized him. Who could have failed to recognize, in that instant, the ugly mis-shapen Quilp! (XXVII, p. 207)

The narrative continues with a similar climactic gothicism, building to the revelation that Quilp and a boy have apparently stolen a trunk. Shortly thereafter, Nell is awakened from "dreams of falling from high towers" (Quilp lives in a bower on Tower Hill) to find her grandfather in precisely the same kind of ominous and stealthy activity, stealing from Nell their remaining gold pieces. Even the tone of Nell's reflections on her grandfather's thievery encourage us to identify him with Quilp:

---

19. Pearson, p. 84, feels that Quilp's nocturnal vigil, and the increasingly red glow of his fiery cigar are oblique descriptions of Quilp's sexual voraciousness, "as close as we get to downright copulation in a Victorian novel."

> but the man she had seen that night, wrapt in the game of chance, lurking in her room, and counting the money by the glimmering light, seemed like another creature in his shape, a monstrous distortion of his image, a something to recoil from, and be the more afraid of, because it bore a likeness to him, and kept close about her, as he did. (XXXI, p. 230)

Thus Nell's grandfather's singular obsession acquires symbolic connotations that identify him with the unbridled licentiousness of Quilp.[20]

Moreover, when we juxtapose the narrator's pointed observation of Nell's bravery in remaining alone at night (it is her solitude that first causes his concern) with the equally pointed observation of Mrs. Quilp's fear of remaining alone, the novel seems to be moving the two figures together. Mrs. Quilp's fear both separates her from, and identifies her with Nell.[21] The configuration of the Quilps is in a sense an exaggeration of the configuration of Nell and her grandfather. Quilp represents a total viciousness which plagues and manipulates a relatively innocent female, just as Nell's grandfather is a singular vice that dominates the life and freedom of an entirely innocent female.

Very early in the novel Mrs. Quilp informs us of her husband's irresistible charms:

> "Quilp has such a way with him when he likes, that the best-looking woman here couldn't refuse him if I was dead, and she was free, and he chose to make love to her." (IV, p. 32)

Subsequently, Nell's identification with Mrs. Quilp, combined with her recurring obsessive dreams of Quilp, subtly undermine Nell's much-insisted purity and perfection. The dreams hold out an oblique and tantalizing suggestion that Nell is responding subconsciously to the carnality of Quilp. At one point Nell's flight is described as leading "her sacred charge farther from guilt and shame" (XLIV, p. 333). The abstract, moralistic diction here almost invites the reader to augment the meaning of "sacred," "guilt," and "shame" with certain very familiar Victorian connotations: The *sacred* charge of chastity and the "guilt" and "shame" that accrues to the fallen woman. Earlier our view of Nell and her meaning has

---

20. To insist that Grandfather's thievery is mainly a matter of its "anticlimactical effects, and creation of gothic atmosphere," passes by the structural relevance of his similarity to Quilp. See Earle R. Davis, *The Flint and the Flame*, p. 91.

21. Kincaid, "Laughter and Pathos," p. 73, sees but does not discuss an even closer connection between Nell and Mrs. Quilp: "Now Betsy Quilp is very nearly Nell's double."

been complicated by the part she plays in what is very ambiguously described as her grandfather's "desperate passion" (XXIX, p. 223):

> She was the innocent cause of all this torture, and he, gambling with such a savage thirst for gain as the most insatiable gambler never felt, had not one selfish thought! (XXIX, p. 224)

Ultimately, any complete reading of the novel is obliged to cope with the kaleidoscopic way that the purity and innocence of Nell is sporadically and temporarily undermined by such oblique suggestions. She is entirely pure and innocent, but at the same time the cause of her grandfather's destructive passion. She is repulsed by the powerful carnality of Quilp, but she dreams of him obsessively.[22] She loves her grandfather dearly, yet she hates his amplified image in Quilp.

Despite the ambiguity surrounding Dickens' original intention in the matter of Nell's death, Dickens' obvious preoccupation with death eventually overcomes the possibility of Nell's living happily ever after. But Dickens colors the pathos of his death theme with a comic irony. The Manichaean vision of the novel, the sanctimonious moral perfection of Nell versus grotesquely comic moral perversity of Quilp, yields up two perspectives on the world that are essentially irreconcilable. Rhetorically the appeal of Nell's melodrama can survive neither the onus of the fairy-tale world that surrounds it, nor the parallels which undermine it.

The Old Curiosity Shop shows Dickens' continuing reliance on conflicting narrative postures that shape his earliest stories and sketches. Because of the differences inherent in those postures, the novel sets at odds conflicting visions of the world. On the one hand we have the world of Quilp, with its sardonic comedy, its grotesque celebration of things gone awry, its substitution of cynicism and absurdity for moral consequence. On the other hand we have the world of Nell, with its maudlin sentimentality, its compassionate apologetics for the vulnerability of absolute virtue, in a world where goodness leaves its mark whether or not it wins the day.

Just as in the preceding works, in *The Old Curiosity Shop* Dickens produces a novel which embodies his divergent attitudes, and satisfies his basic ambivalence. Nell is human perfection entrapped in a malevolent world she never made; but again she is not all that perfect; and for the most

---

22. See Steig, "The Central Action of *Old Curiosity Shop*," pp. 163–70, where he compares Nell's sexuality to the fear of sexual awakening depicted in Blake's *Book of Thel*; Thel's unresolved conflicts and personal failings cause her to refuse to enter the Vales of Har, the realm of sexual experience.

part the malevolence of her world is really quite funny. Rhetorically the novel makes an explicit request for our tears; but it also makes an implicit demand on our laughter; it deprecates the way of the world while chuckling that the world will have its way. The novel bemoans the victim of an evil that produces tragic consequences, but at the same time, celebrates the inconsequence of the evil it depicts.

vi Martin Chuzzlewit *and nature*

There are ten years between Dickens' debut as a short story-sketch writer and the publication of his sixth novel, *Martin Chuzzlewit*. Though the early stories and sketches continue to influence the content of *Martin Chuzzlewit* and all the rest of Dickens' novels, this continuity of themes, subjects, characters, and situations is not nearly so important as the continuity of process, of Dickens' way of representing the world, its problems and their solutions.

The significance of the early stories and sketches resides in the style of thinking that they reveal. They show us a mind beset with conflicting impulses, a mind whose stories move towards the reduction of the world to transparent and unheroic banalities, where simplistic, mechanistic, idiosyncratic characters play out their fates in an indifferent environment. Yet the same mind creates sketches which suggest an entirely different vision; in the sketches we are given a world that tries to go beyond the negativistic simplicity of the stories; the sketch world examines people, places, situations within the contemporary scene, and while confronting limitations, inadequacies, and injustices, tries to suggest the essential order, coherence, and benignity of the world described.

Dickens' art in effect flows from the tensions between two such divergent postures. The effects of that tension are seen in the rhetorical complexities of the novels. Dickens' rhetoric requires that in the novels several mimetic systems operate simultaneously in order to accommodate his ambivalent vision. He asks us to accept a Manichean world which operates according to the principles of poetic justice, but at the same time he sets in motion structures which create a mockery of that vision.

Dickens' novels inherit the ambivalence of the *Sketches by Boz*. They imitate the structures by which Dickens masked the many contradictions and paradoxes which lie at the center of his early work. And as we shall see in turning to a close examination of *Martin Chuzzlewit*, even when Dickens attempts to build a novel around an idea, the idea is refracted by the rhetoric of an artist who finally cannot make up his mind.

The ambivalent tone that characterizes the novels preceding *Martin*

Chuzzlewit becomes, if anything, even more pronounced here. Few of Dickens' stoutest supporters would be so bold as to argue his consistent excellence as a philosophic thinker, but in *Martin Chuzzlewit* Dickens wrestles in his characteristically ambivalent fashion with the philosophic problem of *nature*. Reminiscent of the writing of the eighteenth century, Dickens' novelistic presentation pursues a definition of *the natural* — with all the variety and multiplicity of meanings that the word implies: Nature — as the name given to the great out-of-doors; nature — as the essential qualities of men, the generic human nature; nature — as the inborn character, innate tendencies, inherent dispositions of individual men; nature — as the system of relations that governs man's harmonious connection with the world and other men; nature — as the primitive uncorrupted state of man; and conversely nature — as the primitive unregenerate and therefore uncivilized state of men. All of these conflicting meanings and more are operative in *Martin Chuzzlewit* as Dickens struggles to present a novelistic vision of *the natural*.

The novel opens with a scene set against the quiet repose of autumnal nature — an overture that asserts the essential harmony of the change of seasons:

> The fallen leaves, with which the ground was strewn, gave forth a pleasant fragrance, and subduing all harsh sounds of distant feet and wheels, created a repose in gentle unison with the light scattering of seed hither and thither by the distant husbandman, and with the noiseless passage of the plough as it turned up the rich brown earth, and wrought a graceful pattern in the stubbled fields. (II, p. 7)

Here, both form and content offer us a vision of the natural, with man represented in his immemorial agrarian occupation; and the selection above is only part of a much longer one in which Dickens consciously manipulates a lyrical flow of word, cadence, and rhythm to achieve a quiet rhapsody in his approval of the equipoise of autumn. But very soon the tone shifts as Dickens undertakes a burlesque dramatization of the Pecksniffs and the many fronts of their battle against all that could be called nature and natural. The leaves continue to blow:

> But the oddest feat they achieved was, to take advantage of the sudden opening of Mr. Pecksniff's front door, to dash wildly into his passage; whither the wind following close upon them, and finding the back-door open, incontinently blew out the lighted

candle held by Miss Pecksniff, and slammed the front-door against Mr. Pecksniff who was at that moment entering, with such violence, that in the twinkling of an eye he lay on his back at the bottom of the steps. Being by this time weary of such trifling performances, the boisterous rover hurried away rejoicing, roaring over moor and meadow, hill and flat, until it got out to sea. (II, pp. 9–10)

Here we see a satiric dramatization of nature's playful attempt to reclaim the Pecksniffs; their house is filled with leaves, their lights blown out, and Pecksniff himself flattened out by an animated nature wryly intent on asserting its superiority.

Having comically dramatized the Pecksniffs' fundamental disharmony with the forces of nature, the novel allows Pecksniff to inaugurate a discussion of other kinds of nature and the natural, a discussion to which all of the action and all of the characters eventually contribute. Pecksniff tries to represent himself as the benign intuitive philosopher whose understanding of human nature transcends the freaks and shocks his flesh is heir to. Thus, he exonerates himself from the need for self-appraisal when his student Pinch disappoints him, actually by showing his good sense in choosing John Westlock for a companion:

"But Mr. Pinch has disappointed me: he has hurt me: I think a little the worse of him on this account, but not of human nature. Oh, no, no!" (II, p. 17)

Elsewhere, Pecksniff uses reflections on human nature to insulate himself from the wily hypocrisy of his own conduct:

"Ah, human nature, human nature! Poor human nature!" said Mr. Pecksniff, shaking his head at human nature, as if he didn't belong to it. (XXX, p. 471)

Because Pecksniff so frequently reflects on various kinds of nature, the narrator tries to suggest a principle for understanding Pecksniff's view of the natural: ". . . he always said of what was very bad, that it was very natural; and that he unconsciously betrayed his own nature in doing so" (III, 34).

Yet Pecksniff's view of what is natural lacks both the clarity and consistency of such a simple inversion. On the one hand he is able to plead to old Martin Chuzzlewit, ostensibly on behalf of his namesake, that "young Martin . . . has the strongest natural claim" on his grandfather (III, p. 41) — particularly when that claim might deliver a tuition fee to Pecksniff's purse. But on the other hand, Pecksniff also deems it natural that Old Martin would entirely disinherit his ward and companion Mary, that some "means might be devised of disposing our respected relative to listen to the promptings of nature, and not the siren-like delusion of art" (IV, p. 59) — a characterization of the situation that strikes any reader as especially ludicrous in the light of Mary's truly enervating lack of art, and most other nameable qualities of personality. Pecksniff's radically selfish view of the world leads him to project a very unusual interpretation of the inequities of the human situation; he finds the inequities a "quite natural, and a very beautiful arrangement" (VIII, p. 116). He enjoys immensely feeling "in keen weather, that many other people are not as warm" as he is, since such an observation leads him to "gratitude . . . one of the holiest feelings of our common nature" (VIII, p. 116).

To the very end of the novel Pecksniff insists on his inherent goodness: "Mine is a trusting nature" (LII, p. 811). Accordingly he sees young Martin as an "unnatural young man" (LII, p. 806), and he congratulates himself for having ejected him from his house "after hearing of his un-natural conduct" (XLIII, p. 669) from Grandfather Martin's lips. Though Pecksniff protests that the world does not "quite understand [his] nature yet" (XXIV, p. 386), the action of the novel moves towards unmasking the perversity of that nature; Mary voices the moralistic attitude of the novel in eventually proclaiming, "I know your real nature and despise it." She hates him for having "warp[ed] and change[d]" Old Martin's "nature," having hardened a "heart naturally kind" (XXX, p. 482).

vii Several views of nature

With respect to the protagonist young Martin, whose evolution we have discussed previously, Dickens' chief concern is to move Martin from a position in which he views his own psychological nature as a morally self-vindicating fact, to one in which he recognizes the precedence of generic human nature as a moral category; he must submit the needs of the self to the much more compelling and universal obligations to others. Thus, in the opening of the novel Martin questions the generosity of Westlock, incapable of understanding that Westlock's feelings for the rustic Tom Pinch are more important than the inequality of their social standing. Martin puzzles, "Is it natural?" (VI, p. 91), when Westlock continues to correspond with his old friend. Similarly Martin tries to justify his vindictiveness by appealing to his own psychological nature:

"After the old man's arbitrary treatment of me, I had a natural
desire to run as directly counter to all his opinions as I could."
(VI, p. 96)

Or, embarked on the venture in Eden, Martin takes Mark Tapley's indus-
triousness for granted while justifying his own laziness:

"It's no trial to *you*, Mark, to make yourself comfortable and to
bustle about. It's as natural for you to do so under the circumstances as it is for me not to do so." (XV, p. 252)

But after Martin has endured the chastening experience of Eden, he
recognizes the moral precedence of his obligations to a collective human
nature over his own idiosyncratic needs. Because of this, later on he is
reluctant to suggest to his Grandfather that Jonas Chuzzlewit is a parricide:

Martin could not endure the thought of seeming to grasp at this
unnatural charge against his relative, and using it as a stepping-
stone to his grandfather's favour. (XLVIII, p. 744)

The unnaturalness of the situation, the disillusionment it would cause his
grandfather, far outweigh the benefits that would accrue to young Martin.
Whereas earlier Martin had justified his spitefulness as a "natural desire,"
upon his return to England Martin is ready to give over his self-
righteousness in favor of the "natural" relations that should prevail between
grandfather and grandson: "Let the voice of nature and association plead
between us, Grandfather; and do not, for one fault, however thankless,
quite reject me" (XLIII, p. 669). As the novel draws to a close, Martin
announces that all disorders have been rectified; things are natural now.

In contrast to Martin, who comes to understand the proper priorities
of the natural, we are given his cousin Jonas who is the embodiment of the
perverse and the unnatural. Reminiscent of his treatment of Pecksniff,
Dickens shows us that Jonas is out of touch with the natural world:

It was a lovely evening in the spring-time of the year; and in the
soft stillness of the twilight, all nature was very calm and beautiful. (XX, p. 330)

Dickens follows this with a detailed description of the breezes and fra-
grances of the evening, benign and harmonious nature, which only leads

Jonas to declare: "Precious dull . . . it's enough to make a man go melancholy mad." Elsewhere Jonas mistakenly conceives the "natural" relationship between father and son as an economic one in which the father guarantees the economic well-being of his son:

> "Buy an annuity cheap, and make your life interesting to yourself.
> . . . But no, that wouldn't suit *you*. That would be natural
> conduct to your own son, and you like to be unnatural, and to
> keep him out of his rights." (XVIII, 299)

Throughout the novel Jonas is seen as possessing idiosyncratic qualities which make his peculiar nature a thing apart from other men, different from more common examples of human nature. Thus when Tom Pinch delivers the letter that arrests Jonas' shipboard flight, we are told that Jonas is "unnaturally self-possessed" (XLI, p. 634). But such unnatural self-possession is seen as entirely natural to Jonas, and his attempted flight itself is called "nothing more natural" (XLI, p. 637). As Jonas' desperation increases, the perversity of the inner man begins to dominate the usually controlled façade of the exterior one; he makes very boisterous responses in an interview with Montague Tigg, leading the narrator to see his demeanor as especially unnatural (XLI). In all, Jonas' actions support the narrator's declaration that "violence was natural" to the mind of Jonas (LI, p. 773). Thus the novel exposes the extensive unnaturalness of Jonas: out of touch with mother nature, reducing parental relations to a self-serving economic arrangement, gradually revealing the core of malevolent idiosyncrasy that explains the father killer and suicide.

But even here we see that the novel presents us with two primary but conflicting notions of the natural. On the one hand the plot moves towards a restoration of the proper and harmonious relationships between men, and between men and the world, establishing and endorsing a kind of pervasive natural law. But while the good characters and events move towards this harmonious condition, other elements produce a counter-movement, insisting that the unnatural and the perverse *are* the natural condition — inborn characteristics, innate tendencies, inherent dispositions — of some men, namely Jonas and Pecksniff. Even on its most serious level *Martin Chuzzlewit* is shot through with such ambivalence.

Dickens is still working within a Manichean system, and accordingly attitudes towards general human nature, one's own nature, and the nature of others parallel and reinforce the moral dichotomy of the novel. All of the evil characters follow Pecksniff in appealing to nature or human nature as a justification of their actions. Thus Chevy Slyme announces his independence from any obligation of human gratitude precisely at the same time he reaches out for a loan:

> "let 'em know that I possess a haughty spirit, and a proud spirit, and have infernally . . . touched chords in my nature, which won't brook patronage." (VII, p. 108)

Similarly, Mrs. Gamp justifies her neglect of her patients by agreeing, "Use is second nature" (XIX, 314). Later she continues defending her ways by appealing to nature:

> "may be Rooshans and others may be Prooshans; they are born so, and will please themselves. Them which is of other naturs thinks different." (XIX, 317)

Or, again, the corrupt medical officer in Montague Tigg's company (who claims to "know a few secrets of nature" [XXVII, p. 436]) rationalizes his illegality by insisting that Jobling "has done more . . . to reconcile me to human nature, than any man alive or dead" (XXVII, p. 440). The appeal to nature is so pervasive that even the narrator uses it, sarcastically and ironically to highlight the aggravated jealousy and spitefulness that shapes the whole relationship of Pecksniff's daughters to one another:

> They had no idea of it. They no more thought or dreamed of it than Mr. Pecksniff did. Nature played them off against each other: *they* had no hand in it, the two Miss Pecksniffs. (II, p. 12)

Inversely, the good characters in the novel are all obliged to refine their understandings of human nature and to correct and relinquish self-vindicating flaws in their own natures. For example, old Martin is forced to confront and correct the unnaturalness that he has fostered among his relations. Initially he bemoans the effects that his wealth has had on the individuals in his family:

> "I have so corrupted and changed the nature of all those who have ever attended on me, by breeding avaricious plots and hopes within them." (III, pp. 39–40)

As a result, old Martin has developed a "suspicious nature" (XXIV, p. 390) which misleads him in his moral judgment of both his grandson and the entirely guileless Tom Pinch, whom he mistakenly sees as a "deceitful, servile, miserable fawner" (XXIV, p. 390). The novel forces the old man to reexamine his pronouncements on human nature. He attains a proper moral perspective when he can see the innocence of his grandson and wrathfully proclaim the essential corruption of his cousin Pecksniff: "Pandering to the worst of human passions was the office of his nature" (LII, p. 805).

Tom Pinch whose only fault is a blindness to Pecksniff, quite appropriately perceives and understands the naturalness of situations; he finds Martin's love for Mary "quite natural" (VI, p. 95) and he declares it "natural and right" (VI, p. 98) that Martin should encounter complications and difficulties in pursuing his love. Quite generously, Pinch does "homage to the natural endowments of young Martin." Towards the end of the novel, Tom and his sister discuss extensively the naturalness of their respective loves (L, pp. 767–769). Because of his inherent goodness, because he is only flawed by an excess of generosity, Tom's pronouncements of other people's natures and human nature are the most accurate ones in the novel. As Westlock very early tells Pinch,

> "Pecksniff traded in your nature and . . . your nature was to be timid and distrustful of yourself, and trustful of all other men, but most of all, of him who least deserves it." (II, pp. 23–24)

Once Tom realizes the truth of Westlock's judgment, he attains a position of moral purity unmatched in the novel.[23] As the novel closes Dickens appropriately crescendoes in his use of the word natural: all is "as natural as possible" (LIII, p. 819), Westlock tells Ruth Pinch, and he encourages her to "do . . . whatever is natural to you" (LIII, p. 820). The final pages abound in references to the "natural" because the "good" characters in the novel have all been schooled, recognizing the proper balance between their own natures and the obligations placed on them by human nature.

Despite the clarity of the moral scheme, we are still in the presence of paradox. The novel argues for a coincidence between actions, relations and postures that are good and those that are natural. But running alongside is the contradictory notion that perversity, malevolence and evil are also natural to some people.

viii Nature in America

The action of *Martin Chuzzlewit* continues to sort the problem of each man's individual nature and its relation and obligations to a generic human

---

23. For a psychoanalytic interpretation of Pinch's moral evolution, see Steig, *"Martin Chuzzlewit:* Pinch and Pecksniff." Steig sees Pinch and Pecksniff as the embodiments of self and selflessness, Oedipal repression of self at odds with egotistic expansion of self.

nature; but just as in the preceding novels, Dickens parodies both the events and conclusions of his central characters' lives by juxtaposing them to comic and inverted redactions of their own situations. Thus while the main action of the novel insists that respect, generosity, and consideration of others are the base of the system that should govern our harmonious connections with other men and the world, elsewhere he shows us the total impossibility of that situation. The harmonies of being natural in England — a kind of Wordsworthian surrender to the "power that rolls through all things" — disappear in America — when the protagonist comes up against something much more like Tennyson's "nature red in tooth and claw."

To begin with, mother nature, heretofore so benign and solicitous, becomes a savage force, a predator proclaiming survival of the fittest as her first rule:

> Three or four meagre dogs wasted and vexed with hunger; some long-legged pigs, wandering away into the woods in search of food; some children, nearly naked, gazing at him from the huts; were all the living things he saw. A fetid vapour, hot and sickening as the breath of an oven, rose up from the earth, and hung on everything around; as his foot-prints sunk into the marshy ground, a black ooze started forth to blot them out.
>   Their own land was mere forest. The trees had grown so thick and close that they shouldered one another out of their places, and the weakest, forced into shapes of strange distortion, languished like cripples. (XXIII, p. 381)

Martin and Mark learn painfully what it means to have "Every sort of nateral advantage" connected to the land in Eden. "No end to the water!" (XVII, p. 282).

Moreover, while the action in England seems to dramatize the moral superiority of innocence guided by intuitive principles, the chapters in America show the total inadequacy of innocence when called upon to meet the rigors of nature. Eden is populated by simple but incompetent folk:

> Farmers who had never seen a plough; woodmen who had never used an axe; builders who couldn't make a box; cast out of their own land, with not a hand to aid them: newly come into an unknown world, children in helplessness, but men in wants, with younger children at their backs, to live or die as it might happen! (XXII, p. 372)

By the end of Martin's stay in Eden, the novel has entirely repudiated that sense of being natural that is implied in domestic primitivism. Thus while the novel insists that our relations to other men must be guided by what is natural — a system of natural law governing civilized human interactions — our ability to survive in the world cannot be an inherent human quality. The American chapters move us toward another typically Dickensian paradox: The state of nature is the state of civilization; to be natural is to be civilized; even mother nature, the natural forces, are civilized in England.

In keeping with the terms of this paradox the Americans are presented as *natural men*, men existing in the primitive, unregenerate, and uncivilized state. As we might expect, the corrupt Americans, like the corrupt Englishmen, appeal to human nature in justifying their conduct. Though the action in America is primarily a demonstration of American rudeness, dishonesty, and greed, Congressman Pogram speaks the universal American rhetoric in insisting that Americans are the

> "model of a man, quite fresh from Natur's mould . . . child of Natur', and a child of Freedom; and his boastful answer to the Despot and the Tyrant is, that his bright home is in the Settin Sun." (XXXIV, p. 534)

America is described as

> "that . . . land, where there were no noblemen but nature's noblemen, and where all society was based on one broad level of brotherly love and natural equality." (XVII, p. 286)

Yet this land of equality and brotherly love sees no contradiction in maintaining the practice of slavery, since "there is a natural antipathy between the races" (XVII, p. 287).

Moreover, like those morally culpable Englishmen, the Americans designate as unnatural anything that displeases them. Thus Martin is asked about the condition of England with the loaded question "how's the unnat'ral old parent by this time?" (XXI, p. 345). And the British are accused of "jealousy and pre-judice" and a "nat'ral unfitness . . . to appreciate the ex-alted Institutions" of America (XXXIV, p. 534). Martin's refusal to offer an opinion on America before his ship has landed is seized on as unnatural conduct, evidence of the "prejudices of human nature" (XVI, p. 257).

Because the Americans presume a monopoly on "the natural," their grievances with England are seen as arising from the unnatural nature of British institutions:

"the natur' of British Institutions [is] their tendency to suppress
. . . popular inquiry and information." (XXI, p. 347)

Or again, exploding the whole issue with superb parody, Martin is informed that a dungeon, "Your Tower of London . . . is nat'rally your royal residence" (XXI, p. 347).

ix Symbolic reinforcement of the dichotomy of nature

The opposition between natural-unnatural is repeated in varying degrees of abstraction through the use of several different symbols throughout the novel. As with the "eyes" and "legs" in *Nicholas Nickleby*, here the different symbols parallel the basic moral dichotomy in the novel. First of all, as an offshoot of the discussion of domestic primitivism, many of the characters make pronouncements on the idea of savagery (never allowing for noble savagery) and frequently attributing the condition of savagery, defensively, to another character. Thus, very early in the novel Pecksniff calls Westlock a "beast" and a "savage" — epithets that eventually revert to their user (II, p. 20). Or later on, Martin discusses American dinner manners, claiming that they are a "question of losing the natural politeness of a savage" (XXXIV, p. 537). And Mrs. Lupin comments on Mark's folly in having undertaken his American adventure by saying,

> "Why didn't he go to one of those countries where the savages eat each other fairly, and give an equal chance to every one." (XLIII, p. 657)

Most appropriately, Jonas Chuzzlewit is frequently described as a "low savage" (XXIV, p. 399); he has a "savage sneer" (XLI, p. 637) and a "savage mirth" (XLII, p. 648). At one point he is said to set upon Tom "like a savage" (XLVI, p. 713). Thus the novel reinforces its endorsement of the civilized and the humanely sophisticated as the proper mode for human conduct. The quality of civilized action even shapes the manner of a good English butcher:

> There was nothing savage in the act, although the knife was large and keen; it was a piece of art, high art; there was delicacy of touch, clearness of tone, skilful handling of the subject, fine shading. It was the triumph of mind over matter; quite. (XXXIX, p. 601)

On still another level, the basic opposition in the novel is again repeated in the discussions of slavery. The American chapters rhetorically promote an antipathy to the unnatural institution of slavery, and accordingly, the idea of slavery becomes another vehicle for evaluating characters morally. Merry Chuzzlewit, as yet unreformed through pain and submission, mistakenly thinks that her coquetry makes "a perfect slave" (XXIV, p. 398) of Jonas. But it is Jonas whose unnatural energies gain the upper hand in the struggle for dominion. Disdainfully he proclaims, "I'll know who's master, and who's slave" (XXVIII, p. 458). He admits to the perverse motivation for his marriage — inhuman mastery:

> "I hate myself, for having been fool enough to strap a pack upon my back for the pleasure of treading on it whenever I choose." (XXVIII, p. 458)

Jonas conceives all relationships in terms of master-slave. Thus he contemptuously derides Tom Pinch in language that echoes the actual conditions of slavery as seen in America:

> "You haven't a right to any consideration. You haven't a right to anything. You're a pretty sort of fellow to talk about your rights, upon my soul! Ha, ha! Rights, too!" (XXIV, p. 391)

Elsewhere, Jonas's sister-in-law Cherry refuses to accept a subordinate position comparable to her sister's, contemptuously insisting "I am not his slave" (XLVI, p. 711).

In addition to the symbolic use of savagery and slavery, Dickens uses animal images to reinforce the dichotomy that runs through the novel. Thus, while Americans brag that they are the "cream of human natur', and the flower of moral force" (XXXIII, p. 522), they ironically go on to describe themselves in qualities that sound most bestial:

> "Our backs is easy ris. We must be cracked-up, or they rises, and we snarls. We shows our teeth, I tell you, fierce." (XXXIII, p. 522)

The "Great American Eagle," highly prized for its "talons" is symbolically appropriate for a country that has achieved a national character from a number of nasty traits. The eagle is a

> Bat for its shortsightedness . . . Bantam for its bragging . . . a Magpie for its honesty . . . Peacock for its vanity . . . Ostrich for

its putting its head in the mud, and thinking nobody sees it.
(XXXIV, p. 547)

And the list of American attributes is topped off by equating the national
character with "a Phoenix, for its power of springing from the ashes of its
faults and vices, and soaring up anew" (XXXIV, p. 547). American contempt for the "savage nature" of the British lion only seems ironic, since it
comes juxtaposed to the heinous insults Americans hurl toward the idea of
"Nigger emancipation" (XXI, p. 361).

All of the evil characters are at one time or another identified with
animals. Pecksniff's attempted seduction of Mary is equated with the "em-
brace of an affectionate boa-constrictor" (XXX, p. 481), and later we are
told that Mary

> would have preferred the caresses of a toad, an adder, or a serpent:
> nay, the hug of a bear: to the endearments of Mr. Pecksniff.
> (XXX, p. 483)

The most perverse Jonas admits to identifying himself with the grotesquely
fantastic (and unnatural) animal, "a griffin" (XXIV, p. 399; XXVIII, p.
458). In opposition to the righteous might of the British lion, we are given
Montague Tigg's "Anglo-Bengallee Disinterested Loan and Life Assurance
Company" and its symbolically appropriate "preserve of tigers" (XXVII, p.
430). Even the malevolent nonconsequence of Mrs. Gamp registers itself in
a symbolic twisting of an animal proverb:

> "Rich folks may ride on camels, but it ain't so easy for 'em to see
> out of a needle's eye. That is my comfort, and I hope I knows it."
> (XXV, p. 407)

Despite elements that align themselves and give an appearance of a
consistent and cohesive structure, here, as in the previous novels, Dickens
seems to work against himself undermining many of his own distinctions.
We have already observed several paradoxes in his treatment of nature: all
men must learn to live naturally; for some men the unnatural is natural;
natural conduct is civilized conduct; a natural world is a civilized one. But
comparable paradoxes invade other parts of the novel.

x Repeating the pattern

It would seem that the whole impulse of the American chapters is
satiric, an attempt to distill and amplify the critique of those who persist in

unnatural conduct under the guise of its naturalness. Thus we are invited to scorn the arrogant claims of Americans who perversely boast they have bested nature, "whipped the universe" (XVI, p. 265). Similarly we are meant to see the irony of the braggart claims of the superiority of American institutions over British ones: "'Yes, sir,' returned the Colonel, 'but some institutions develop human natur': others re-tard it'" (XVI, p. 271). And in view of the profligate degeneracy of American ways we are led to disagree with General Choke's rhetorical insistence "'What are the Great United States for, sir'. . . 'if not for the regeneration of man? But it is nat'ral for you to make such an enquerry.'" (XXI, p. 349)

Yet, when we look at what the action does, as opposed to what it seems to say, again we encounter the characteristic Dickensian ambivalence. The fact is, despite many appeals to the contrary, that we are forced to agree that Martin's human nature is developed by his encounter with America; his prior selfishness — a case of retarded development — is cured by the trials of Eden. The rampant savagery of the new world does prove to operate "for the regeneration of man" in Martin's case. The action and the rhetorical thrust of the novel are at odds. The biggest lie becomes the greatest truth.[24]

The same kind of paradoxical inversion operates in our judgments of Anthony Chuzzlewit and Old Martin as father figures. Supposedly the action of the novel demonstrates that Old Martin has been unnatural in suspicions, indifference, and hostility to his grandson; the action moves both Martins towards a more "natural" conduct. Yet in the end, just as with the cruelties of America, we are asked to concede that Old Martin's cruelties to his grandson are more conducive to the natural scheme than are the generosities which we intuitively consider the natural impulse of parents. Old Martin makes this clear in bewailing the irony of the "natural end" (LI, p. 781) of his brother's parental precepts; that he should be murdered by his own son, the creature of his "rearing, training, teaching, hoarding, striving for" (LI, p. 781). The cruel parent figure, like the cruel environment, seems necessary to the final establishment of natural relations between the Martins.

Such a pattern is by now a familiar one. We have seen it in the *Sketches by Boz*, where Dickens operates simultaneously as the social critic and the social apologist; we have seen it in his revision of the periodical papers for

---

24. Barbara Hardy, *The Moral Art of Dickens*, pp. 100–121, points to related contradictions in insisting on the essential disunity of the novel; she emphasizes the lack of causality in the connections between characters, their sudden changes, and the thematic discontinuity. She opposes recent attempts to impose coherence on the novel.

his collected *Sketches*; we have seen it in the tonal shift in *Pickwick*, and in the ambivalent characterizations and structures of *Nicholas Nickleby* and *The Old Curiosity Shop*. It is perhaps the primary Dickensian mode of meaning: to say, and to unsay; to advance one way rhetorically and to retreat another symbolically, or vice versa.[25]

xi A cluster of symbolic paradoxes

Dickens' manipulation of Chuffey and a whole cluster of images associated with Chuffey further illustrate his tendency toward contradiction, paradox, and parody — devices that ultimately undermine the clear statements that shape the surface of the novel. In the beginning of *Martin Chuzzlewit*, Chuffey simply appears as a faithful but senescent old employee of the Chuzzlewits. He is initially identified as "nothing," but as the novel progresses we learn that — in a manner reminiscent of Lear's "nothing will come of nothing" — this nothing is an enormous something. Chuffey's gradually diminishing awareness of the world, his loss of his senses, becomes a metaphor for a kind of basic confrontation of the world and self which enables the characters to come to terms with all the varieties of nature.

A related image occurs fairly early in the novel, when Mark Tapley describes the sea. The terms of his description are strikingly like the language that has previously been used to describe Chuffey:

> "the sea is as nonsensical a thing as any going. It never knows what to do with itself. It hasn't got no employment for its mind, and is always in a state of vacancy." (XV, p. 247)

But of course neither the sea nor Chuffey are ultimately nonsensical. Mark painfully learns the logic of the sea's energies in the agonized crossing to America. Both Mark and Martin have a preview of the rampant force of nature which later, as settlers in Eden, will bring both men into a confrontation with their own natures, and finally reconcile them to their obligations to other men and to human nature.

Most significantly, the nonsensical state of Chuffey and the sea, the appearance of having lost one's senses, becomes a symbolic state through which many of the characters pass in the course of their moral evolution.

---

25. Raymond Williams, "Dickens and Social Ideas," pp. 77–98, provides an interesting general discussion of the problem of contradictions in Dickens. Williams suggests that we consider the possibility of the contradictions being a conflict between external belief and artistic expression.

Anthony Chuzzlewit never has the time to complete the process, but he begins to approach Chuffey's state:

> "I grow deafer every day, Chuff," said Anthony, with as much softness of manner, or, to describe it more correctly, with as little hardness as he was capable of expressing.
> "No, no," cried Chuffey. "No, you don't. What if you did? I've been deaf this twenty year."
> "I grow blinder, too," said the old man, shaking his head.
> "That's a good sign!" cried Chuffey. "Ha! ha! The best sign in the world! You saw too well before." (XVIII, p. 300)

Quite clearly the loss of his senses means the acquisition of new senses for Chuffey. But as Anthony slides toward death, Chuffey's senses remain lost:

> But Chuffey, Heaven help him! heard no sound but the echoes, lingering in his own heart, of a voice for ever silent. (XIX, p. 324)

He emerges from his state only for a moment when Anthony is buried: "'I loved him' cried the old man, sinking down upon the grave when all was done." (XIX, p. 324)

Similarly as young Martin approaches his purgative physical and psychological crisis, he too begins to enter the Chuffey state: he "complained that his sight was dim, and his voice feeble" (XXIII, p. 381). Eventually the transformation is complete:

> Martin gave him no answer. He had sat the whole time with his head upon his hands, gazing at the current as it rolled swiftly by; thinking, perhaps, how fast it moved towards the open sea, the high road to the home he never would behold again. (XXIII, p. 382)

And again, in England, Old Martin is also being transformed into a Chuffey:

> As one trait disappeared, no other trait sprung up to take its place. His senses dwindled too. He was less keen of sight; was deaf sometimes; took little notice of what passed before him; and would be profoundly taciturn for days together. The process of this alteration was so easy, that almost as soon as it began to be observed it was complete. (XXX, p. 475)

Old Martin's situation appears to be permanent.

But in the design of the novel, the symbolic senility and the idea of "nothing" are played against each other, producing the opacity which the denouement of the novel attempts to dissolve. We see various kinds of "nothing," but the task of the novel is to distinguish them from one another. There is the "nothing" of the senile Chuffey, but this is very different from the "nothing was the matter" (XXVI, p. 426) that Chuffey pronounces in hiding the dark secret of Jonas' parricide, and different again from the "nothings" of the various characters who imitate Chuffey.

A much more literal kind of "nothing" is the "nothing" of Pecksniff, a quality that several of the characters point to.[26] Tom Pinch is the first to see that his submission to Pecksniff has been — like the symbolic senility of the other characters — a state of existing without his sense of seeing: The "star" of Tom Pinch's boyhood becomes a "putrid vapour":

> Tom's blindness . . . had been total and not partial, so was his restored sight. (XXXI, p. 493)

Pecksniff becomes synonymous with a void:

> But there was no Pecksniff; there never had been a Pecksniff, and the unreality of Pecksniff extended itself to the chamber, in which, sitting on one particular bed, the thing supposed to be that Great Abstraction had often preached morality with such effect that Tom had felt a moisture in his eyes, while hanging breathless on the words. (XXXI, p. 502)

Mark Tapley also sees that the only proper way to treat Pecksniff is to act on the knowledge that he doesn't exist:

> "Why, I wouldn't see the man myself; I wouldn't hear him; I wouldn't choose to know he was in company. I'd scrape my shoes on the scraper of the door, and call that Pecksniff, if you liked; but I wouldn't condescend no further." (XLIII, p. 663)

And in turn, young Martin ceases to allow that Pecksniff exists:

---

26. But the symbolic equivalence of Pecksniff with "nothing" should not cause us to lose sight of what A. E. Dyson calls his "radiance." Dyson says that Pecksniff's radiance colors our apprehension of almost all the evil in the novel. The mixed humor and joy in Pecksniff and in Mrs. Gamp negate their moral dimensions (*The Inimitable Dickens*, pp. 71–96).

he evinced no knowledge whatever of that gentleman's . . . existence . . . there might have been nothing in his place save empty
air. (XLIII, p. 666)

The confrontations with "nothing" and the symbolic senility that the
characters undergo are finally important to what Dickens wants to say and
his characteristic way of saying it. Since the whole cluster of symbolic
images — "nothing," "the sea," the "lost senses" — flows from Chuffey's
appearance in the novel, fittingly it is Chuffey who dramatizes the central
paradox created by those images. Chuffey bursts through what appeared to
have been a total senility and establishes Jonas' guilt (cf. LI, 776 ff).
Chuffey's righteous accusation of Jonas, the speech of a character who has
been identified as a mute, is the dramatization on a serious level of a
situation which Dickens has earlier foreshadowed on an ironic one. Just as
in the previous novels, Dickens anticipates a serious symbolic event with a
parody of that event. Shortly after Anthony Chuzzlewit has died, Pecksniff
sings Jonas' praises to Mary:

> "Shall I be backward in doing justice to that young man, when
> even undertakers and coffin-makers have been moved by the con-
> duct he has exhibited; *when even mutes have spoken in his praise*, and
> the medical man hasn't known what to do himself in the excite-
> ment of his feelings!" (XXIV, p. 387, my italics)

With a double irony, Pecksniff's speech above foreshadows the end of the
novel, a "mute" does "sing" Jonas's praises, and Jonas recognizes that such
is the way of the world; he cannot escape his fate because

> there would rise some new avenger front to front with him; some
> infant in an hour grown old, or old man in an hour grown young,
> or blind man with his sight restored, or deaf man with his hearing
> given him. (LI, p. 787–88)

Such is the paradoxical view of the world that the novel really wants to
advance. Jonas learns what all the characters have learned, that "the
genuine Freedom is dumb, save when she vaunts herself" (XXXIII, p.
520); freedom is speechless except when she speaks.

Thus a comparable close reading of many of Dickens' novels comes to
the same kind of paradoxical situation. Here we have seen the novel attempt to demonstrate that the natural is the civilized, that the abysmally

perverse and cruel can lead to the natural and kind, senility is wisdom, the dumb and blind can regain sight and tongue.

The world of *Martin Chuzzlewit* like the world in the earlier Dickens' works tries to transcend that which is seen and recorded — a recognizable reality with its poverty, cruelty, senility, death, murder — by a far more ideal and fantastic vision — generosity, kindness, senility reversing itself, justice and liberty finally coming to preside in human events.[27] Though Dickens so clearly sees, records, and makes us feel all that is wrong with the world, finally he does not want to surrender to what he sees. On the one hand his perception leads him to present a comically grotesque and brutal naturalistic world, but inevitably, he marries that world to a fairy tale.

---

27. Dyson, *"Martin Chuzzlewit*: Howls the Sublime,"* points to the paradoxical nature of the novel in a number of passages; it is the "most sparkling" of the novels, yet its themes are "among the darkest." The novel "comes closest to creating a holiday out of evil." The novel offers "comedy poised over the tragic abyss," yet there is a "transforming exuberance at work."

CHAPTER NINE
CONCLUSION

IN CONCLUDING, I should like to draw together several strands of my argument, and to point it outward towards later Dickens novels that have not been touched upon here.

This study has used initial observations about Dickens in his earliest writings as a way of apprehending pervasive tendencies in his revisions of those writings and his later novels. I began by describing Dickens' earliest short stories in which the characters consist almost entirely of idiosyncrasies; the characters' lives are a humiliating progress through a negatively simple mythic world. But Dickens grows to the point where he offers us a seemingly complex and effectively paradoxical vision which contains and masks the simpler sardonic view of his earliest short stories, while purporting to offer us a vision far more consoling and affirmative. Though it would be pointless to claim that Dickens had reached his full creative potential with the early novels, by the time he completed *Martin Chuzzlewit* in 1843 it is clear that he had achieved the rhetorical form for containing the ambivalence of his vision.

Dickens had yet to solve the problem of his wooden heroes and heroines. But in the novel following *Martin Chuzzlewit*, *Dombey and Son*, Dickens hit upon a device for making his hero or heroine more like his other characters, for putting his conception of them in touch with that of the rest of his novel world. The solution to the problem of the hero had been implicit in his very first short story, in all the short stories by Boz, and in the myriads of characters in the first novels. Until *Dombey* the central figure had been insulated from the essence of Dickensian vivacity by Dickens' willingness to submit his hero or heroine to a conventional moral perfection; even Martin Chuzzlewit, though he must work to attain it, becomes a stock figure. But the heroine who follows Martin, Florence Dombey, is very different from her predecessors. Florence is, in effect, a Dickensian idiosyncratic character who has taken over the center of a novel. Florence's obsession with gaining her father's love gives her an identity with the idiosyncratic population of the Dickens' world. With her, the opposition between the central figure shifts its base from a difference of *kind* — conventional perfection versus the idiosyncratic world — to a difference of *degree* — a psychologically debilitating idiosyncrasy, internally and sympathetically rendered, versus other idiosyncrasies, externally and comically rendered.

It might seem hard to stress the difference between Florence and Little Nell, but dealing with the two girls at their most general level of conception helps to highlight the point. Nell is simply maidenly perfection encumbered with external problems that lead her to the necessity of making strategic choices if she wishes to avoid the encroaching tragedy. Florence, on the other hand, though no less perfect a maiden, is defined by the degree to which she has internalized a problem which does permeate every aspect of her being, and the reader's consciousness of her. When we think of Nell, we think of encumbered perfection; when we think of Florence, we think of a young woman struggling to attain the parental love taken for granted as the birthright of the species.

Florence is the first of Dickens' heroines or heroes to have a distinct psychic shape, and as such she is the first to have an idiosyncratic dimension which presents us with a continuing perspective on her past, present, and future life. With Florence, Dickens has found a way both to go beyond static novel convention, and to make his principal character more like the characters who surround them, thereby integrating them with the essential quality of Dickens' novel world.

Most of the heroes and heroines who follow Florence are similar in conception: Esther Summerson's anxiety over the mystery of her birth, Sissy Jupe's faith in reunion with her father, Amy Dorrit's ongoing consciousness of prisons, David Copperfield's omnipresent awareness of painful youthful experiences, Pip's illusions of expectations, Eugene Wrayburn's melancholic indeterminateness, are all redactions of the idiosyncratic hero-heroine whose consciousness shapes the mature Dickens' novels.

i Continuing myths and metamorphosis

With the introduction of the idiosyncratic hero or heroine, Dickens' novels acquire a consistent texture that had been lacking previously. Sub-

The Gin Shop

jective experience of the hero or heroine shapes much of our apprehension of the novel, making for a kind of blending of the subjective and objective planes — characteristic of myth; that is, the consciousness of the idiosyncratic hero or heroine's needs shapes the narrative presentation of the novel world, objectifying psychic phenomena in the external world. Thus Florence's need for love, Amy Dorrit's consciousness of prisons, or Pip's illusions of expectations are made to invade other characters and to color the very shape of reality as presented in the novel.

Florence Dombey's desperate need for love makes her potentially a more believable representation of human personality than her predecessors; but, at the same time, the exaggeration of that idiosyncrasy contracts her humanity into a lifelessly objectified personality. She floats through the novel with her aura of agonized pathos, an emblem of incompleteness, in a myth about the attainment of completion.

Though the tonality of the central character in the mature novels is radically different from the tone in those early stories by Boz, in conception the two are much alike, both veritably exhausted by their idiosyncrasies. Yet even with the achievement of a new mode for his central figure, Dickens' novels continue to be the curious blend of a mythic vision, undercut by rhetorical ambivalence. As a writer, Dickens wanted to objectify and clarify the rites of passage, to act as an affirming apologist of a knowable world, to write myths.

Thus the world of Dickens' novels continues to be one in which reality has been processed by a myth-making mind. The objects in that world continue to carry moral meanings and embody energies that border on the animistic. The clocks that open *Dombey and Son*, the trains that represent both a levelling onslaught of the industrial world and a paradoxically demonic embodiment of poetic justice are all part of a vision that reaches for the magical and fantastic. Old Dombey, deserted, frozen, amidst the splendor of his mansion is just one more object in the Midas-moral world that his tragedy represents. We willingly accept the brilliance of Dombey as a psychological portrait; the man who has drained off his life in getting and spending, the man whose known self has precariously merged with a gilded shield mistakenly erected to protect a vulnerable core from the burdens of human connection. Yet while we all walk in a world peopled with Dombeys, where the dehumanizing objectification of self turns people into their possessions and obsessions, not many of us believe in a magical event that can reverse the process as it does for Dombey.

But such metamorphosis is an omnipresent possibility in the Dickens world, whether it be John Dounce becoming a lover, Nicholas Nickleby becoming an actor, or Mrs. Nickleby becoming a sage. The patriarchal tyrant Chuzzlewit who becomes the benevolent father and the senile Chuffey who recovers to sing Justice's song are the antecedents of numerous Dickens' characters who undergo a metamorphosis. Sometimes, like Florence Dombey's eventual groom Walter, or Dr. Manette in *A Tale of Two Cities*, or John Rokesmith in *Our Mutual Friend*, the metamorphosis takes the form of a symbolic resurrection from the dead. Elsewhere, as with Rouncewell or even Lady Dedlock in *Bleak House*, Gradgrind in *Hard Times*, the father of *Little Dorrit*, Pip of *Great Expectations*, or Boffin of *Our Mutual Friend*, characters undergo a moral metamorphosis, achieving new selves which have very little connection with the old. And the agency of these changes persists in being almost magical. Thus, though Pip's overview of himself begins to suggest a kind of continuity in explaining the change from the smug would-be gentleman to the contrite, self-contained gentleman-blacksmith, it is his encounter with Magwitch, the criminal sustainer of his illusory expectations, and Pip's ritualistic bathing that are the only clear explanations of the changes he undergoes. That Dickens never really gives up this impulse towards magical transformation is made clear in his last complete novel. There it is Boffin, who inherits the dustpiles, apparently transforming his innate generosity into a miser's greed that ultimately changes again into a self-effacing generosity willing to suffer ignominy and ill-repute in order to effect the moral transformation of others. His change from good to evil to good is effected almost magically and it is such a magical world that at least one part of Dickens wants to write about.

ii Hard Times

Dickens' novels offer us a world where character and object merge; where symbolic identifications are more than comments on human personality; character and symbol merge in an almost totemic system. Thus in a book like *Hard Times* we get the premetamorphosized Gradgrind whose physical being — square jaw, square coat, square index finger — is part of the relentlessly angular, inhumanly brittle, coldly logical system of utilitarianism to which he subscribes. Gradgrind with his totally symmetrical house is a walking piece of utilitarianism. And in opposition to his murderously dissecting intellection (not intellectualism) the novel poses the world of the circus with its warmly human "loopholes," its curves of human compassion, and its arabesques of imaginative flight. At its most abstract level, the novel is a myth about the battle between the square and the circle, where geometric shapes become the repository and symbols of conflicting value systems.[1] In keeping with this objectification of human personality, each of the main characters is given at least one symbolic identification that embodies his personality and subsumes his identity into an object. Thus we have Gradgrind's squareness, and the ashes that cover the potentially human fire of his children. Bounderby becomes a man of brass, swollenly sounding the evacuation of his own brazen wind; Bitzer is a transparent and colorless embodiment of the abstraction and vacuity of his mind and spirit. Stephen Blackpool is the embodiment of the pessimism, confusion, and martyrdom implied in his name. Rachael is identified with a star, the only glimmer of light in the black pool of Stephen's life, the symbol of light that casts its rays even into the old Hellshaft that eventually swallows the "Blackpool." And so on. Hovering above and competing with the literal mimetic intentions of the novel, the reader apprehends a mythically simple conflict of symbols, the story of the "square man" and "brass man" who turn children into ashes, who change the colors of rivers, who reduce men to hands that are obliged to tend their snakes and elephants, who muddle the world into a blackpool that they sink into a hellshaft. On this level, the novel is perhaps its clearest, because such a symbolic discussion is by its very nature absolved of most of the burdens of a more literal mimetic representation.

Although Dickens' symbolic system is elaborate and the novel purports to argue for the necessity of the imagination, it culminates in paradox and confusion in a typically Dickensian fashion. All of the good characters are entirely prosaic and unimaginative: Sissy, Louisa, Stephen Blackpool, Rachael, Sleary of the circus never show an iota of imagination. They argue for the necessity of the imagination as embodied in the circus, literature, fantasy, and amusements, not as exercises conducive to the liberation of the spirit, but as consolations and ameliorations of the spirit's entrapment. "People must be amused." On the other hand, the hard-nosed utilitarians are all fantasists of the first order. With their imaginations they remake both the world and their own lives. Thus we have the bizarre setting of Coketown, with its red and purple rivers, with its people given over to the maintenance of the snakes and elephants of Bounderby's factories, with the factories themselves appearing like an illuminated fairyland at night. We have Bounderby who makes the prosaic facts of his upbringing into an elaborate fairy tale of desertion and self-made success, who sees his work-

---

1. I find belatedly that much of what I say here about the symbolic structure of *Hard Times* (and most of what I would say in amplification of this discussion) has been anticipated by David Sonstroem in "Fettered Fancy in *Hard Times*."

men "as hands," who knows that the working class aspires to venison and golden coaches; ironically, he is far more imaginative than any of the "good" spokesmen for the imagination. Similarly Mrs. Sparsit with her illusions of grandeur, with her self-consciously aristocratic bearing of her Coriolanian nose, with her mystical visions and dreams of staircases, is a powerful demonstration of an imagination at work. A detailed examination of the novel would show that all the characters who profess a belief in a pragmatic utilitarianism are actually given over to perverse exercise of very expansive imaginations. Conversely the proponents of the imagination show nothing but their humdrum, mundane, and utilitarian capacities for dealing with the difficulties, the compromises, the disappointments and inequities of ordinary experience. The novel exalts the imagination only to demonstrate the necessity of purging it. The *indulgence* of the imagination, i.e., attending the circus, telling and reading stories, seeking amusements, becomes the primary instrument of leading the good and utilitarian life. The *exercise* of the imagination becomes the pathway leading to corruption, deception, and inhuman indifference.

iii Bleak House

The complexity of Dickens' novels continues to be achieved by extension and amplification of techniques he had developed as a sketch writer. Thus, for instance, in the world of *Bleak House*, the rhetorical force of the opening description of London, the billowing fog, ubiquitous, separating and joining everything in its opacity and confusion, is undercut by the symbolic equivalents of that confusion that occupy different strata of reality within the novel.[2] The fog has many comparative equivalents in the novel: the "log-jam" of Chancery, the morass of Jarndyce and Jarndyce, the Jumble of Krooks', within which nestles the idiosyncratic peculiarities of Miss Flite and the mysterious secret convolutions of Nemo. These are joined by the pathetic degradation of Tom-all-Alone's, the domestic confusion of the Jellybys and its echo in the self-righteous misapplication of charity at the Pardiggles.

Additionally, the symbolic equivalent of fog hovers over most of the principal characters, making each of their consciousnesses subject to the aura of confusion in the novel. Thus we are confronted with the deadlock between the fiery interior and the icy facade of the Lady who is Esther's

---

2. For a detailed discussion of the fog in *Bleak House*, and its symbolic equivalents, see J. Hillis Miller, *Charles Dickens: The World of His Novels*, pp. 160–224.

mother, and the frozen humanness that aristocratic tradition and ceremony impose, first figuratively and then literally, on her husband, Sir Leicester Dedlock. Esther Summerson quietly endures the confusion of her origins; Richard and Ada pursue opposing paths in their own relationship to Jarndyce and Jarndyce with self-debilitating involvement and dispassionate indifference respectively. Mr. Gridley is swallowed in the confusing abyss of his own case in Chancery. Skimpole compounds his infantile self-indulgence with his willful blending of aesthetic amorality and parental irresponsibility. Poor Jo wanders confusedly, the bottom of the human scale that projects confusion and opacity as a common denominator.

Yet despite the fact that the parallels are so clear, the novel culminates in a typically Dickensian paradox and contradiction. First of all, the numerous characters that the novel draws together as examples of the confusion that has come to dominate both private and institutional life do not occupy the same strata of reality, and accordingly are incapable of sustaining their equivalence of conception, either as moral or rhetorical devices. These apparently similar characters exist on different moral and mimetic strata of the novel. For the most part, the seriousness of moral consequence for the characters is directly proportional to the mimetic density of their particular stratum in the novel. That is, where character has been reduced to idiosyncrasy, as in Miss Flite, who is much like a character out of a short story by Boz, or Mr. Turveydrop, whose aging model deportment is even more reminiscent of those stories, there are no consequences to their actions that the novel takes seriously, mainly because such characters inhabit different levels of reality from the main characters. Miss Flite expends half a lifetime in the treacherous, ostensibly life-consuming courts of Chancery, and lives to free her birds with impunity. Turveydrop continues exhibiting his narcissistic deportment about town, granted a special license to parasitically live off of his daughter-in-law without moral repercussion. Miss Jellyby can transfer her charitable allegiances from Africa to women's rights while continuing the irresponsibilities that make such a demeaning confusion of her domesticity. The pathos and melodrama of the victims of the general social confusion, Jo, the people at Tom-all-Alone's, cannot be integrated with the comic nonconsequence of the willful confusions created by people such as the Jellybys and the Pardiggles. The parasitical Skimpole, whose amoral irresponsibility disorders all who surround him, is granted an immunity from the consequences of his actions.

Moreover, while the novel bemoans the irrational confusions that shape the world, it sacrifices to that confusion all who try to rationally dispel it. The rational pursuit of order, of understanding, becomes the prelude to disaster for all who undertake it. Lady Dedlock succumbs in trying to retie the broken strands of her motherhood. Richard Carstone and Gridley lose themselves in pursuing a modern minotaur in the labyrinth of Chancery. Illiterate Krook combusts spontaneously in his stultified and drunken attempts to cipher out the meaning of the mystery that he houses in his "little Chancery."

The paradigm of the orderly house seems to be the central moral metaphor that shapes the novel. Yet the novel does not imagine or project possibilities for order beyond a very limited domesticity. Esther, Mrs. Bagnet, Caddy Jellyby Turveydrop, can each create a locus of order in their own domesticity; Mr. Jarndyce, Boythorn, Woodcourt, Mr. George Rouncewell can each slightly amplify his own ordered domesticity through random acts of kindness to those unfortunates who cross their paths. But for a novel that undertakes a critique of social institutions, societal structures, that are by definition *rational* and programmatic, the reader finds himself woefully disappointed in anticipating solutions. The possibilities of rational action are entirely subsumed by the intuitive and the spontaneous. In the way of solution we are left with either the abstract and unrealizable accomplishment of a domestic order on the national scale — with no explanation of what this would mean or how it would happen — or we can accept the "Krook solution" — allowing the confusion to go on accumulating until it combusts spontaneously in fires of purgation.

Bleak House itself becomes the perfect symbol for the paradox that the novel advances. If we are to erect an enduring house, to shelter our humanity, it will have to arise from programs of restoration; but it cannot be rebuilt at once; its design must be enriched through time, through additions, through the implementations of changing conceptions of how the structure will be used, and adapted to the needs of its inhabitants. It must have many rooms, many passages, many exits, many levels, many accesses to refreshing gardens. It must be a house that while retaining some sign of its former degeneration, its Bleakness, can triumph over it, becoming a house of joy.

But the Bleak House that is presented in the novel is at best the diminished and undetailed model for a much greater "house," an architectural idea without blueprints, without the scale which would enable us to transpose from the model to the much larger structure it points toward. It remains a spot of order in a world of chaos and confusion. It portends the promise of sanity and decency in a world both indecent and insane, where the Jos, the Bricklayers, the Tom-all-Alone's continue to fend for themselves in a system that is, and remains, out of control.

iv Rearranging the world

Almost all of Dickens' writing retains a plasticity of time which moves it towards the mythic and away from the expectations of realistic fiction. Though a number of his heroes and heroines are initially presented to us as children, neither their evolution into adults, nor their initial presentation as children, are processes that can be explained and accounted for with reference to time. For instance, Florence Dombey, Esther Summerson, Sissy Jupe, David Copperfield, Little Dorrit, are all "children" in the opening of their respective stories. But of what age? It really doesn't matter, because Dickens has no desire to represent children with respect to real and recognizable differences in their psycho-emotional development. Instead, each of these children is an archetype of innocent displacement in a world that he cannot understand. For Dickens the confusions of a four-year-old and a ten-year-old and a sixteen-year-old are much the same. We are dealing with a kind of emotional time in which Esther Summerson's adolescent remembrance of telling her dolly "we are not very clever," Sissy Jupe's inability to define a horse as a "gramnivorous quadriped," Pip's confusion over the spacial-spiritual location of his dead parents, or Amy Dorrit's peripatetic excursions from prison in search of a livelihood, are all equivalent events in Dickens' time-world. The reader never apprehends a time-voice geared to a specific sense of the character's age. Instead we are given an emotion-voice geared to the internal psychic shape of the character, his idiosyncracies and preoccupations.

Moreover as each of these characters moves through time, whether in first-person flashback (Esther Summerson and David Copperfield) or through a narrator's voice (Florence Dombey, Sissy Jupe, Amy Dorrit), their lives unroll as a series of remotely connected events, in which there is at best a single strand of continuity in personality through time. Thus, the inept waif, such as Sissy Jupe, Esther Summerson, Pip, is capable of evolving into the shaper of others' destinies, or the moral-order maker, because, though each of these characters preserves an idiosyncratic psychic shape, that shape is an internalized and subjective fact which, while coloring the shape of the external world, says very little about how or what that character will do in meeting the world. The sense of fragility, incompetence, or even stupidity in the children who become Dickens' heroes and heroines, is never debilitating. Though rarely rendered as dramatically as some of the secondary characters in his novels, the central character frequently retains quasi-magical-metamorphic possibilities with respect to his movement through the external world and time. When we contrast Dickens' children-heroes with those of other Victorian novelists, the difference is clear. Becky Sharp's aggressively clever femininity, Maggie Tulliver's headstrong passionate nonconformity, Tom Tulliver's puritanical and righteous orderliness, Ernest Pontifex's natural aesthetic generosity, Jude Fawley's morbid intellectual alienation, are all part of those characters from the moment they present themselves. They carry their childish personalities and capabilities with them, through time, in a manner very different from Dickens' central figures. Dickens' children-figures retain their emotionally idiosyncratic way of apprehending the world — their highly stylized internal life — but the outward signs of person can change radically while providing no coherent links between selves.

Where other novelists attempt to align age and personality in their character's movements through time, Dickens retains a plasticity which tends to diminish the sense of empirical time. Even where he gives us specific time referents — Esther Summerson's nine-year history in *Bleak House* for instance — time becomes at best a container for, but not an explainer of, human events. The sense of linear time with a continuous density, so conspicuous in other Victorian novelists, in Dickens becomes a kind of emotional time with a subjective psychic posture providing the continuity for the various forms that the self takes. Pip the confused child, Pip the coerced thief, Pip the fawning courter of expectations, Pip the masquerading gentleman, Pip the harborer of criminals, Pip the chastened realist, is a collection of selves with a very tenuous unity incapable of explaining the changes in the external man.

A corollary to Dickens' basic detachment from empirical time emerges in his frequent inversions of usual parent-child relationships. Almost all of the characters in the novels who have parents go through only two stages: first there is the stage of parental dependence, frequently omitted from the narrative in the case of central characters (Nicholas Nickleby, Amy Dorrit, Lucie Manette, Lizzie Hexam); secondly, there is a stage of parental responsibility in which literally "the child is father of the man." Any character in the novels, major or minor, who has gone beyond the stage of parental dependence is likely to have dependent parents, dependent in ways that far exceed an economic obligation. Nicholas Nickleby, Florence Dombey, Caddy Jellyby, Prince Turveydrop, Sissy Jupe, Louisa Gradgrind, Amy Dorrit, Lucie Manette, Pip and Estella, Lizzie Hexam, Bella Wilfer, all have adult figures (actual parents or surrogates) towards whom they play a parental role. This tendency is also pronounced among minor characters, perhaps reaching its most grotesque amplitude in the crippled seamstress of *Our Mutual Friend*, who constantly refers to her father as a "naughty boy," frequently requiring punishment and chastisement. The prevalence of these inverted relationships amounts to what is almost a time rupture in the Dickens universe, as though there were some magic possibility of rearranging time so that children could father their parents. In an oblique way, this pervasive time rupture can be explained as an outgrowth of the vision of the short stories by Boz. Those stories offer us a world in which human incompetence, bumptiousness, sham and pretense are constantly at odds with the exposing forces of a humiliating world. The children in those stories are inevitably subjected to the incompetencies that emerge from their parents' encounters with that world. But correspondingly, the children of the novels, children who "father" their parents, become another device for redressing the negative story vision and for containing the fundamental ambivalence we have seen in Dickens. Thus while the parents retain and dramatize the incompetence so pervasive in the stories by Boz, the novel-children project and dramatize the contrary principle, embodying in their economic, social and moral superiority the mythic affirmation that finally creates the paradoxical vision of Dickens' novels.

I have attempted to account for some of the qualities of that vision by studying Dickens' earliest publications in detail. Throughout this study my focus has been on the curious ambivalence that characterizes Dickens' writing from the first year of his publishing career. On the one hand he seems to offer us a very cynical vision of experience, where human motives are transparent and mechanical, where heroism and grandeur are at best illusions cast abroad to service the forces of a sardonic and humiliating world. Yet on the other hand Dickens wants to insist that the world makes sense, that a conscientious program of Christian virtue will lead to a good life and shelter and solace from an ever-threatening disorder. The center of his mature novels consistently treats the compromises, settlements, half-measures, limitations, that voracious egos, desperate for love and fulfillment, must formally accept as "human expectation, paid in full." But the structural and logical counterpoints to this dulcet-toned deception inevitably cry out for a more complex statement about the world. Through a variety of devices Dickens tells us that human beings are as generous as they are petty, as fluid and spontaneous as they are mechanical, as complex and impenetrable as they are simple, as sane and rational as they are crazy. Dickens lights a candle in the darkness and celebrates the sunshine of his creation with firm reminders that it is night. A trick worth doing.

BIBLIOGRAPHY

Secondary Sources Relating to
Sketches by Boz

Adrian, A. "The Demise of the Strange Gentleman." *Dickensian*, 51 (1955), pp. 158–60.

Allen, M. L. "The Black Veil: Three Versions of a Symbol." *English Studies*, 47 (1966), pp. 286–89.

Bausch, Reinhold. "Studien uber Thackeray's *Sketches and Travels* in London, und Dickens' *Sketches*." Diss. Leipzig University, 1907.

Boll, Ernest. "The *Sketches by Boz*." *Dickensian*, 36 (1940), pp. 69–73.

———. "Charles Dickens and Washington Irving." *Modern Language Quarterly*, V (1944), pp. 453–67.

Browning, Robert. "*Sketches by Boz*." *Dickens and the Twentieth Century*. Gross, John, ed. London, 1962.

Butt, John and Kathleen Tillotson. *Dickens at Work*. London, 1957.

Carlton, W. J. "The Old Lady in *Sketches by Boz*." *Dickensian*, 49 (1953), pp. 149–52.

———. "Portraits in a Parliamentary Sketch." *Dickensian*, 50 (1954), pp. 100–109.

———. "'Captain Holland' Identified." *Dickensian*, 57 (1961), pp. 69–77.

———. "'Boz' and the Beards." *Dickensian*, 58 (1962), pp. 9–21.

Collins, P.A.W. "Dickens and the Prison Governor George Laval Chesterton." *Dickensian*, 57 (1961), pp. 11–26.

———. "Dickens and Popular Amusements." *Dickensian*, 61 (1965), pp. 7–19.

Cox, Charles B. "Comic Viewpoints in *Sketches by Boz*." *English*, 12 (1959), pp. 132–38.

Darton, F.J.H. *Dickens: Positively the First Appearance: A Centenary Review.* London, 1933.

Darwin, B. "New Discoveries of Charles Dickens: His Earliest Writings in Maria Beadnell's Album." *Strand*, 84 (1935), pp. 574–79.

Dean, F.R. "Dickens as a Reporter: Further Facts Now Revealed." *Dickensian*, 29 (1933), pp. 91–95.

De Leeuw, Margaret L. "The Significance of Humor in the Early Works of Charles Dickens." *Dissertation Abstracts*, 21 (1960), pp. 872–73.

Dexter, W. "A Dinner at Poplar Walk: A Facsimile of Dickens's First Story." *Dickensian*, 30 (1934), pp. 4–10.

———. "The Genesis of *Sketches by Boz*." *Dickensian*, 30 (1934), pp. 105–11.

DeVries, Duane K. "Dickens' *Sketches by Boz*, Exercizes in the Craft of Fiction." *Dissertation Abstracts*, 25 (1964), pp. 5273–74.

———. "Two Glimpses of Dickens' Early Development." *Dickens Studies Annual*, 1, Ed. Robert B. Partlow. Carbondale, 1970, pp. 55–64.

Dickensian. "Dickens' First Contributions to the *Morning Chronicle*." 31 (1935), pp. 5–10.

———. "The Strange Gentleman, Sept. 1836." 33 (1937), pp. 81–85.

———. "The Metropolitan Magazine and Dickens' Early Work." 33 (1937), pp. 93–96.

———. "Macrone and the Reissue of *Sketches by Boz*." 33 (1937), pp. 173–76.

Fitzgerald, Percy. "Bozland." *Gentleman's Magazine*, Nov. 1894, pp. 447–66.

Ganz, Margaret. "Humor's Alchemy: The Lesson of *Sketches by Boz*." *Genre*, 1 (1968), pp. 290–306.

Gottshall, James K. "Dickens' Rhythmic Imagery: Its Development from *Sketches by Boz* through *Bleak House*." *Dissertation Abstracts*, 19 (1958), pp. 797–98.

Hamilton, R. "Dickens and Boz." *Dickensian*, 36 (1940), pp. 242–44.

Hill, T. "Notes on *Sketches by Boz*." *Dickensian*, 46 (1950), pp. 206–13.

———. "Notes on *Sketches by Boz*." *Dickensian*, 47 (1951), pp. 41–48, 102–7, 154–58, 210–18.

———. "Notes on *Sketches by Boz*." *Dickensian*, 48 (1952), pp. 32–37, 90–94.

———. "Boz." *Dickensian*, 49 (1953), p. 44.

Hollingsworth, Keith. *The Newgate Novel, 1830–1847.* Detroit, Wayne University, 1963.

Johannspeter, Wilhelm. "Handlungs-, Charakter-, und Situations- Kontrast in den jugendwerken von Charles Dickens (*Sketches by Boz*, *Pickwick Papers*, *Oliver Twist*, *Nicholas Nickleby*)." Diss. Halle University, 1914.

Jugler, Richard. "Uber die Technik der Charakterisierung in den Jugendwerken von Charles Dickens (*Sketches by Boz*, *Pickwick Papers*, *Oliver Twist*, *Nicholas Nickleby*)." Diss., Halle University, 1912.

Kaplan, Fred. "The Development of Dickens' Style." *Dissertation Abstracts*, 27 (1966), pp. 747–48A.

Kitton, F. G. "The Inimitable Boz." *The Library Review*, Feb. 1893, pp. 778–84.

Lascelles, T. S. "Transport in the Dickensian Era." *Dickensian*, 57 (1962), pp. 75–86, 152–60.

McNulty, J. "First and Last." *Dickensian*, 46 (1951), pp. 83–87.

Marble, Anne Russel. *Pen Names and Personalities*. New York and London, 1930.

Morley, M. "Plays and Sketches by Boz." *Dickensian*, 52 (1956), pp. 81–88.

————. "Private Theatres and Boz." *Dickensian*, 59 (1963), pp. 119–23.

————. "Revelry by Night." *Dickensian*, 60 (1964), pp. 97–101.

Nielsen, H. "Some Observations on *Sketches by Boz*." *Dickensian*, 35 (1938), pp. 243–45.

New Monthly Belle Assemblee. "Sketches by Boz." London, May, 1837, pp. 263–64.

Pacey, W.C.D. "Washington Irving and Charles Dickens." *American Literature*, 16 (1945), pp. 332–39.

Peyrouten, N. C. "Boz-Town Conference." *Dickensian*, 57 (1962), pp. 7–8.

————. "Some Boston Abolitionists on Boz: A Lost American Note." *Dickensian*, 60 (1964), pp. 20–26.

Philips, George L. "Dickens and the Chimney-Sweepers." *Dickensian*, 59 (1963), pp. 28–44.

Quarterly Review. "*Pickwick Papers* and *Sketches by Boz*." Oct. 1837, pp. 484–518.

Rathburn, Robert C. "Dickens' Periodical Essays and Their Relationships to the Novels." *Dissertation Abstracts*, 17 (1957), p. 2002.

Seawin, G. "A Newly Discovered Dickens Fragment." *Dickensian*, 54 (1958), pp. 48–49.

Shyvers, W. "Positively the First Appearance." *Dickensian*, 40 (1948), pp. 89–93.

Stedman, J.W. "Boz and Bab." *Dickensian*, 58 (1962), pp. 171–78.

Stevenson, L. "An Introduction to Young Mr. Dickens." *Dickensian*, 29 (1933), pp. 111–14.

Stott, R. Toole. "Boz's *Memoirs of Joseph Grimaldi*, 1838." *Book Collector*, 15 (1966), pp. 354–56.

Tillotson, K. "Dickens and a Story by John Poole." *Dickensian*, 52 (1956), pp. 64–70.

Vallance, Rosalind. "From Boz to the Uncommercial." *Dickensian*, 63 (1966), pp. 27–33.

Viebrock, Helmut. "The Knocker: Physiognomical Aspects of a Motif in Hoffman and Dickens." *English Studies*, 43 (1962), pp. 396–402.

Wegelin, Christof. "Dickens and Irving: the Problem of Influence." *Modern Language Quarterly*, 7 (1946), pp. 83–91.

Wright, James A. "The Comic Imagination of the Young Dickens." *Dissertation Abstracts*, 20 (1959), p. 294.

ABOUT DICKENS AND HIS OTHER WORKS

Selected Bibliography
of Secondary Sources

Adrian, Arthur A. "The Cheeryble Brothers: A Further Note." *Modern Language Notes*, 44 (1949), pp. 269–70.

———. "Nicholas Nickleby and Educational Reform." *Nineteenth Century Fiction*, 4 (1949), pp. 237–41.

Askew, H. "Edward Smith, The Prototype of Smike." *Notes and Queries*, (Dec. 9, 1933), p. 402.

Axton, William F. *Circle of Fire*. Lexington, 1966.

———. "Dramatic Style in Dickens' Novels." *Dissertation Abstracts*, 22 (1962), pp. 2788–89.

———. "Unity and Coherence in *The Pickwick Papers*." *Studies in English Literature*, 5 (1965), pp. 663–76.

Bagehot, Walter. *Literary Studies*. London, 1895.

Ball, Roy A. "The Development of Smike." *Dickensian*, 57 (1966), pp. 125–28.

Barrett, Edwin B. "Charles Dickens: The Essential Fable, Character Idea, Form, and Diction in Four Novels of His Maturity." *Dissertation Abstracts*, 22 (1962), p. 2789.

Bell, Vereen M. "Parents and Children in *Great Expectations*." *Victorian Newsletter*, 27 (Spring, 1965), pp. 21–24.

Bennet, W. C. "Clothes as an Index to Character." *Dickensian*, 35 (1939), pp. 184–86.

———. "The Marchioness and Little Nell." *Dickensian*, 36 (1939), pp. 7–8.

Bergler, Edmund. "Little Dorrit and Dickens' Intuitive Knowledge of Psychic Masochism." *American Imago*, 14 (1966), pp. 371–88.

Bergonzi, Bernard. "Nicholas Nickleby." *Dickens and the Twentieth Century*. Ed. John Gross and Gabriel Pearson. Toronto, 1962, pp. 65–76.

Berman, Ronald. "Human Scale: A Note on *Hard Times*." *Nineteenth Century Fiction*, 22 (1967), pp. 288–93.

Birkett, Lord. "The Versatility of Dickens." *Listener*, 15 (1962), p. 282.

Blount, Trevor. *Dickens: The Early Novels*. London, 1967.

———. "Sir Leicester Dedlock and 'Deportment' Turveydrop: Some Aspects of Dickens' Use of Parallelism." *Nineteenth Century Fiction*, 21 (1966), pp. 149–65.

Bodelson, C. A. "Some Notes on Dickens' Symbolism." *English Studies*, 40 (1960), pp. 420–31.

Boege, Fred W. "Point of View in Dickens." *PMLA*, 45 (1950), pp. 90–105.

Bort, Barry D. "A Study of Dickens' Heroes From Oliver Twist to Jasper." *Dissertation Abstracts*, 23 (1962), pp. 1666–67.

Bradby, K. "Social Wrongs in Bleak House." *Dickensian*, 38 (1942), pp. 228–30.

Brogunier, Joseph. "The Dreams of Montague Tigg and Jonas Chuzzlewit." *Dickensian*, 62 (1962), pp. 65–70.

Butt, John and Tillotson, Kathleen. *Dickens at Work*. London, 1957.

Carter, John Archer, Jr. "Dickens and Education: The Novelist as Reformer." *Dissertation Abstracts*, 17 (1957), pp. 628–29.

Carter, J. A. "The World of Squeers and the World of Crummles." *Dickensian*, 58 (1962), pp. 50–53.

Cary, Joyce. *Art and Reality: The Clark Lectures*. London, 1956.

Cassirer, Ernst. *The Philosophy of Symbolic Forms*: Vol. II, *Mythical Thought*. Trans. Ralph Manheim. New Haven, 1955.

Chesterton, G. K. *Charles Dickens*. London, 1913.

———. *Criticism and Appreciation of the Works of Charles Dickens*. London, 1933.

Cockshut, A. O. J. *The Imagination of Charles Dickens*. New York, 1962.

Colburn, W. E. "Dickens and the 'Life Illusion'." *Dickensian*, 54 (1958), pp. 110–18.

Collins, Phillip Arthur William. *Dickens and Adult Education*. Leicester, 1963.

Collins, Phillip. *Dickens and Crime*. London, 1961.   •

Coolidge, Archibald, Jr. *Charles Dickens as Serial Novelist*. Ames, 1967.

————. "Dickens and Latitudinarian Christianity." *Dickensian*, 59 (1963), pp. 53–60.

————. "Dickens and the Philosophic Basis of Melodrama." *Victorian Newsletter*, 20 (Fall, 1961), pp. 1–6.

————. "Dickens' Complex Plots." *Dickensian*, 57 (1961), pp. 174–82.

————. "Dickens's Humor." *Victorian Newsletter*, 18 (Fall, 1960), pp. 8–15.

Coppock, A. "Smike." *Dickensian*, 35 (1939), pp. 162–63.

Cotterell, T. "The Original of Quilp." *Dickensian*, 43 (1946), pp. 39–40.

Cross, A. E. B. "Some By-ways in *Nicholas Nickleby*." *Dickensian*, 34 (1938), pp. 5–9.

Davis, Earle R. "Dickens and the Evolution of Caricature." *PMLA*, 55 (1940), pp. 231–40.

————. *The Flint and the Flame: The Artistry of Charles Dickens*. Columbia, 1963.

Dexter, Walter. Ed., *Mr. and Mrs. Charles Dickens*. London, 1935.

Dickens, Charles. *The Letters of Charles Dickens*. 3 vols. Eds. Arthur Waugh, Hugh Walpole, Walter Dexter, and Thomas Hatton. Bloomsbury, 1938.

————. *The Letters of Charles Dickens*. Vol. I, 1820–1839, Ed. Madeline House and Graham Storey. London, 1965.

Dyson, A. E. "*Hard Times:* The Robber Fancy." *Dickensian*, 65 (1969), pp. 67–69.

————. *The Inimitable Dickens*. London, 1970.

————. "*Martin Chuzzlewit:* Howls the Sublime." *Critical Quarterly*, 9 (1967), pp. 234–53.

Easson, Angus. "Dickens Household Words, and a Double Standard." *Dickensian*, 60 (1964), pp. 104–14.

Egan, Pierce. *Real Life in London*. London, 1821; rpt: London, 1905.

Engel, Monroe. *The Maturity of Dickens*. Cambridge, 1959.

————. "The Politics of Dickens Novels." *PMLA*, 71 (1956), pp. 945–74.

Fielding, K. J. *Charles Dickens*. London, 1958.

————. "Dickens and the Critics." *Dickensian*, 58 (1962), pp. 150–151.

————. "Hard Times for the Present." *Dickensian*, 63 (1967), pp. 149–52.

————. "The Weekly Serialisation of Dickens's Novels." *Dickensian*, 54 (1958), pp. 134–41.

Finlay, I. F. "Dickens in the Cinema." *Dickensian*, 54 (1958), pp. 106–9.

Fleissner, Robert F. *Dickens and Shakespeare.* New York, 1965.

Ford, George H. *Dickens and His Readers.* (1955; rpt. New York, 1965), pp. 55–71.

———— and Lane, Lauriat. Eds., *The Dickens Critics.* Ithaca, 1961.

Frye, Northrup. *Anatomy of Criticism: Four Essays.* Princeton, 1957; rpt.: New York, 1966.

Garis, Robert. *The Dickens Theatre.* Oxford, 1965.

Gerson, Stanley. "Dickens's Use of Malapropisms." *Dickensian*, 61 (1965), pp. 40–45.

Gibson, John W. *"The Old Curiosity Shop:* The Critical Allegory." *Dickensian*, 60 (1964), pp. 178–83.

Gilmour, R. "Manchester Men and Their Books," *Dickensian*, 63 (1967), pp. 21–24.

Gimbel, Richard. "An Exhibition of 150 Manuscripts, Illustrations and First Editions of Charles Dickens." *Yale University Library Gazette*, 36 (1962), pp. 46–93.

Gissing, George. *Critical Studies of the Works of Charles Dickens.* New York, 1924.

Goodheart, E. "Dickens's Method of Characterisation." *Dickensian*, 54 (1958), pp. 35–37.

Graham, W. "The Cheerybles and the Cogglesbys." *Dickensian*, 45 (1949), pp. 23–25.

Gray, Paul E. Ed., *Twentieth Century Interpretations of Hard Times: A Collection of Critical Essays.* Englewood Cliifs, 1969.

Greene, Graham. "The Young Dickens." *The Lost Childhood and Other Essays.* New York, 1966.

Grob, Shirley. "Dickens and Some Motifs of the Fairy Tale." *Texas Studies in Literature and Language*, 5 (1964), pp. 567–79.

Gross, John and Pearson, Gabriel. Eds., *Dickens and the Twentieth Century.* London, 1962.

Haight, Gordon S. "Dickens and Lewes on Spontaneous Combustion." *Nineteenth Century Fiction*, 10 (1955), pp. 53–63.

Hardy, Barbara. "The Change of Heart in Dickens' Novels." *Victorian Studies*, 5 (1961), pp. 49–67.

————. "The Complexity of Dickens." *Dickens 1970.* Ed. Michael Slater. London, 1970.

————. *The Moral Art of Dickens.* London, 1970.

Harris, Stephen L. "The Mask of Morality: A Study of the Unconscious Hypocrite in Representative Novels of Jane Austen, Charles Dickens, and George Eliot." *Dissertation Abstracts*, 25 (1965), p. 4669.

Harvey, William R. "Four Character Types in the Novels of Charles Dickens." *Dissertation Abstracts*, 27 (1966), p. 1056a.

Hill, T. W. "Notes on *Nicholas Nickleby.*" *Dickensian*, 45 (1949), pp. 98–102, 153–66.

———. "Notes on *Nicholas Nickleby.*" *Dickensian*, 46 (1950), pp. 42–48, 99–104.

———. "The Oyster: A Close-up." *Dickensian*, 36 (1940), pp. 139–46.

Holloway, John. "Dickens's Vision of Society." *Listener*, 73 (1965), pp. 287–89.

Hood, Thomas. *The Works of Thomas Hood.* Ed. by his Son and Daughter. London, 1969.

Hook, Thomas. *Choice Humorous Works.* London: John Camden, n.d.

House, Humphrey. *The Dickens World.* London, 1941.

Hunter, R. A., and Macalpine, I. "A Note on Dickens's Psychiatric Reading." *Dickensian*, 53 (1957), pp. 49–51.

Hynes, Joseph A. "Image and Symbol in *Great Expectations.*" *English Literary History*, 30 (1963), pp. 258–92.

Jackson, T. A. *Charles Dickens: Progress of a Radical.* London, 1937.

Johnson, Edgar. *Charles Dickens: His Tragedy and Triumph.* 2 vols. New York, 1952.

———. "The Paradox of Dickens." *Dickensian*, 50 (1954), pp. 149–58.

———. "The Paradox of Dickens." *Dickensian*, 51 (1955), p. 23 ff.

———. "The Present State of Dickensian Studies." *Victorian Newsletter*, 7 (April, 1955), pp. 4–9.

Kelty, J. M. "The Modern Tone of Charles Dickens." *Dickensian*, 57 (1961), pp. 160–65.

Kieft, Ruth M. Vande. "Patterns of Communication in *Great Expectations.*" *Nineteenth Century Fiction*, 15 (1961), pp. 325–34.

Kincaid, James R. "Laughter and *Oliver Twist.*" *PMLA*, 83 (1968), pp. 63–70.

———. "Laughter and Pathos: *The Old Curiosity Shop.*" *Dickens Studies Annual*, 1 (1970), pp. 65–94.

Kitton, Frederic G. *The Novels of Charles Dickens.* London, 1891.

Lane, L., Jr. "Dickens and the Double." *Dickensian*, 55 (1955), pp. 45–55.

Leacock, Stephen. *Charles Dickens: His Life and Work.* London, 1933.

Leavis, F. R. *The Great Tradition.* London, 1948.

MacLean, Robert S., "Putting Quilp to Rest." *Victorian Newsletter*, 34 (1968), pp. 29–33.

Manning, John. *Dickens on Education.* Toronto, 1959.

Marcus, Steven. *Dickens: From Pickwick to Dombey.* New York, 1965.

Marshall, William H. "The Conclusion of *Great Expectations* as the Fulfillment of Myth." *The Personalist*, 44 (1963), pp. 337–47.

McCabe, Bernard. "Taking Dickens Seriously." *Commonweal*, 82 (1965), pp. 244–47.

McLean, Robert S. "Charles Dickens' Villainous Characters: A Study in Ethical Values and Esthetic Control." *Dissertation Abstracts*, 27 (1966), pp. 183a–84.

McMaster, R. D. "Dickens and the Horrific." *Dalhousie Review*, 38 (1958), pp. 18–28.

———. "Man into Beast in Dickensian Caricature." *University of Toronto Quarterly*, 31 (1962), pp. 354–61.

Meckier, Jerome. "The Faint Image of Eden: The Many Worlds of *Nicholas Nickleby*." *Dickens Studies Annual*, 1 (1970), pp. 129–46.

Miller, J. Hillis. *Charles Dickens: The World of His Novels.* Cambridge, Mass., 1958.

Monod, Sylvere. *Charles Dickens.* Paris, 1958.

Morley, Malcolm. "Where Crummles Played." *Dickensian*, 57 (1962), pp. 23–29.

Nelson, Harland S. "Dickens' Plots: 'The Ways of Providence' or the Influence of Collins?" *Victorian Newsletter*, 19 (Spring 1961), pp. 11–14.

Orwell, George. *Dickens, Dali and Others: Studies in Popular Culture.* New York, 1946.

Page, Norman. "A Language Fit for Heroes: Speech in *Oliver Twist* and *Our Mutual Friend*." *Dickensian*, 65 (1969), pp. 100–107.

Pakenham, Pansy. "Dickens and the Class Question." *Victorian Newsletter*, 16 (1959), p. 30.

Partlow, Robert B., Jr. "The Moving I: A Study of the Point of View in *Great Expectations*." *College English*, 23 (1961), pp. 122–31.

Patten, Robert L. "The Interpolated Tales In *Pickwick Papers*." *Dickens Studies*, I (1965), pp. 86–89.

———. "Plot in Charles Dickens' Early Novels 1836–1841." *Dissertation Abstracts*, 26 (1966), p. 4670.

Pearson, Gabriel. "*The Old Curiosity Shop*." *Dickens and the Twentieth Century*. Eds. John Gross and Gabriel Pearson. Toronto, 1962, pp. 77–90.

Phillips, George L. "Dickens and the Chimney Sweepers." *Dickensian*, 59 (1963), pp. 38–44.

Phillips, Walter C. *Dickens, Reade, and Collins: Sensation Novelists.* New York, 1919.

Pondered, M. "Dickens the Rebel." *Dickensian*, 29 (1933), pp. 101–9.

Price, Martin. *Dickens: A Collection of Critical Essays*. Englewood Cliffs, 1967.

Raleigh, John Henry. "Dickens and the Sense of Time." *Nineteenth Century Fiction*, 13 (1958), pp. 127–37.

Roulet, Ann. "A Comparative Study of *Nicholas Nickleby* and *Bleak House*." *Dickensian*, 60 (1964), pp. 117–24.

Sonstroem, David. "Fettered Fancy in *Hard Times*." *PMLA*, 84 (1969), pp. 520–29.

Spilka, Mark. *Dickens and Kafka*. Bloomington, 1963.

Starr, H. "Dickens' Parody of Gray's Elegy." *Dickensian*, 51 (1955), pp. 186–87.

Stedman, Jane W. "Child-Wives of Dickens." *Dickensian*, 59 (1963), pp. 112–18.

Steig, Michael. "Erotic Themes in Dickens' Novels." *Dissertation Abstracts*, 24 (1964), pp. 4704–5.

———. "The Central Action of *Old Curiosity Shop*." *Literature and Psychology*, 15 (1965), pp. 163–70.

———. "*Martin Chuzzlewit*: Pinch and Pecksniff." *Studies in the Novel*, 1 (1969), pp. 181–87.

Stewart, D. H. "Dickens's Contribution, Then and Now." *Dickensian*, 56 (1960), pp. 71–75.

Stoehr, Taylor. *Dickens: A Dreamer's Stance*. Ithaca, 1965.

Stone, Harry. "Dickens and Interior Monologue." *Philological Quarterly*, 38 (1959), pp. 52–65.

———. "The Novel as Fairy Tale: Dickens' *Dombey and Son*." *English Studies*, 47 (1966), pp. 1–27.

Strange, E. H. "Notes of the Bibliography of *Nicholas Nickleby*." *Dickensian*, 33 (1937), pp. 30–33.

Sucksmith, Harvey Peter. *The Narrative Art of Charles Dickens*. Oxford, 1970.

Tedlock, E. W. J. "Kafka's Imitation of *David Copperfield*." *Comparative Literature*, 52 (1955), pp. 52–62.

Thale, Jerome. "The Imagination of Charles Dickens: Some Preliminary Discriminations." *Nineteenth Century Fiction*, 22 (1967), pp. 27–43.

Thompson, Leslie M., "Mrs. Nickleby's Monologue: The Dichotomy of Pessimism and Optimism in *Nicholas Nickleby*." *Studies in the Novel*, 1 (1969), pp. 222–29.

Times Literary Supplement. "Little Nell." Sept. 4, 1937, p. 640.

———. "*The Old Curiosity Shop*: Dickens and Disney." April 6, 1940, p. 167.

Van Ghent, Dorothy. *The English Novel: Form and Function*. New York, 1958.

Walbank, A. "With a Blush Retire." *Dickensian*, 57 (1961), pp. 166–73.

Watt, William W. Ed. Introduction to *Hard Times* by Charles Dickens. New York, Rinehart, 1965.

Williams, Raymond. "Dickens and Social Ideas." *Dickens, 1970*. Ed. Michael Slater. London, 1970.

Wilson, Edmund. *The Wound and the Bow*. London, 1952.

Wing, G. D. "A Part to Tear a Cat In." *Dickensian*, 64 (1968), pp. 10–19.

Winters, Warrington, "Dickens and the Psychology of Dreams." *PMLA*, 43 (1948), pp. 984–1006.

Yanko, Anne. "Technique and Vision in *Bleak House, Little Dorrit*, and *Our Mutual Friend*." *Dissertation Abstracts*, 23 (1962), p. 2143.

Zabel, Morton. *Craft and Character: Vocation in Modern Fiction*. New York, 1956.

INDEX

Actor. *See* Symbol; Theme

Ambiguity: in *The Sketches By Boz*, 100; in *The Old Curiosity Shop*, 187

Ambivalence: toward theatre, 9, 143; in *The Sketches by Boz*, 99–100; problems of, 121; of early writings, 135; toward acting, 143; in *Nicholas Nickleby*, 143, 158, 159, 160, 162–163, 167, 202; of Dickens' humor, 148 n; of Dickens' vision, 169; in *The Old Curiosity Shop*, 172, 184, 202; in novels, 188; toward nature, 193; characteristic, 201; contained by rhetoric, 207; fundamental, 218

America, 195–198, 200

Animal images. *See* Symbol

Anti-hero: in short story, 82; Pickwick as, 125, 130; use of, 130; in *Nicholas Nickleby*, 167

Apositive. *See* Devices

Archetypes: elderly type, 4; middle-class British, 15, 121; uncle-figure, 22; mother, 28, 93; bachelor, 28; wayward son, 75, 75 n, 93; swaggering clerk, 93; stereotyped characters as, 158; children as, 216

"Astley's": as prototype, 6–7; people as actors in, 9, 93; sense of theatre in, 10; clothing as symbol in, 10; power of object in, 33; ambivalence toward actors in, 143

Athenaeum, 117 n20

Atlas, 116 n14

Bachelor. *See* Archetypes

Bagnet, Mrs., 215

Bagshaw, Alick: as prototype, 23; mentioned, 19, 21

Bagshaws: as antithesis to Minns, 19–21; later change in name, 19 n

Barker, William, 104–105

"Baron of Grogswig," 152

"Bellamy's": as prototype, 2; excluded from *First Series*, 102; revised, 103

Bell's Life in London and Sporting Chronicle: sketches and stories contained in, 96; mentioned, 92, 97, 103–104

Bell's Weekly: sketches and stories contained in, 95; mentioned, 86 n

Bentley's Miscellaney, 109

Billsmethi, Signor, 5

Bitzer, 212

Blackpool, Stephen, 212

Blackwood's Magazine, 14, 14 n2, 15 n4, 16

"The Black Veil," 75 n

Bleak House: characters foreshadowed, 5; use of oysters in, 39 n; view of minor characters of, 153 n; metamorphosis in, 211; extension of techniques, 213–215

"Bloomsbury Christening, The": as

231

24–25; actors in, 93; illustration of,
112; ambivalence toward actors, 143
"Mr. Watkins Tottle," 49–50
Myth: mythic literature, defined, 31;
discussion of mythic literature,
31–34; mythic view, defined, 32;
mythic literature, Dickens', 37–45;
and causality, 39; versus irony,
48–54; mythic vision, 121; type of
metamorphosis, 134; and characters,
148–149; in *Nicholas Nickleby*,
166–167; and hero-heroine, 210; of
novels, 210; affirmation of, 218

Narrator: third-person, 16–17, 45;
double narrative frame, 122–123;
traits of, 130; of sketches compared
with stories, 132; of short story, 170
"National Distress," 61–63
Nature. *See* Theme
Nature, human. *See* Theme
Nemo, 213
New Monthly Magazine: first-person
narrative in, 16
Nicholas Nickleby: use of oysters in,
39 n; rhetoric in, 122, 136, 143,
165; as "Dickensian" novel,
129–133; limitations of, 130;
dialogue in, 131; parody in, 131,
165; use of gesture in, 132;
characterization in, 134–135;
paradox in, 135, 151, 202;
ambivalence of, 135, 159; first
movement, 135–138; business as
theme in, 136–137, 149, 154, 163;
second movement, 138–144; actor as
symbol in, 143; third movement,
144–148; conflicts in, 148–151;
structure of, 136 n, 151; irony in,
152, 165; view of minor characters
of, 153 n; acting joined to business,
154; eyes as symbol, 159; legs as
symbol, 160; city in, 163–164;
hero-heroine, 165; compared to
The Old Curiosity Shop, 172, 177,
179, 181, 184; compared to *Martin
Chuzzlewit*, 198; mentioned, 109
Nickleby, Godfrey, 136

Nickleby, Kate, 132, 139–146 *passim*,
153–154, 157, 160
Nickleby, Mrs.: paradox of, 160–162;
mentioned, 4, 141, 156, 159,
162 n, 165, 211
Nickleby, Nicholas: foreshadowed, 22;
as heroic character, 130–137, 171;
evolution of, 137–139, 144–147; as
actor, 142–144, 148; mirrored by
Smike, 149–151; and death,
152–153; as lover, 156–157, 165;
parodied, 157–159; eyes as symbol,
159; legs as symbol, 160; and city,
163–164; compared to Nell, 170;
child-parent relationship, 217;
mentioned, 141, 154, 161, 162,
166, 210
Nickleby, Nicholas, elder, 136
Nickleby, Ralph, 132, 134, 136, 141,
144, 146, 149–160 *passim*
Noggs, Newman, 132, 140, 141, 154
Novels: paradox in, 205–206;
compared with short story, 210
Nubbles, Kit, 179, 183

Object: power of, 33–34; people as, 41,
42
"Old Bailey, The": use of
comparison, 73–78; confessional tone
in, 74; later changes, 74, 77 n;
changing tone in, 74–77; archetype
in, 75; use of tone in, 94; excluded
from *First Series*, 102 n; ambivalence
toward actors, 143. *See also* "Criminal
Courts"
Old Curiosity Shop, The: rhetoric in, 122,
180, 184, 187, 188; heroine in,
169–170; reality in, 179; fairy tale
in, 179–184, 187; business as theme
in, 180; compared with the short
story, 182; syntax in, 182; tone of,
182; ambivalence in, 184; compared
to *Nicholas Nickleby*, 184; parodies of,
184–188; ambiguity in, 187;
compared with short story and
sketch, 187; irony, 187; Manichean
vision of, 187; paradox in, 203;
mentioned, 176 n11

antecedents, 1–7; revealing the youthful Dickens, 7–11; relation to originals, 13; use of oysters in, 39 n; publication chronology, 86–94; recurrence of theme in, 92; in original periodical groupings, 94–97; as periodical numbers, 105–109; periodical numbers of, contents, 106–108; illustrations of, 109–115; reception of, 115–117; contrasted with *Pickwick*, 122–127; use of dialogue, 131–132; idiosyncrasy in, 134; structure of, 151; compared with *Nicholas Nickleby*, 166; similarities with novels, 188; pattern of paradox, 201–202; mentioned, 143, 148
—*First Series*: tone in, 94; new sketches in, 96; first book, 97–102; contents, 98; ambivalence in, 99–100; ambiguity in, 100; organization of, 100–102; revisions in preparation of, 101–102; exclusions in preparation of, 101–102, 102n;
—*Second Series*: tone in, 94; new sketches in, 96; contents, 103; mentioned, 103,104,105
Skimpole, 214
Slavery. *See* Symbol
Sleary, 212
Slyme, Chevy, 194
Smike: as mythic character, 149; as symbol, 149–150; compared with "The Phenomenon," 150–151; mentioned, 138, 142, 142 n, 149 n11,12, 152, 155–156, 160, 162, 163
Snevelicci, 133, 134
"Some Account of an Omnibus Cad," later form of, 92, 102 n, 104–105. *See also* "Last Cab-Driver and the First Omnibus Cad, The"
Space-time coordination: in Dickens, 44; in Eliot, 45
Sparkins, Horatio, 24, 25
Sparsit, Mrs., 213
Spontaneous combustion, 5–6, 5 n, 215

Squeers, Miss, 132, 160
Squeers, Mrs., 153
Squeers, Mr., 133–160 *passim*
Stereotype: "Love and Oysters" as, 17; in characters, 26–27; of perfection, Nell as, 170
"Street Sketches," 86 n4
"Streets — Morning, The," 5, 102 n, 108
"Streets — Night, The," 108
Summerson, Esther, 208, 213, 214, 215, 216
Sun, 115, 116 n14,15
Sunday Herald, 115, 116 n14, 117 n16,19
Swiveller, Dick, 175–176, 176 n11, 183
Symbol: flight, 7; clothing as, 10–11; Dotheboys Hall as, 137–138; actor as, 143; Smike as, 149–150; Lillyvick-Petowker marriage as, 154; eyes as, 159; in *Nicholas Nickleby*, 159–160, 165; legs as, 160; Quilp as, 185; savages as, 198; dichotomy of nature as, 198–200; slavery as, 199; animal images as, 199–200; versus rhetoric, 202; paradoxes as, 202–206; anticipated by parody, 205; in *Hard Times*, 211–212, fog as, 213, 213 n; *Bleak House* as, 215
—*Theatre*: ambivalence toward, 9–10, 143; mentioned, 139 n4,5, 140
Syntax: in the short story, 52–53; Egan's use of, 59; in *Nicholas Nickleby*, 150; of Nell and Quilp, 180; of *The Old Curiosity Shop*, 182

Tapley, Mark, 171–172, 192, 196, 198, 202, 204
Tale of Two Cities, A, 211
Theatre. *See* Symbol
Theme: first present in *The Sketches by Boz*, 6; middle-class, 6; actors, 9, 93, 139–144, 148; dinner scenes, 23; recurrence of, in *The Sketches by Boz*, 92; transportation, 92–93, 109; business as, 136–137, 149, 153, 163, 180; business united with

Q5